The China Triangle

THE CHINA TRIANGLE

Latin America's China Boom and the Fate
of the Washington Consensus

KEVIN P. GALLAGHER

OXFORD
UNIVERSITY PRESS

OXFORD
UNIVERSITY PRESS

Oxford University Press is a department of the University of Oxford. It furthers
the University's objective of excellence in research, scholarship, and education
by publishing worldwide. Oxford is a registered trade mark of Oxford University
Press in the UK and in certain other countries.

Published in the United States of America by Oxford University Press
198 Madison Avenue, New York, NY 10016, United States of America.

Library of Congress Cataloging-in-Publication Data
Names: Gallagher, Kevin, 1968– author.
Title: The China triangle : Latin America's China boom and the fate of the
    Washington consensus / Kevin P. Gallagher.
Description: Oxford ; New York : Oxford University Press, 2016. | Includes
    bibliographical references and index.
Identifiers: LCCN 2015028973 | ISBN 9780190246730 (hardback) | ISBN 9780190246747
(ebook)
Subjects: LCSH: China—Foreign economic relations—Latin America. | Latin
    America—Foreign economic relations—China. | United States—Foreign
    economic relations—China. | China—Foreign economic relations—United
    States. | United States—Foreign economic relations—Latin America. |
    Latin America—Foreign economic relations—United States. | Economic
    development—China. | Economic development—Latin America. |
    China—Economic policy. | Latin America—Economic policy. | United
    States—Economic policy. | BISAC: POLITICAL SCIENCE / Government /
    Comparative.
Classification: LCC HF1604.Z4 L2935 2016 | DDC 337.8051—dc23 LC record available at
http://lccn.loc.gov/2015028973

9 8 7 6 5 4 3 2 1
Printed by Sheridan, USA

CONTENTS

LIST OF FIGURES AND TABLES

Figures

Tables

The first time I visited China, in 2001, I left from Mexico and not my native Boston, Massachusetts. In Mexico I was visiting the El Colegio de Mexico (COLMEX), which was having a conference on the performance of the North American Free Trade Agreement (NAFTA) in Mexico. NAFTA, then the biggest regional trade deal in history, went into force in 1994 and economically integrated Mexico with the United States. By 2001 exports to the United States had surged, and investment from the United States did too. At the COLMEX conference we were trying to figure out why the NAFTA-led surge in exports and investment had not translated into broader prosperity for Mexico's economy, its people, and the natural environment there.

I boarded a plane in Mexico City en route to Beijing, China. The Chinese government had asked me to participate in a workshop to help them think about how to evaluate the economic and environmental impacts of the first big trade agreement they were about to join—the World Trade Organization (WTO). I knew next to nothing about China, but had devised some economic models on how to think about such impacts and also had a lifelong curiosity about China and its people so I jumped at the chance—thinking that they such opportunities would be few and far between. Little did I know that over the next decade I would visit China numerous times as part of a broader effort to understand how the emergence of China in the global economy (in no small part due to its entry into the WTO) would impact the development prospects in Latin America.

I have written, supervised, commented on, been part of, and read countless academic studies on the China–Latin America economic relationship for more than a decade. This book is my attempt to synthesize and analyze those findings for a broader audience, given the fact that the China–Latin America relationship is at a crossroads and needs considerable dialogue and rethinking on the part of China, Latin America, and even the United States to ensure that the relationship continues to evolve in a way that can bring prosperity to both China and the Western Hemiphere.

While this book is written for a broader audience, it draws on extensive scholarly work with my team at Boston University's Global Economic Governance Initiative (GEGI), as well as the work of other colleagues and friends. It is my aim that general readers and policymakers will find this book useful, as well as scholars and students.

At GEGI we have a research program titled "China's Global Reach." Over the years I have led GEGI's research on China's lending to Latin American governments, China's trade and investment policy with the region, the impact of China on manufacturing export competitiveness in Latin America, and the environmental dimension of China in Latin America. While I have led this work, it has benefited from the collaboration and assistance of a number of colleagues and students. Roberto Porzecanski and I wrote a number of technical papers on the competiveness issues when we both were affiliated with the Global Development and Environment Institute at Tufts University, and published them as a book with Stanford University Press in 2010.

Another former student whom I have published extensively with on China and Latin America, and who is now a GEGI research associate, is Amos Irwin. With Katherine Koleski, Amos and I produced the first estimate of Chinese policy bank lending in Latin America, and compared the environmental safeguards of Chinese banks with those of other development banks working in the region. Amos and I have also written extensively on the environmental impacts of Chinese foreign direct investment in Peru.

More recently I have greatly enjoyed working with Rebecca Ray, a GEGI fellow and budding economist. Becky and I have done extensive analysis on the social and environmental impacts of Chinese trade, investment, and finance across the Americas. Indeed, we help steer a working group that has published eight country studies on the subject, soon to be an edited book. In addition to Becky, I have highly benefited from collaborating with Cynthia Sanborn of the Universidad de Pacifica in Lima, Peru, and long-time collaborator Andres Lopez from the University of Buenos Aires in Argentina. I also thank Julian Donaubauer, Daniela Ramos, Alejandra Saravia López, Adam Rua Quiroga, Philip Fearnside, Adriano M. R. Figueiredo, Nicola Borregaard, Annie Dufey, Guillermo Rudas, Mauricio Cabrera Leal, Adam Chimienti, Claudia Schatan, Diana Piloyan, Jeronim Capaldo, and Victoria Chonn Ching for collaborating with GEGI on this important work.

Most recently I have been collaborating with Fei Yuan on work related to the environmental and social safeguards of Chinese development finance in Latin America. Thank you Fei for helping to prepare this manuscript as well. Christian Estrella, Yuechan Lu, Jill Richardson, and Victoria Puyat are others affiliated with GEGI who have been enormously helpful as we work on these issues.

I have also collaborated with scholars outside GEGI on China and Latin America. My first paper on the subject was with Juan Carlos Moreno-Brid at the United Nations Economic Commission for Latin America and the Caribbean. With Juan Carlos I analyzed the extent to which Mexican firms were losing out to their Chinese counterparts in the US market.

With Enrique Dussel Peters from the National Autonomous University of Mexico, I extended the work with Juan Carlos and examined the extent to which firms from the United States were threatened by China in Mexico. Enrique is the pioneer on China–Latin American studies. By far he has done the most research on the subject (as the endnotes to this book reveal!). He has also done a great service by founding a network of scholars across the Western Hemisphere and in China that work on these issues.

I have also learned a lot from and benefited from Margaret Myers at the Washington-based Inter-American Dialogue (IAD). IAD published the working paper version of our estimates on Chinese finance in Latin America. Margaret and I then came up with the idea to annually publish the data on an interactive web page housed at IAD as the China–Latin America Finance Database. The collaboration has been a great success—helping to bring a more empirical-based understanding of China in Latin America for policymakers, the media, and the general public.

I am also indebted to the following individuals whom I have collaborated with in some way or whose insights I have benefited from: Carol Wise, Barbara Stallings, Rhys Jenkins, Eva Paus, Michele Chan, Jiaming Ju, Paulina Garzon, Denise Leung, Hu Tao, Li Zhu, Gregory Chinn, Yu Yongding, Ming Zhang, Jose Antonio Ocampo, Jiaming Ju, Riordan Roett, Fran Hagopian, Harley Shaiken, Sun Hongbo, Pieter Bottelier, Kirsten Sternbusch, Ricardo Ffrench-Davis, Janine Ferretti, Evan Ellis, Rose Niu, Jose Antonio Ocampo, Adrian Ahearn, Erik Bethel, Matt Ferchen, Bo Kong, Andres Lopez, Cynthia Sanborn, Alicia Garcia-Herrero, Mauricio Mesquita Moreira, Chai Yu, Andres Soares, Jorge Dominquez, Ben Schneider, Matias Vernengo, Daniela Prates, Eric Helleiner, Osvaldo Rosales, Michael Shifter, Athena Ronquillo-Ballesteros, and many more.

I must give special thanks to Deborah Brautigam. Deborah is the world's leading scholar on China and Africa, and we met in

China when she was giving lectures for her pathbreaking book *The Dragon's Gift: The Real Story of China in Africa*. We have gone on to do comparative analyses of China in Africa and in Latin America together. Deborah graciously hosted me as a visiting scholar in her International Development Program at Johns Hopkins University's Paul Nitze School of Advanced International Studies, where the bulk of this book was written.

I also greatly benefited from two other visiting scholarships during the research stage of this book. In 2010 I was a visiting professor at the School of Public Policy and Management in China's Tsinghua University. I thank Xue Lan and Su Jun for hosting me there. In 2012 I lived in Argentina and was hosted by the Center for the Study of State and Society. I thank Leonardo Stanley and Ricardo Frenkel for that opportunity.

The research and writing of this book, and the many research projects that came before, could not have been conducted without the generous support of a number of private foundations. I thank the Smith Richardson, and Allan Song in particular, for the support to write this book. The Charles Stewart Mott Foundation, the MacArthur Foundation, and the Rockefeller Brothers Fund have supported many of the research programs that came before. I thank Sandra Smithey, Traci Romine, Amy Shannon, Steve Cornelius, Jorgen Thomson, and Thomas Kruse.

Boston University continues to be a great home for research, writing, and teaching. Our newly endowed Frederick S. Pardee School for Global Studies is a perfect environment for such work. I also greatly benefit from affiliations with the Center for Finance, Law, and Policy, the Pardee Center for the Study of the Longer Range Future, and the Latin American Studies Program. I thank Adil Najam, Joe Fewsmith, Cornel Ban, William Grimes, Scott Palmer, Susan Eckstein, Cornelius Hurley, Anthony Janetos, Cynthia Barakatt, Edward Cunningham, Dilip Mookerjee, Jon

Simon, Bruce Larson and countless others who have helped me better understand China, Latin America, and the global economy.

I am deeply indebted to John Wright. John serves as my literary agent and helped me craft a book proposal that led to the contract with Oxford University Press for this book. I thank John and David McBride, editor at Oxford, for their support, encouragement, and acceptance. I thank my colleague Andrew Bacevich for introducing me to John.

Let me share with you a secret. One of the reasons why I seized the opportunity to start examining China in Latin America had nothing to do with scholarship. It had to do with family. My wife of fifteen years now, Kelly Sims Gallagher, is a Tufts University professor and expert on China's energy and environmental policy. After writing a few papers on China and Latin America, I realized that this was an essential relationship to understand for scholars concerned about the political economy of Latin American development. I also realized that it was a way to travel with my wife and family. Our converging interests allowed us to bring our entire family to Tsinghua in 2010, with my son Theo even learning some Chinese. Kelly, Theo, and daughter Estelle are the inspiration for my life's work. I thank and dedicate this book to them.

LIST OF ABBREVIATIONS

BANDES	Venezuelan Economic and Social Development Bank
BNDES	Brazilian National Development Bank
BOC	Bank of China
BRICS	Brazil, Russia, India, China, and South Africa
CAF	Development Bank of Latin America
CCB	China Construction Bank
CCT	Conditional Cash Transfer
CDB	China Development Bank
CELAC	Community of Latin American and Caribbean States
CHEXIM	China Export-Import Bank
CHINALCO	Aluminum Corporation of China
CNOOC	China National Offshore Oil Corporation
CNPC	China National Petroleum Corporation
CCP	Communist Party of China
ECLAC	Economic Commission for Latin America and the Caribbean
EITI	Extractive Industries Transparency Initiative
EMBI+	Emerging Markets Bond Index Plus
FCCV	China-Venezuela Joint Fund
FDI	Foreign Direct Investment
FEES	Economic and Social Stabilization Fund

FOCAC	Forum on China-Africa Cooperation
FONDEN	Venezuelan National Development Fund
FTAA	Free Trade Area of the Americas
GDP	Gross Domestic Production
IBRD	International Bank for Reconstruction and Development
ICBC	Industrial and Commercial Bank of China
IDB	Inter-American Development Bank
IFI	International Financial Institution
ILO	International Labor Organization
IMF	International Monetary Fund
ISDS	Investor-State Dispute Settlement
ISI	Import Substitution Industry
LAC	Latin America and the Caribbean
LGFV	Local Government Finance Vehicle
LIBOR	London Interbank Offered Rate
MEP	Ministry of Environmental Protection
MIT	Massachusetts Institute of Technology
MOFCOM	Ministry of Foreign Commerce, China
NAFTA	North American Free Trade Agreement
NDRC	National Development and Reform Commission, China
OECD	Organization for Economic Cooperation and Development
OFDI	Overseas Foreign Direct Investment
PAE	PanAmerican Energy
PBOC	People's Bank of China
PRC	People's Republic of China
SEC	Securities and Exchange Commission, US
SINOPEC	China Petroleum and Chemical Corporation
SWF	Sovereign Wealth Fund
UN	United Nations

UNESCO	United Nations Educational, Scientific and Cultural Organization
US	Ex-Im United States Export-Import Bank
WTO	World Trade Organization

"Mo zhe shi tou guo he 摸着石头过河": "Crossing the river by feeling for stones"

"hu hui dai kuan 互惠贷款": mutual benefit loan

"shiyou, xindai, gongcheng yi lanzi hezuo xiangmu 石油信贷工程一揽子项目": cooperation package of oil, credit, and construction projects

The China Triangle

1

The China Triangle

Back in 2003, I was in Panama briefing negotiators to the Free Trade Area of the Americas—a trade pact that would have spanned the entire Western Hemisphere. One day en route to a breakfast meeting, I was struck by what appeared to be a thickly populated neighborhood buzzing with people looking Chinese but speaking Spanish. I asked my driver to say more, and he informed me that this was a neighborhood of Chino-Panameños, or Chinese Panamanians. At the end of the nineteenth century, the Panama Railroad Company imported thousands of Chinese workers to lay the tracks for the railway lines that would later lead to the construction of the Panama Canal. They settled in Panama afterward and live in these enclaves today. Hadn't I heard of Bruce Chen, one of the most famous Chino-Panameños, the driver added? Being a Bostonian, I asked if he could possibly be referring to the Bruce Chen who played for our Boston Red Sox for a short spell. The driver was so thrilled with Panamanian pride, and that I knew who Bruce Chen was, that he offered me my ride for free.

Over a century after they came to the Americas as laborers on large infrastructure projects, the Chinese are back in Latin America. This time, rather than coming to the Americas as laborers on such projects, the Chinese are now the bankers that are financing them. To name but a few, Chinese policy banks and entrepreneurs are pouring billions of dollars into the Twin Ocean Railroad Connection, a 5,000 km high-speed rail project that will connect Brazil's Atlantic coast to the Pacific coast of Peru, and into a controversial new canal through Nicaragua. These and many other projects will help get Latin America's soybeans, iron ore, copper, and petroleum to China faster, help China sell its products to Latin America, and gain new trading routes for both China and Latin America alike.

Latin America experienced a "China Boom" from 2003 until about 2013, when it started to taper. As luck would have it, during that time Latin America had just the natural resources that China needed to feed and fuel the Chinese growth miracle that started in the late 1970s. During the China Boom Latin America's economies grew by 3.6 percent per year, the best spurt since the region's state-led industrialization period that stretched from the 1930s until 1982. The China Boom couldn't have come at a better time, as the region's economies experienced slow growth and financial instability for over two decades under the so-called Washington Consensus. Indeed, the China Boom helped erase the increases in inequality in Latin America that accrued during the Washington Consensus period. The China Boom also helped many Latin American economies recover from the global financial crisis of 2008–2009. As the United States and Europe struggled to recover from the crisis, Latin American trade and investment with those partners waned. China filled the gap.

Latin America's economic prospects are taking a turn, however. China's voracious appetite for Latin American natural resources has begun to decline as China balances its economic model from export-led industry toward a more consumer-based economy. Latin American countries will have to consolidate gains made during the China Boom and implement sorely needed reforms that should have been put in place during the boom period. In so doing, Latin American leaders will not be operating in a vacuum. Latin America will have to navigate the China Triangle. At the top of the triangle tips is the United States, while China and Latin America form a new base of cooperation from left to right. But China has its own delicate relationship with the United States. The United States has a longstanding connection to the Americas. In addition to reforms at home, Latin American capitals will need to retool alliances with China to be more consistent with those reforms. At the same time, China's new alliance with Latin America is seen as a challenge to the United States, a nation that has long considered the Americas its backyard. To be successful, then, Latin America's reforms will have to operate in a manner that simultaneously builds on its relationships with China and the United States alike rather than picking one over the other. The benefits from such an approach would far exceed the costs of the escalating economic and political storm that otherwise could stir.

The China Boom in Context

Latin America's China Boom marks a new era of economic history in the Americas. As I note in the next chapter, from the turn of the nineteenth century to the Great Depression Latin America was a winner of what has been referred to as the "commodity lottery" period. Latin America had many of the key natural resources and commodities that were needed for Western Europe to boom into its industrial revolution. Silver, gold, coffee, wool, bananas, and more were exported from Latin America to Europe—and not only for consumption. This exporting also enabling the European peasantry to leave the farms for new factories. Indeed, Latin American governments and companies couldn't get those commodities out of the ground and overseas fast enough. Thus European (and US) companies invested heavily in Latin American railroads, infrastructure, and other activities to extract commodities out of the region and ship them back to to Europe. During the so-called commodity lottery Latin America's economies grew by 3.4 percent per year.

When the Depression hit in the United States the rest of the Americas were also badly hurt. Leading Latin American economists of the time, notably Raul Prebisch of the Central Bank of Argentina, observed that the prices of commodities were falling over the longer term. At the same time, the more advanced economic countries were fountains of industrial innovation whose products, at least initially, would be relatively more expensive. Prebisch and others saw these trends as a trap for Latin America. Given that the prices of Latin American exports would never match those of their imports, countries in the region would become ever more dependent on international debt flows to finance a modern way of living.

Prebisch's observations kicked off the second modern era of Latin American economic development, that of state-led industrialization. From the Great Depression until the early 1980s, the nation-state played a major role in laying infrastructure and boosting industries that would substitute for the imports from the United States and Europe. The hope was that Latin America would produce consumer goods for consumption and export, and thus break the cycle of dependency feared by Prebisch and others. The state-led industrialization period remains the best period on record in terms of growth—at almost 5 percent per annum. However, the period was also associated with accentuated inequalities, both economic in terms of wealth and income and politically in terms of dictatorships and a lack of democracy. What is more, macroeconomic mismanagement during the period ultimately led to a financial crisis in the 1980s that swept the whole region and led to the demise of the state-led period.

In response to the crises of the 1980s the region was forced to adopt the Washington Consensus, the dominant economic paradigm that ended with a major financial crisis in Argentina in 2002. Still very much alive in some countries and political parties in Latin America to this day, the basic tenet of the Washington Consensus was to reduce the role of the state in economic affairs. By pushing the government aside and opening up to global trade and finance, the idea was that markets would develop and thrive, and lead to prosperity. The Washington Consensus has been extremely controversial both economically and politically. In economic terms growth in this period was slowest of the eras mentioned, at just 2.4 percent per year, with inequality accentuating even more than in the state-led industrialization era. However, during the Washington Consensus period Latin American governments put an end to high inflation and fiscal irresponsibility. What is more, the period ushered in a return to democracy—the region's hallmark achievement of the late twentieth century. Nonetheless, the policies of the Washington Consensus left the region very vulnerable to external shocks, and at the end of the century a wave of financial crises hit the region—in Mexico, Brazil, Uruguay, Argentina, and beyond. In response to lackluster performance and crisis, many of the region's newfound democracies threw the beacons of the Washington Consensus out of office.

Despite the controversies surrounding the Washington Consensus in Latin America and the fact that it has fallen out of favor in most academic circles, official policy from the US government has become more steadfast for the Washington Consensus, not less. After bailing out Latin American countries in the 1980s, Washington-based financial institutions such as the International Monetary Fund and World Bank conditioned such loans on privatization, liberalization, and deregulation. In the 1990s and 2000s Washington minted the Washington Consensus into numerous and binding trade and investment treaties—most notably the North American Free Trade Agreement (NAFTA) and treaties with Chile, Peru, Central American countries, and more. Despite a mixed record of these treaties, the United States pressed the region for a full-blown treaty of the entire hemisphere—the Free Trade Area of the Americas (FTAA). Eventually the region said enough is enough. But the United States keeps pressing on. When Xi Jinping traveled to Latin America in 2013 with a big financial package for many of the region's governments, the United States sent Vice President Joseph Biden and offered yet another trade agreement. The region's leaders have been reluctant to further bind their economies to Washington Consensus policies—in large part because they believe they have an alternative in China.

Latin America's China Boom

China came to the rescue, at least for many South American countries. Like Latin America during the Washington Consensus, China has been opening its economy to global market forces since the late 1970s and early 1980s. Unlike Latin America, however, China was able to do so on its own terms. China did not reform in reaction to a major external crisis in the way that Latin America did, and did not have Washington-based experts dictating what the reforms should look like. China's was a globalization centered around the saying of its great reformer, Deng Xiaoping—"Crossing the river by feeling for stones" (Mo zhe shi tou guo he 摸着石头过河). Instead of diving head first into globalization as Latin America did, China sequenced the liberalization of some sectors of its economy while fostering other sectors until they were ready to compete on a global basis.

China's strategy paid off. China grew at over 10 percent per year for over 30 years, the fastest and strongest growth ever recorded. In

2001 China entered the World Trade Organization (WTO) and soon began purchasing and selling with the rest of the world at a breakneck pace as well. Latin America was no exception. As China has risen, it has been guzzling oil from Venezuela, Ecuador, and Mexico to fuel its expanding fleet of cars, trucks, and container ships. China has wired more than half the world's consumer electronics products with copper from Chile and Peru. Much of the steel in China's new cities is made with iron ore from Brazil at their core. As standards of living have risen, the Chinese eat more beef from cattle that are fed soya beans from Argentina and Brazil. In turn, Chinese companies have flocked to the Americas to invest in these commodities, backed by China's state-run development banks.

At the turn of the twenty-first century, Latin American trade with China was only 1 percent of total Latin American trade, $12 billion. By 2013 it was $289 billion and China stood as the number one trading partner for many of Latin America's biggest economies such as Brazil, Peru, Chile, and others. China's demand for Latin American commodities had double that impact, however. Because China's consumption of these goods made those goods more scarce, the prices of such goods went up in the global marketplace, allowing the region to enjoy a massive commodity boom. The commodity boom triggered investment in the region's commodity sector by Chinese companies and other global firms alike. The rate of new trade and foreign investment into the region was both remarkable and welcome.

Perhaps most remarkable is that China has provided massive amounts of finance to Latin American governments for infrastructure, mining, and energy projects. According to the China–Latin America Finance Database that I publish with the Washington-based Inter-American Dialogue, China has provided upward of $119 billion in loans and lines of credit to Latin American governments since 2003.

In many ways China's appetite for Latin American commodities has been a savior for the Americas, especially in the wake of the global financial crisis when trade and finance from the West dried up. Latin America rode the coattails of the boom in China, growing at an annual rate of 3.6 percent from 2003 to 2013. This return to economic growth brought a rise to an emerging middle class in many Latin American countries. What is more, for the first time in a century Latin American governments started to put a dent in rising inequality. That stands in stark contrast to the previous two decades dominated by the Washington Consensus. Under the Washington Consensus growth was a much slower 2.4 percent, and inequality increased.

In the wake of the 9/11 attacks and then after the global financial meltdown that originated in the United States, Washington turned to other shores. Most of the countries in Latin America had made a strong transition to democracy, did not harbor terrorists, and had been following Washington's economic orders. While the United States wasn't paying attention, Latin America quickly became of the utmost strategic importance for China—as a source for many of the key natural resources it needs to grow its economy and the appetites of more than a billion people.

Saving the China Boom

This book tracks Latin America's China Boom in context and argues that Latin Americans have not capitalized on the China Boom in many ways. As the infamous "resource curse" predicts, during commodity booms money pours into the commodity sector. Commodity booms create windfalls for the commodity sector, but few jobs. What is more, it causes the exchange rate of countries to appreciate, making noncommodity exports more expensive.

That's what happened in many Latin American countries during the China Boom. Money poured in, commodity producers got rich, and noncommodity exports became less competitive. Indeed, 78 percent of Latin American manufacturing was under threat from their Chinese counterparts in world markets during the boom.

What is more, the infrastructure, energy, and mining projects that were the source of so much investment from the Chinese and beyond are endemic to environmental degradation and social conflict in Latin America. The World Bank estimates that the economic costs of environmental degradation during the China Boom were an annual 8.6 percent of GDP. As Chinese, US, European, Canadian, and other companies have flocked to the region for its resources they deforested the Amazon, polluted waterways, and sometimes mistreated indigenous and local communities while Latin American governments turned a blind eye.

The curse has a cure, but the Latin Americans squandered much of the opportunity. Nations such as Norway have navigated their way through the curse by parking windfall profits into special funds to be reinvested into export competitiveness, financial stability, environmental protection, and long-run growth. Not so in Latin America. According to the International Monetary Fund (IMF), Latin Americans saved less from this boom than in past ones at the margin, and United Nations calculations show that government fiscal revenue did not increase in proportion to the windfall either. It is thus no surprise that investment in the region was so low overall. Economists say that nations need to invest 25 percent of their gross domestic product per year to achieve stable and strong growth (China has invested well over 40 percent per year over the past 30 years), but Latin Americans averaged a paltry 20 percent— less than one percentage point more than during the Washington Consensus period.

The lack of investment in long-run growth and sustainable development will hurt the region as the headwinds that carried the Americas for a decade start to turn. The Chinese economy is making a shaky transition toward a more consumer-based economy. For one, this brings a more modest level of growth. Whereas China was growing at 10 percent a year, that figure is now closer to 6 or 7 percent per year. Second, China will eventually be shifting toward more consumer-based products, rather than natural resources. It is not clear if Latin American manufacturing exports will be competitive enough to seize the opportunity to meet Chinese demand for such products. Finally, China's transition will prove to be a tricky one, and has been marked with financial instability. Slow growth, different growth, and increasing instability have put fear into the finance ministries of Latin America.

Time for Reform

There is still time for Latin America to put in place the proper reforms in order to finally sustain stable growth and capitalize on China's rise. It would be foolish to replace the Washington Consensus with a Beijing Consensus. In many ways Latin America was *already there* during its state-led industrialization period, and is *beyond* that now. Modern Latin American economic history is characterized by periods where there was arguably too much state involvement in the economy—the state-led industrialization period—and then too little state involvement under the Washington Consensus. It is now time to take the best from both and embed the state in a way that enables a well-functioning marketplace that can deliver growth, employment, inclusion, and sustainable development. Key to doing so will be building on the region's comparative advantage in primary commodities and strengthening institutions to capture more of the windfall during boom times. The proceeds will have to be invested into three clusters: sustainable infrastructure, innovation and competitiveness, and people and the environment.

Governments will have to capture the windfalls through fiscal reforms. The fruits of reform to be invested into infrastructure, innovation, and the environment can flow through commodity stabilization and sovereign wealth funds, national development banks, and targeted fiscal expenditure. The target and design of all new investment should be the product of a process where the state and the private sector jointly identify the binding constraints for economic opportunities and craft policy to break those constraints loose in an inclusive and sustainable manner. Perhaps the biggest challenge is for the region to put in place the proper checks and balances alongside reforms. Both the private sector and the state have to be made more accountable for reforms to move ahead and work.

Latin America's China Triangle

Any serious reform will have to engage with the outside world and global economy. That means navigating the China Triangle: capitalizing on and strengthening ties to the two largest economies of the world, China and the United States.

In January of 2015 the Chinese sat down with the Latin American region as a whole and put together a cooperation plan with the region that on paper could be a perfect complement to Latin American reform. China pledged to boost trade to $500 billion and investment to $250 billion over the next decade. To demonstrate that it means business, China created a new set of funds of upward of $35 billion for infrastructure investment in Latin America.

China's pledge of new trade and finance will be key for the region to draw on during the downturn. After the decade-long China Boom, the IMF put the region's growth for 2014 at less than

1.3 percent, for 2015 at less than 1 percent, and estimates that Latin America's economy may not improve much more over the next half decade. In addition to trade, new financing might even provide Latin America with the fiscal space it needs for infrastructure investment—which has been prescribed by the IMF as a key target for investment during the downturn. Indeed, according to United Nations, the region faces an annual infrastructure gap—a need for new and upgraded roads, ports, energy systems, and communications networks—that amounts to 6.2 percent of GDP. What is more, Chinese finance comes with few strings attached. China may tacitly require that Chinese companies have a hand in some projects, but has avoided meddling in domestic policy. This is an attractive feature for many Latin American governments, but the onus is on them to put it to productive use.

The new joint cooperation plan also puts a premium on cooperation on science, technology, and innovation policy (later in 2015 establishing a $30 billion dollar fund to execute these goals). In addition to the sharing of technology, China pledges to start a dialogue about the establishment of Chinese industrial parks across Latin America. If similar agreements with Africa are an indication, China means business, having established at least six industrial parks in that continent by 2015, modeled after the special economic zones that were an engine of the Chinese growth miracle. If Latin America puts in place the proper reforms that enable such zones to benefit the broader economy, China's industrial parks can help diversify Latin American economies and make them more competitive. Latin American exchange rates will be depreciating relative to their China Boom peaks as well. That will make the prices of Latin American exports more affordable across the world—and their industries more competitive. New industrial opportunities, competitive exchange rates, and an increasing demand for consumer goods in China can be harnessed into diversified growth for Latin America.

China's cooperation plan with Latin America also boasts a built-in dialogue on environmental cooperation. Recognizing the environmental and social impacts of its trade and investment with the region, this can be a forum to enable China's firms and financial institutions to upgrade their social and environmental safeguards. Such an outcome will not only benefit people and the environment across the Americas, but also help China's bottom line. Environmental and social conflict in the Americas can trigger costly delays and shutdowns that cut into profits and the image of China's vision for South–South cooperation.

The Latin America–United States economic relationship will need to be transformed from a patronage to a partnership. The United States has to let go of the notion that Washington is the place to devise economic policy in Latin America. In so doing, Latin American governments should re-engage with the United States, benefiting from the more diverse economic opportunities the United States has to offer, as well as the social and environmental norms that the United States practices when at its best. The United States has put one good foot forward when it reformed its Cuba policy, taking that nation off official terrorist lists and reaching out a hand of partnership. The United States has also made more realistic gestures with respect to immigration reform. In these moves, the United States has set a higher bar for itself moving forward—and it will have to live up to that bar to foster successful relationships with the region in the future.

Over 80 years ago, when the United States was concerned about rising European influence in Latin America, the US Export-Import Bank was established. The bank has been not only providing financing Latin American governments for industrial and infrastructure projects all this time; it provides opportunities to strengthen ties among US exporters and Latin American importers, thus strengthening value chains in the Western Hemisphere. At the bank's founding there was a consensus among those in the Roosevelt administration concerned about geopolitical aspects of Europe in Latin America, and a private sector that wanted access to Latin America's capital goods markets. In this context Nelson Rockefeller, a Republican, led an effort on the bank that led to a tripling of its financing to Latin America. Ironically, today the US Export-Import Bank is under threat from Congress to be eliminated—at a point when there should be a renewed discussion about reinvigorating it.

At this writing, the composition of US–Latin American trade and investment is more diverse and thus more supportive of necessary Latin American reforms than China's trade with the region. China's economic relationship with Latin America remains one that is based on natural resource–based commodities. It is also important to note that for Mexico and Central America, US trade with those areas dwarfs that of China. What is more, Latin America is integrated into US value chains in the manufacturing sector, as well as in services.

In keeping with the need to upgrade social and environmental safeguards, the United States also has a lot to offer. The US-backed World Bank and Inter-American Development Bank now have some of the strongest social and environmental safeguards operating in the world economy, as does the US Export-Import Bank. What is more, through a new executive order by President Barack Obama, the United States has pledged that all its development finance will be more climate-change resilient.

The diversity of US–Latin American trade and the social and environmental safeguards of US best practice could be more beneficial for Latin America if reforms were made to many of the trade and investment treaties that the United States has with Latin American countries. Written during the Washington Consensus period, these treaties leave countries without the proper flexibility needed to invest in innovation and export competitiveness. Also, unlike arrangements under the WTO, US treaties grant US companies the right to pursue legal claims against host governments looking to upgrade social and environmental regulations in their countries. Under US treaties, US companies have taken Latin American countries to task for putting in place taxes on the windfall profits from commodities exports and for reducing toxic pollution and deforestation in the Amazon—the very pillars of needed reform. A new era of US trade policy should ensue that gives both sides the breathing space they need to diversify and grow, while upgrading social and environmental policy.

While China and the United States can help Latin American reforms meet their objectives, only Latin America can put in place the reforms themselves. It is not every day that a country like China rises in a manner that just so happens to demand increasing amounts of Latin American resources. In fact, the last time it happened was over 100 years ago when Latin America won the commodity lottery that formed the backdrop of the industrial revolution in the West. If Latin America wants to truly win the China lottery in a manner that can help put the region on a long-run path for sustainable development, governments in the region will have to put in place major reforms while navigating the China Triangle.

2

A Tale of Two Globalizations

In early 2006 I took my mother to visit descendants of our ancestors in Italy. There we were told that about half of our ancestors
went to Argentina at the turn of the nineteenth century, and the
other half went to the United States. That was typical, as the
prospects for Latin America seemed as promising as those of
the United States at the time. Latin America was booming in the
late nineteenth century, and over 6 million Europeans migrated
to the region to get in on the action.[1] Migration wasn't limited to
migrants from Europe, however. As already noted, some of the
first Chinese came to the Americas to help build the Panama Canal
in the late 1800s.

At the turn of the seventeenth century China was the hegemon of the Eastern world, enjoying similar standards of living to
those of Latin America's colonizers. Latin America was then in the
throes of Western colonization. Since that heyday China has been
looking to regain its place at the top of the world economy, while
Latin America has been searching for an economic path that will
help the region catch up to the rest of the world once and for all.
Latin America's quest has remained elusive. China's growth miracle is the most successful on record.

But we are getting ahead of ourselves. Let's rewind a bit. Latin America and China have had similar economic policy goals since the middle of the twentieth century. From midcentury to the late 1970s, most Latin American countries and China both attempted to transform their agrarian societies into industrial ones via an inward-looking strategy of import protections and a heavy hand for government in the economy. By the early 1980s both China and Latin America had scrapped that strategy for one that looked to globalize with the world economy. Each moved to make the invisible hand of the market guide the economy, and looked to integrate with world markets as a way forward.

By the turn of the twentieth century Latin America was still striving for that goal, though it made some notable improvements. At the same time, China's domestic reform made it poised to jump into the world economy and leapfrog over Latin America to become the biggest economy of the world by 2015. Indeed, China overshot its goal, and must work to clean up some of the mess that came with the fastest and strongest growth miracle in world history. As China reformed and grew, however, Latin America was able to ride China's coattails.

Latin America's Elusive Quest for Growth

Latin American economic history from the late nineteenth to the twenty-first century can be divided into three distinct eras. In every era, nations in the region developed a new recipe for economic prosperity that policymakers thought held great promise for the region. Each era had some notable accomplishments, but each largely failed to fully deliver on its promise. Table 2.1 lists the three eras of Latin American economic history: the commodity lottery period from 1870 to the Great Depression, the period of state-led

Table 2.1 Latin America's Growth Record

Period	GDP growth	GDP per capita growth
Commodity Lottery (1870–1929)	3.4%	1.5%
State-led industrialization (1930s–1980)	4.9%	2.2%
Washington Consensus (1980–2002)	2.4%	0.5%
China Boom (2003–2013)	3.6%	2.4%

industrialization that followed, and the Washington Consensus that ended the twentieth century.

The Commodity Lottery

The late nineteenth and early twentieth centuries are known as the period of the great Northern European "takeoff" from the rest of the world that was soon followed by an even greater takeoff by the United States. The magnitude of economic growth by the West during this period had been unrivaled. The world marveled as the West rapidly industrialized its economies—and countries across the world rode on the back of this success.[2] The industrial revolution in the West caused a great "supercycle" of demand for energy and raw materials that also shot prices up to new highs.[3] Latin America was a winner of the commodity lottery that ensued. Latin America's geography met Western economic demand. As the West took off so did its demand for copper and iron ore from Peru and Chile, beef and hides from Argentina, fertilizers from Peru, coffee from Brazil, sugar from Cuba, cocoa from Venezuela and Ecuador, tobacco from Colombia, and beyond.[4]

This triggered a modest takeoff in Latin America as well. Relative to the income growth from independence in the 1820s up to 1870 (which was only 0.3 percent per year), the region's 1.5 percent annual growth in incomes was significant.[5] More telling is the total growth rate, of 3.4 percent. Per capita incomes are the total amount of GDP divided by the population of a country. Latin America was (and is) a highly unequal place, so some pockets were among the richest in the world. Indeed, the Latin American commodities sector was in such high demand that Latin Americans alone could not get enough of the commodities to market fast enough. Latin American countries lacked the infrastructure to get products to market, and lacked the laborers to do the work.

The period thus marked the first significant surges in foreign investment and migration to the region in modern times. The British, the Europeans, and later the North Americans laced the Americas with railways to help get commodities to port. In 1840, there were only 478 kilometers of rail across Latin America. By 1913 there were 107,266 kilometers of rail across the region—enough to circle the entire earth close to two and a half times. In 1913, one fourth of the entire world's rail was located in Latin America.[6]

The commodity lottery period is notable given that the region integrated with the world economy in terms of trade, investment, and migration. However, the commodity lottery period locked Latin America into the commodity dependency that started during the colonial period and continues to this day. It is also seen as the period when the region locked in its grave levels of inequality. Based on income and wealth surveys, economists use an indicator referred to as the "GINI coefficient" to measure inequality. Ranging between zero and one, the closer a measure is to one, the more unequal it is. In 1870 Latin America was already considered highly unequal and had a GINI of 0.58. By 1920 the GINI for Latin America was 0.72. Since that era Latin America has been the most unequal region on earth.[7]

State-Led Industrialization

Have you ever flown in a smaller, regional, passenger jet? Whether you went from New York City to Washington, DC, from Buenos Aires to Montevideo, or from Shanghai to Beijing, there is a very good chance that you were aboard a plane manufactured by the Brazilian aerospace giant Embraer. Embraer is the third largest airplane maker in the world, and has corned the market for smaller commercial, corporate, and military aircraft. Embraer got its wings from the Brazilian government during the state-led industrialization era. Whereas the invisible hand of the global marketplace tugged Latin American economies along during the commodity lottery era, the heavy hand of the government transformed Latin American economies into producers of manufactured goods and services, industrial cities, and middle classes.

Relative to the globalizing turn that ended the nineteenth century, many of the world's nations turned inward after the Great Depression and World War II.[8] In the West, the post–World War II era until the late 1970s is seen as a period of "embedded liberalism." Free markets were acknowledged to be the best way to allocate resources, but markets were reined in by strong financial regulations to prevent and mitigate financial crises, by strong wage and labor standards to ensure domestic demand for a growing production base, and by limits on global trade and financial flows.[9] The period is still looked back at as the "golden age of capitalism," where economic growth soared and social protection increased.[10]

Interestingly, Latin Americans spawned their own brand of state-led capitalism during that period—though Latin America's version had a heavier hand for government and had less interest in global trade. Two economists from Latin America born at the end of the nineteenth century, Raul Prebisch from Argentina and Arthur Lewis from Saint Lucia, developed a set of ideas that set Latin America apart from the Western embedded liberal tradition. Prebisch was concerned that the terms of trade between developing and industrialized nations would lock the developing world into backwardness unless significant structural transformation occurred across the developing world. Prebisch saw the industrialized nations as booming markets with high wages and increasingly sophisticated manufactured and consumer goods. In the lottery of the global marketplace developing countries stood to gain only insofar as they supplied cheaper and less sophisticated commodities to the rich countries to use in their factories and homes. There would be no way, then, according to Prebisch, for developing nations to ever afford a modern set of goods and services by paying for them through commodity exports. Thus, said Prebisch and others, Latin Americans and other developing countries needed to breed their own manufacturing sectors and shield them from competition from rich country companies until they were strong enough to compete on their own. Markets alone would not make such a transformation, so the state had to step in.[11]

Arthur Lewis saw the world economy in a similar manner and argued that the solution was for the state to create an environment where a modern sector of manufacturing and other capital-intensive economic activity could flourish. If the wages in that sector were sufficiently higher than in the bloated rural sector, then laborers would flock from the countryside into newfound factories and boost production. With strong regulations on foreign competition, and regulations that gave incentive for the new capitalists to reinvest their profits back into the modern sector rather than investing it in (more profitable) enterprises in the West, a nation could eventually build up industrial capacity to compete and prosper.[12] Lewis went on to win the Nobel Prize in economics.

Harvard University economists Hollis Chenery and Albert O. Hirschman further developed these ideas by pinpointing the kinds of industries that would be the most appropriate for the state to support. These authors stressed the need to target and develop sectors of the economy such as automobiles and steel plants—given the large and increasing number of inputs into those sectors that could enable markets to develop and link to other dynamic parts in an economy.[13] Chenery also worked for the US Agency for International Development and went on to become a vice president at the World Bank. Hirschman was an advisor to each of those institutions and to nations such as Colombia. These ideas became mainstream, with the United Nations, the World Bank, and the United States advocating for and financially supporting state-led industrialization in Latin America and beyond.[14]

The United States publicly supported state-led industrialization in Latin America, and not just on paper. Prominent US Treasury officials at the time stated that "the standard of living of the Brazilian people cannot, in our opinion, be raised until or unless Brazil embarks upon these productive investments."[15] What is more, in 1938 the United States declared a "financial Monroe doctrine" for Latin America—not only supporting Latin America's state-led model in public, but providing long-term loans for industrial projects across the region. The United States had just created the US Export-Import Bank, which with Congressional approval financed steel mills in Brazil and beyond. The rationale for the United States was threefold. First, the Roosevelt Administration looked to export its New Deal policies through a "good neighbor policy with the region." Second, it saw Latin American prosperity as a way to maintain the Monroe doctrine and stem the threat of European (especially German) influence growing in the region. Third, Roosevelt, Republicans, and the private sector alike saw a growing and industrializing Latin America as a future source for US capital exports.[16]

With the support of its northern neighbor, Latin America ran with these ideas and created an elaborate set of institutions, many of which survive to this day. Countries across the region attempted to manage the prices of primary commodities through domestic policy and global treaties to limit supply. By limiting supply, they could ensure that prices and profits were relatively high and hoped to escape the massive price drops that followed depression and war. With profits from commodities they created state-owned enterprises and supported private companies by providing cheap credit from central banks or newly formed national development banks. They further protected and supported the industrialization effort by encouraging foreign direct investment into strategic sectors, by protecting new sectors from foreign competition, and by steering profits back into productive sectors rather than allowing it to flow abroad.[17]

By many counts, this era was a great success. In terms of economic growth and the diversification of the economy away from primary commodities, the era remains the most successful for Latin America. During the period the region grew at 4.9 percent per year, and productivity growth sped at 2 percent per year. Brazil and Mexico emerged as the powerhouses of the era, growing their economies at 7 and 6.6 percent respectively.[18]

The state-led industrialization period was also plagued by major mistakes and shortcomings. Macroeconomic mismanagement was rife, especially after the discovery of new oil fields in the 1970s. Seeing endless profits from high oil prices, Mexico, Brazil, and others went on a borrowing spree to fund state-led industrialization. Global banks, flush with petrodollars deposited by oil-rich nations in the Middle East making windfall profits from high prices, were more than happy to accommodate. When the cost of borrowing shot up and prices for oil plummeted in the early 1980s, the region suffered a financial crisis that devastated Latin America—even more so than the Great Depression. The 1980s is always referred to as Latin America's "lost decade."[19]

Although Latin America's state-led period can be credited for structural transformation and technological learning relative to Latin America's past, the region did poorly relative to the other nations that also embarked upon state-supported industrialization. Indeed, Asian nations such as Japan, South Korea, and Taiwan all had higher rates of growth and transformation during the period and under a similar model. While Asian nations also relied on the heavy hand of government, they relied less on domestic demand to fuel the expansion of industrial production. Where the Latin Americans were "export pessimists," the Asian tigers focused more on exports. Indeed, government support was conditioned on exporting. This had the advantage of breeding even more techno-logical sophistication and international competitiveness.[20]

Exports as an ultimate goal helped put a lid on corruption in Asia, which was much more prevalent in Latin America. Brazil incubated computer companies and thrust them on the domes-tic market. While the computers were never competitive enough to export, with no other choice, Brazilians preferred their subpar computers over pen and paper! But sole reliance on the domestic market put a drag on government resources as more and more of those resources went into companies and cronies. Moreover, the lack of competition in the Brazilian computer market gave little incentive to innovate. When Brazil finally opened the sector to foreign competition, the Brazilian computer companies were wiped out in a second. South Korea and Taiwan's computer giants like Samsung and Acer also received significant support from their governments. While they each had their share of cronyism and corruption, they also had to produce their goods at the technological frontier in order to export. When state support was let go in the Asian case, the firms could already compete.[21]

The period of state-led industrialization for many countries in Latin America was also characterized by bloody dictatorships that suppressed workers and human rights in the name of power and industrialization. The political fallout and legacy of that era plagues many Latin American nations to this day and accentuated many of the built-in social inequities such as poverty and inequality.

Washington to the Rescue

The financial crises of the 1980s put Latin American countries on their knees. One by one, most countries in the region turned to Washington for money and ideas. Hence the next two decades were the era of the Washington Consensus. The World Bank, the International Monetary Fund, the US Treasury, and even the White House repeatedly stepped in to provide financial support across the Americas—on condition that each country undergo a series of neoliberal reforms aimed at reducing the role of the state in economic affairs.[22]

Table 2.2 boils these policies down to five key characteristics. First, in exchange for rescue packages Latin American governments agreed to limit government budget deficits, to dismantle national development banks, and to shift subsidies away from big industrial projects. Second, central banks in the region also kept their interest rates relatively high to tame inflation. Third, nations fully liberalized all forms of foreign investment flows—not only allowing foreign multinationals to set up factories, but also allowing foreign financial firms to enter and exit stock, bond, currency, and later derivatives markets. Fourth, nations moved to fully floating exchange rates. Rather than fixing the value of a nation's

Table 2.2 A Tale of Two Globalizations: Core Policies
of Latin America and China

Latin America and the Washington Consensus	China's Managed Globalization
1. Fiscal conservatism and 'horizontal' policy for industry	1. Public investment in infrastructure and strategic industry
2. Inflation targeting, relatively high interest rates	2. Directed credit toward structural transformation
3. Fully open capital accounts	3. Selectively open capital account
4. Floating exchange rate	4. Fixed and competitive exchange rate
5. Free trade and deep integration	5. Free trade

exchange rate, nations allowed the exchange rate of their currencies to be governed by the laws of supply and demand. Fifth, all Latin American members became members of the World Trade Organization and thus committed to free trade. Some nations, such as Mexico, Central American countries, Peru, Chile, and others, also committed to much deeper trade agreements that further slashed regulations on innovation and intellectual property, subsidies, investment, and in other areas. Indeed, many governments in the region even further liberalized and deregulated their economies than Washington prescribed. The Washington Consensus had not gone so far as to recommend the complete openness of Latin American financial systems, and at the time was not recommending fully floating exchange rates.[23]

This package of policies brought considerable benefit to Latin American economies. First and foremost, governments in the region were able to tame the massive budget deficits and runaway inflation that had long plagued the region. Second, Latin American countries abandoned the export pessimism characteristic of the previous period, and began to engage with the world economy again. Indeed, one of the poster children of the Washington Consensus,

Mexico, went so far as to lock in reforms to open trade and investment under the 1994 North American Free Trade Agreement (NAFTA) with the United States and Canada. Third, many social indicators began to improve. By the turn of the century more than 90 percent of Latin Americans had a primary education, and 70 percent had secondary education. Ninety percent had access to safe drinking water, and the mortality rate of children under five was slashed to 25 percent (from well over half).[24]

On the whole, however, the era of the Washington Consensus did not live up to its promise. Economic growth was the slowest of all the eras discussed here, at 0.5 percent per annum. Even if one discounts the lost decade of the 1980s as an adjustment period to the neoliberal regime, per capita GDP growth would still be the lowest on record, at a mere 1.1 percent annually. Mexico saw incomes remain stagnant at 0.8 percent annually during the period, compared to 3.6 percent during the state-led industrialization era. Mexico's productivity levels have also been on the decline since 1990s.[25] And the growth that did occur did not produce the kinds of jobs that give families security and boost domestic demand. By 2002 almost 48 percent of all the jobs in Latin America were in the informal market, such as selling food and consumer goods on the streets in a manner that is untaxed and unregulated.[26] Gone were many jobs in manufacturing. Whereas the manufacturing sector averaged close to a third of the gross domestic product of Latin America in 1978, that share dropped to 16 percent by 2002, and Asia became the hub for manufacturing in the developing world.[27] Moreover, the productivity of manufacturing and economies as a whole was on the decline during the Washington Consensus. The loss of jobs and technological dynamism accentuated inequality during the period—with the few connected to global markets gaining ground while many others lost out. The GINI coefficient, discussed earlier, was at (still high) 0.49 in 1980, and by 2002 had risen again to 0.53.[28]

Finally, the premature deregulation of financial and capital markets in Latin America made the region very prone to external shocks. When global interest rates were low and growth outlooks or commodity prices in Latin America looked promising, foreign finance would surge into the region. While Latin America desperately needed new investment, the investment that came was often too hot to handle—in the form of short-term capital flows into currency, bond, stock, and derivatives markets rather than in roads, factories, and modern services. These surges of inflows tended to push up exchange rates and make Latin American exports less attractive. Strong currencies led to large current account deficits and the need to take on ever-larger amounts of debt. More often than not, the debt would be denominated in US dollars. That seems like a bargain when your currency is strong. When external conditions change, such as interest rate hikes in the United States, there was often a sudden stop of capital inflows into the region's economies, followed by the flight of capital out of the region. These swings would cause Latin American currencies to rapidly depreciate—yet the debt that companies and governments accrued during the boom still would have to be paid in dollars even though the value of the Mexican peso or the Brazilian real would be worth just a fraction of what it was during a boom. By the turn of the century, these surges and sudden stops had become a key characteristic of most of the more dynamic Latin American economies such as Argentina, Brazil, Chile, Colombia, Peru, Mexico, and Uruguay. In many cases such swings triggered financial crises, as was the case in Mexico (1994), Brazil (1998), and Argentina (2001–2002).[29]

Moreover, the relatively high interest rates, free trade policies, and poor policies from the past started a hollowing out of the region's manufacturing industries. Latin American nations, especially powerhouses like Brazil and Mexico, had build up significant domestic industrial bases during the state-led industrialization period. However, many of the firms that benefited from the era were shielded from competition. When countries liberalized their trade regimes and raised interest rates, domestic firms could not compete with new imports and could not obtain credit to invest and upgrade their facilities to compete. The low investment by the private sector was accentuated by the extreme cutbacks in government investment relative to the past period. The result was an investment rate of 20 percent of GDP. Most economists, however, believe that it is necessary to sustain a 25 percent rate for decades in order to accelerate economic growth.

Thus as the century turned, Latin America had made some significant gains but also faced new risks. By the turn of the century Latin Americans could boast fiscal discipline, low inflation, and a commitment to improving social well-being. Yet the region could not live up to its promises because of volatile growth rates, weak levels of investment and productivity, declining levels of industrialization and innovation, weak competitiveness, persistent inequality, and significant environmental degradation.[30] Then, in 2001 a nation of over 1 billion people leaped into the world economy through accession to the World Trade Organization. That country was China—a country that would define the latest era in Latin American economic history.

The Return of the Dragon

China has returned to its status as one of the leading economies on the planet. During the early part of the Qing Dynasty (which spanned from 1644 to 1911), China was the hegemon of the Eastern world and some Chinese enjoyed a standard of living similar to what could be found in Great Britain at the time. For a variety of reasons, by the mid-nineteenth century China was on the decline. By 1950, however, after almost a century of civil strife, foreign conflict, and revolution, China's aims and policies began to mimic those of their Latin American counterparts. Like Latin American countries, from 1950 to the end of the 1970s the Chinese engaged in an inward-looking strategy of heavy industrialization. Like Latin America, by the early 1980s China had shifted more toward free markets and sought to integrate the economy with the rest of the world. China has proven to be a far better globalizer.

Observers tend to forget that China was among the most prosperous and powerful countries in the world in the seventeenth and eighteenth centuries, while Latin America was under colonization. China had a large and self-sufficient domestic market reinforced by selling ceramics, silk, and textiles to the Western World—in exchange for increasing amounts of silver.[31] Indeed, by 1820 China's economy amounted to one-third of the entire economic output of the earth. Latin America, at the time, produced 2.2 percent.[32]

By the middle of the nineteenth century, however, China failed to keep up with the dramatic developments that happened in the West and began to decline. Great Britain discovered large coal deposits that were close to urban centers of manufacturing and fostered rapid technological change. China had substantial amounts of coal, but the coal was far from the centers of power and commerce. Moreover, the West could more easily shift workers from agriculture and crafts into manufacturing because its colonies—such as those in Latin America—could be used as a source of cheap foodstuffs and raw materials to feed people and factories.[33]

As the West's rise spurred a global commodity boom in the nineteenth century, Latin America won the commodity lottery and China lost. Whereas Latin Americans exported the beef, coffee, fertilizers, silver, and other key goods to the West and grew by 3.4 percent per year, China imported opium and saw its vast surplus of silver disappear. Chinese economic growth from 1870 to

1929 is estimated to have been 0.8 percent per year.[34] This reversal of fortune was a factor that triggered internal social strife and military conflict with Britain and Japan. China was being left behind, having gone from 33 percent of world economic output in 1820 to 9 percent in 1913. Latin America's share was still small but was going in the right direction, growing from 2.2 percent in 1820 to 4.4 in 1913.[35]

There was some promise for the Chinese economy during the onset of the young republic, but the country's economic prospects were sidelined by war with Japan and internal revolution. The establishment of the People's Republic of China (PRC) in 1949 led to a completely new model of economic activity aimed to catch up with the rest of the world and regain China's sense of eminence. The PRC's first three decades were a mixed success at best.

Like the Latin Americans, the Chinese realized they needed to transform themselves from a society based on peasant agriculture to one based on modern industry. Also like the Latin Americans, the Chinese thought they would not be able to compete with Western industry and therefore looked inward for the sources of industrialization and growth. China embarked upon a period of what has been referred to as "big push" industrialization, where the primary effort of the socialist government was to coordinate the large-scale industrialization of the economy. The Chinese government accrued and distributed the country's savings into the establishment of state-owned enterprises that were the primary source of economic activity in the country. Large steel mills, smelters, coal plants, and factories began lacing a countryside previously dominated by household-based farms for centuries.[36]

If industrialization alone was all one assessed, China's big push fared far better than Latin America's. In a fairly short amount of time China was able to start along the road that Arthur Lewis outlined as necessary for development—transforming the structure of the economy from one solely based on agriculture to one with a strong manufacturing base. By the late 1970s manufacturing output as a percentage of the total Chinese economy rose to 40 percent, compared to 28 percent in Latin America. China's overall economic growth was similar to Latin America's state-led industrialization period between 1950 and 1978, growing at 5.1 percent annually versus Latin America's 4.9. Given China's rapid population growth, however, per capita income growth was only 0.03 percent per year.[37]

Mao Zedong and the Communist Party of China constantly shifted the policy goal posts during this period. On average growth was strong, but occurred in spurts followed by big busts. One aspect that held constant throughout this period was a neglect of employment and consumption, and an inability of the agricultural system to supply the changing Chinese populace. What stands out in the minds of many Chinese who remember the period is the Great Chinese famine of 1959 to 1961 that may have caused up to 40 million deaths from starvation.[38]

The Great Globalization

By the end of the 1970s both China and most Latin American countries sought to integrate their economies with the rest of the world. In terms of economic growth, China grew faster and stronger than any country in the history of the world—including Great Britain during the Industrial Revolution. As Figure 2.1 shows, in 1990 China's economy was half the size of all of the Latin American economies combined, and the average Chinese person earned less than one-sixth of the annual income that a Latin American earned. By 2013, China's economy was close to twice the size of all the Latin American economies combined and was just shy of matching Latin America's level of average income.

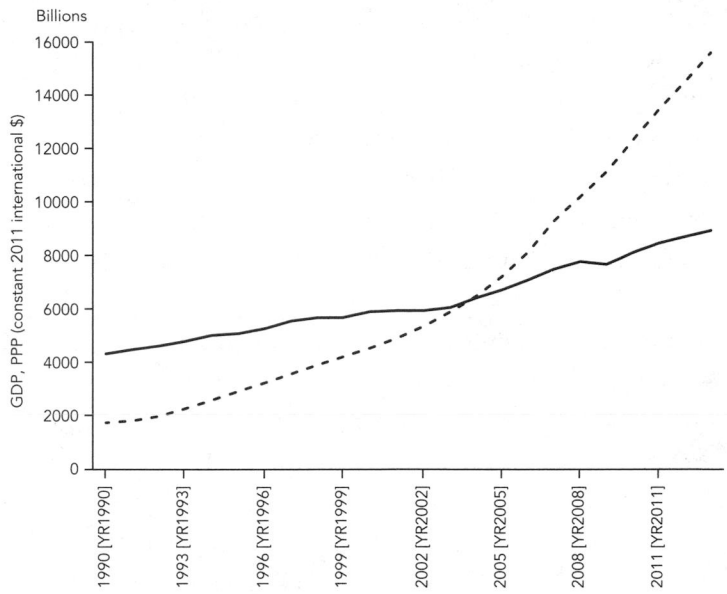

Figure 2.1 China Leapfrogs Latin America

Whereas most Latin American nations took a "big bang" approach and rapidly liberalized their economies across the board between 1980 and 2000, China took a more managed and gradual approach. The Mao era of big push industrialization was replaced by the Deng Xiaoping era of reform, characterized by the saying "Mo zhe shi tou guo he" or "Crossing the river by feeling for stones." China didn't flick a switch and privatize state-owned companies, liberalize trade, and deregulate its financial system as the Latin Americans did in one shocking instant. Whereas Latin Americans stood ready to inflict short-term pain as they adjusted to a new economic model in hopes that it would eventually pay off, China decided that reforms had to produce economic growth immediately, not eventually. Economist and long-time China watcher Barry Naughton writes:

It was never conceivable to Chinese policy-makers that their economy would postpone economic development until after an interlude of system transformation. It was always assumed that system transformation would have to take place concurrently with economic development, and indeed that the process of economic development would drive market transition forward and guarantee its eventual success.[39]

This approach of supporting both the old and the new not only assured sustained growth but also helped politically by giving the state-owned sector a chance to benefit from the reforms and therefore not fight the reforms. In contrast with Latin America's approach in column 1, the second column of Table 2.2 exhibits five core policies of China's gradualist approach to globalization.

First, the Chinese government and government-sponsored "policy banks" played a strong role in the reform process by pouring massive outlays into infrastructure and strategic industrialization policies. Over the past few decades a key engine of this pillar was the China Development Bank (CDB). Headed by the highly influential Chen Yuan from 1998 until 2013, the CDB had a seemingly magical formula for domestic finance. Local governments set up local-government finance vehicles (LGFVs) off of the balance sheets of their fiscal budgets. The CDB would lend through the LGFVs for public infrastructure and industrialization projects. The theory was that infrastructure and industry would raise home and land prices, and thus bring in more government income to pay the loans. Indeed, in some cases the CDB secured loans to land sales. As we will see in chapter 4, this model was also used when the CDB granted finance to Latin American countries.[40]

Second, China's "big four" state banks—the Bank of China, China Construction Bank, Industrial and Commercial Bank of China, and the Agricultural Bank of China—were commercialized but heavily regulated. China managed to regulate in a manner that allowed the big four to make healthy profits and subsidize credit to industry at the same time. The banks were required to keep deposit rates very low and lending rates only a few percentage points higher. Often times the big four banks piggybacked on CDB projects. Given that CDB loans were seen as so risk free, they acted like a triple-A credit rating.[41]

When one travels in China you can't help but notice the difference in infrastructure. China now has the second largest air transportation system in the world, second only to the United States. Brand new bridges and roads are everywhere and in much better shape than their counterparts in the United States and even Europe. By 2005 China had two million kilometers (roughly 1.24 million miles) of new roads, and 75,000 kilometers of new railroads. That is approximately 46,500 miles of rail, now equal in length to—but much newer and faster than—the United States.[42] Linked to all the new infrastructure, China built thousands of economic processing zones loaded with cutting-edge facilities for the manufacture and distribution of shoes, clothing, electronics, cars, and just about every other manufactured good available on the planet.

Third, China put up a "Welcome" sign to foreign investors in strategic sectors so foreign firms would locate in these new manufacturing hubs. Fourth, as an extra bonus to firms and foreigners, China's central bank, the People's Bank of China (PBOC), adopted a competitive exchange rate policy, essentially offering products exported from China at a discount relative to their competitors— in so doing the PBOC had amassed $3.9 trillion dollars in foreign exchange reserves. Fifth, by 2001 China adopted free trade policies by joining the WTO.

As we know, the world's companies flocked to China. By 2013 China had the second largest stock (next to that of the United States) of foreign investment in the world, at roughly $1.8 trillion dollars.⁴³ Upward of 160 million Chinese in the countryside flocked to cities and factory towns to work in the companies—the largest internal migration in human history.⁴⁴ Then China became the biggest trader in the world in terms of having the world's largest amounts of exports and import. What makes China's approach so clever and productive, however, is the deal the Chinese struck with the world's companies. China offered access to the world's largest workforce, the world's largest market (the United States through the WTO), and a newly paved and equipped export platform. In order to get in on that action, foreign companies had to partner with domestic companies and governments in research and development and technology transfer. It was a price, at least in the beginning, that most companies were more than willing to pay, especially given how sophisticated the domestic firms were becoming in China.

An illustrative case is the electronics sector—computers, mobile devices, home appliances, and more. In its "National Industrial Policy Outline for the 1990s," China singled this sector out as a pillar industry where China wanted to eventually have global name brands competing with the world's biggest electronics companies. These kinds of companies not only create jobs but are highly sophisticated in terms of their embodied knowledge and the intricacy of the parts and components used, and can thus link to many other sectors of the economy as well. Foreign firms came and had to participate in the "Transfer of Technology in Exchange for the Domestic Market" program, where foreign firms had to partner Chinese firms and transfer technology. China also created the "Electronics Industry Development Fund" for the domestic firms that handed out $4.87 billion to state and nonstate electronics firms. By 2013 Chinese companies were among the largest electronics makers in the world, and 70 percent of them came through these programs. What is more, most of the companies are now private firms no longer in need of government support. China had similar programs for autos, airplanes, and beyond.[45]

The case of Mexico is the opposite. Guadalajara, a city in the Mexican State of Jalisco, had built the capacities for electronics in the 1970s and 1980s with companies like IBM having a strong foothold in the region and numerous other smaller electronics companies. In the early 1990s Mexico had some policies for electronics that were similar to China's, but under the North American Free Trade Agreement Mexico traded away the ability to forge partnerships between foreign firms and domestic production. Moreover, Mexico's infrastructure is notoriously outdated and weak, and the firms that remained in Mexico could not access credit markets to upgrade. In 2000 both China and Mexico produced about 5 percent of the world's computers; by 2010 China was producing 50 percent of the world's computers and Mexico's share shrank. Where China managed the globalization process by investing in infrastructure and building networks between foreign and domestic firms, Mexico simply opened its doors to foreigners, who put many locals out of business. With few roots in Mexico, some of those foreign firms then moved to China by the 2000s.[46]

Eventually, the dual-track approach of supporting the state sector while focusing on the development of private markets took root and the private sector became the engine of economic growth in China. By 1999 Chinese authorities were referring to the private sector as an essential component of its economy. According to new work by Nicholas Lardy of the Peterson Institute for International Economics, the share of state-owned enterprises in China's industrial output fell from 78 percent in 1978 to 26 percent in 2011. The private sector is also in increasing generator of employment. According to Lardy, 0.2 percent of total employment in China was in private enterprises and individual businesses in 1978. By 2012, 35.6 percent of jobs were in the private sector.

This is truly remarkable given the fact that most of the interest rate and bank credit policies discussed earlier were geared toward local governments and state-owned enterprises. The private sector was more nimble and more productive; productivity grew in the private sector at close to 4.3 percent per year as opposed to 1.7 percent in the state-owned sector. Productivity and profits allowed the private sector to finance much of its activity through retained earnings rather than bank credit. And eventually, the big banks began lending to the private sector as well. Fifty-two percent of bank lending in 2012 went to the private sector in China.[47]

The contrast with the Latin American experience is striking. China has outreformed and outperformed Latin America by almost every score. China's GDP is now close to twice the size of Latin America's, though in 1990 Latin America's economies summed to twice that of China and incomes are becoming remarkably close. The key to this has been the massive amounts of public and private investment. "Gross-fixed capital formation" as a percentage of GDP is economist jargon for the amount of investment in an economy. Conventional wisdom among development economists is that a nation needs many years of sustained investment of over 25 percent of GDP to accelerate the growth process.[48] China's average investment rate was almost 40 percent since 1978, but Latin America's hovered around 20 percent during their reform period. This strong and fast growth in China brought hundreds of millions of its people out of poverty. In 1981 close to 80 percent of all Chinese lived on less than $1.25 per day; by 2011 that share was 6.3 percent. Latin America has done a stellar job of reducing poverty as well, with a poverty headcount ratio of 4.6 percent in 2011, though in 1980 Latin America's rate only stood at 12.6 percent.

Indeed, it is important to note that China was able to make its transition from state-led capitalism to private-sector capitalism on its own terms. Latin America's financial crises in the 1980s and 1990s left the region's countries bankrupt. There is no way they could have amassed the savings and investment necessary for fostering new industries. With the financing Latin Americans did receive from international financial institutions such as the IMF and the World Bank, countries in the region were explicitly restricted from steering finance into industry and innovation. On the domestic front there was also a lack of political will to try a middle and managed road to globalization in Latin America. Latin Americans wholly scrapped the state-led industrialization model rather than making a gradual transition as China did, because the old model was associated with brutal dictatorships that the newly founded democracies did not want to emulate in any way.

As we will see in later chapters, China's growth miracle has also brought new risks to China and may be running out of steam. More money often means more corruption, and the Chinese economy is becoming increasingly plagued by corruption scandals. The divide between the new urban wealthy classes and those in the countryside is growing rapidly, with inequality starting to shoot toward Latin American levels. Massive infrastructure projects, the proliferation of factories, and the energy use to fuel this activity has created an acute environmental crisis in China—China is now the world's largest emitter of greenhouse gas emissions. According to official estimates in China, environmental degradation may be costing China 3 to 4 percent of its GDP in health and other damage costs on an annual basis.[49] China's emphasis on exports has also come at the expense of consumption in the country and has been a cause of imbalances at home and abroad. China's financial system is also very fragile, and if China opens its financial system too quickly and without the proper regulations in place, it could suffer financial crises as Latin American countries did when they prematurely deregulated global financial flows into their countries in the 1980s and 1990s.[50]

Nonetheless, in terms of transitioning from state-led capitalism to private-sector capitalism and sustained economic growth, the far-reaching globalization of China led to the greatest growth miracle on record and brought hundreds of millions of people out of poverty. As we will see in the next chapter, China's rise also helped Latin America enter a new era of economic growth, its best era in over 100 years.

3

Winning the China Lottery

In 2004, Brazil's then-President Luiz Inacio Lula da Silva brought close to 400 Brazilian businesspeople to China on a major trade and investment mission. "Lula," as he has long been referred to, had been in office for just over a year and was keen to accelerate trade relations with the Chinese. Lula had been campaigning for decades against the Washington Consensus. Citing more of the same, Lula was looking to sever negotiations on the Free Trade Area of the Americas (FTAA), a US-led trade deal with Brazil and the majority of other Latin American countries. Eyeing China's rise, Lula thought he could get a better deal by trading with the Chinese. Lula later referred to his China mission as his "greatest trip."[1]

For close to a decade, it would have been hard to find someone who disagreed. As Latin America had won the commodity lottery of the industrial revolution supercycle, it was also a winner in the China lottery of the commodity supercycle spurred by China's growth miracle. By the time Lula left office in 2011 China was Brazil's leading trading partner and his country was making headlines the world over for its newfound growth, emerging middle class, and endless promise. Lula was no fool to be impressed by China's rise. As we saw in the last chapter, no country in the history of the world has grown so fast, for so long, while bringing so many people out of poverty as China has. China's annual growth rate since the early 1980s was 10 percent per annum and accounted for more than a third of total global economic output.[2]

Latin Americans watched as China's export industrial complex surged into the twenty-first century, and new cities expanded around export industries across China. To grow at such a pace China needed significant supplies of natural resources—like oil, iron ore, copper, soybeans, and beef—in order to build those cities, provide inputs to the rapidly expanding factories, and to feed a modernizing nation. That's where Latin America came in.

Latin America rode China's coattails. Brazil and Peru have a great deal of the world's iron ore. Chile and Peru have the copper. Uruguay has the wool. Colombia, Venezuela, Ecuador, Brazil, and Mexico have oil. Brazil, Argentina, and Bolivia supplied the soy and some beef. The Chinese increasingly toast at their meals with Chilean or Argentinean wine. In 2000 Latin American exports to China were just 1 percent of their total exports to the world; in 2013 Latin America sent over 10 percent or $110 billion in exports to China.[3] By 2013, most countries in the region had China as their number one or number two trading partner. Eighty percent of those exports were in oil, soybeans, iron, copper, and wool.

Following the imports, Chinese energy and mining companies started investing in Latin America to get in on the action. Between 2005 and 2013 Chinese companies—backed by favorable credit at home—poured over $50 billion into the region. Firms such as SINOPEC, China National Offshore Oil Corporation (CNOOC), CHINALCO, Huawei, Chery, and Minmetals have started to become household names across the Americas. These firms have not only been supplying investment, but have also been linking Latin America to Asia's accelerating production networks.

Indeed, China became a major contributor to one of Latin America's best growth spurts in decades. The 2003 to 2013 period marks the beginning of Latin America's China Boom. During that period, incomes grew in the region by 2.4 percent annually—despite the global financial crisis of 2008. In fact, Latin American incomes grew faster during the China Boom than during any other period since the region gained independence from colonial powers in the 1800s. And from where Lula sat the China Boom dwarfed the record of Washington Consensus, when Latin American incomes grew by only one-half of 1 percent per annum and the region was struck by numerous financial crises. Perhaps most significant is that the China Boom has enabled Latin American countries to finally stem the rise in inequality that has long plagued the region.

Winning Another Commodity Lottery

When the industrial revolution led the West to take off from China in the nineteenth century, Latin America won the commodity lottery that ensued. Western demand for Latin American coffee, fertilizers, silver, and grains triggered a commodity supercycle that Latin American countries benefited from. Just over 100 years later many Latin American countries were winners of another supercycle, this time set off in large part due to the unprecedented rise of China. Without China, Latin America would have had a very lackluster export performance in the early twenty-first century. Figure 3.1 shows just how dynamic exports to China were with the rest of the world. Exports to China grew by a factor of more than 20 between 2000 and 2013, whereas exports to the rest of the world increased just over two times.[4]

Much of the hoopla surrounding China's trade is the country's incredible penetration of global export markets. But the world's

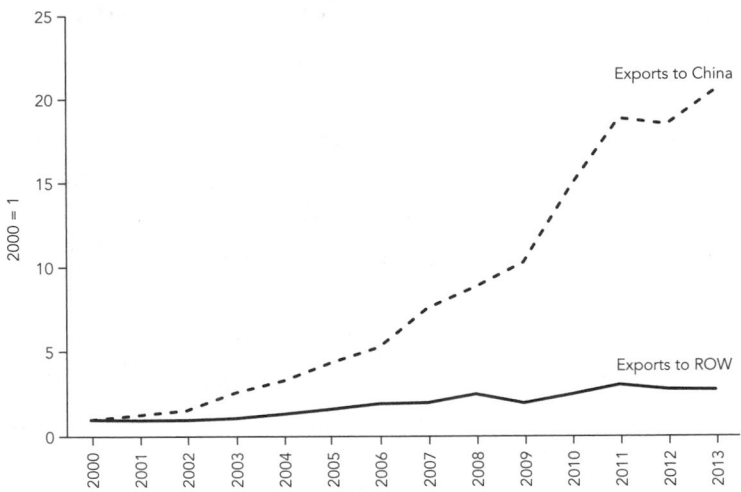

Figure 3.1 Latin America's China Boom
Exports to China Drive Latin American Export Growth

largest trading nation is also a massive *importer* as well. By joining the World Trade Organization (WTO) in 2001, China committed to put foreign country imports on the same footing as its domestic producers. In so doing, China experienced an import boom that is just as spectacular as its export boom. Elizabeth Economy and Michael Levi succinctly put it this way:

> Chinese consumption boomed, and imports rose. Between 1980 and 2010, oil and coal consumption both doubled roughly every dozen years. Natural gas use took longer to accelerate, but between 1995 and 2010 it doubled roughly every five years. From 2000 to 2010, copper use more than tripled; steel production quintupled, driving demand for its main ingredient, iron ore.[5]

Moreover, China's accession to the WTO led to major tariff reductions and the end of state monopolies in agriculture. Agriculture imports increased by 23 percent annually from 2001 to 2010. China became the largest importer of soybeans by 2009, and by 2014 it accounted for 70 percent of global imports of soy.[6]

The jackpot! Oil, gas, copper, and iron ore are among Latin America's most abundant natural resources. By 2011 China became the number one trading partner with all of South America, leapfrogging over the United States and European countries. For the region as a whole, the United States is still the largest trading partner given its large trade with Mexico.[7] The vast majority of Latin American exports to China are in a handful of primary commodities in a small set of countries in South America. Such a pattern of trade with China is quite distinct relative to Latin America's trade patterns with the rest of the world, and China's imports from the rest of the world. Between 2008 and 2012, 86.4 percent of Latin American exports that went to China (over 15 percent of total exports from the region) were in the primary commodities sectors, and 13.3 percent in manufacturing. This stands in stark contrast with the rest of Latin America's export basket, where only 56 percent of exports were in primary commodities and 40 percent are in manufacturing. From where China sits, only 33.7 percent of all its imports were in the primary commodities sectors, and 63.4 percent were in manufacturing. For commodities, anyway, Latin America is a uniquely important source of supply for China.[8]

Iron ore tops the list, and Brazil wins the iron ore lottery for the region. China gets one-third of all its imported iron ore from Latin America, and almost all of it from Brazil. Iron ore has long been one of Brazil's chief exports. Odds are that if you are sitting in a sturdy skyscraper, gliding along on a new high-speed rail, or stuck in Beijing traffic in a car made in China, that at least some of it has been exported from Brazil, perhaps from its flagship iron giant, Vale. In 2012 China imported 600 million tons of iron ore, one-third of that from Brazil.[9]

It is hard to think of China without thinking of soy. Indeed, China is the center of origin for the soybean and soy has long been held as a sacred core of the Chinese diet. The Chinese use soy meal for tofu and other staple foods, and use soy oils in cooking and flavoring. Increasingly soy is also used as a feed for cattle in the growing Chinese cattle industry. Soy seeds may have been introduced to the Americas in the 1800s in the Chinatown that existed in Acupolco, and reached Brazil in the late 1800s.[10] Today Brazil, Argentina, China, and the United States are the largest soy producers in the world.

As the Chinese economy boomed, so did its demand for soy. Latin America won that lottery too, and soy exports to China (both seeds and oils combined) were the region's second largest export to China during the China Boom. Brazil is the region's largest exporter of beans to China, and Argentina is the largest exporter of oils. Colombia, Bolivia, and Paraguay export soy to China as well. In 2009, 58 percent of all Chinese imports of soybeans came from Latin America, mostly from Brazil. In that same year, 95 percent of China's imports of soy oil came from Argentina, representing 73 percent of that country's soy oil exports.[11]

Copper is Latin America's third largest export to China. Like the steel made from iron ore in Brazil, copper from Chile and Peru is often a building material found in China's new cities and factory buildings. Copper is also of course a key transmitter of electricity, and copper from Chile and Peru laces the wires of parts and components in China's vast and growing electronics, telecommunications, and auto industries. Fifty-four percent of China's copper imports come from Chile and Peru. Copper also has another use that is unique to China. In the last chapter we discussed how the China Development Bank (CDB) liked to secure loans to local governments with land. In the next chapter we will learn how Chinese policy banks secure loans to Latin American governments with oil.

In China, copper is also used as collateral for credit or a hedging device. Usually, an importer in China places the value of a copper purchase as a deposit in a bank in exchange for a line of credit for the same amount. The importer then resells the copper in China and uses the proceeds to invest (or speculate) on other asset classes such as real estate. In other cases, copper importers in China purchase copper and store it in a warehouse as collateral for a loan from a foreign bank.[12]

Venezuela, Colombia, Brazil, Ecuador, and Mexico together provide Latin America's fourth largest export to China—petroleum. In 2013, China consumed 10.7 million barrels of oil per day but produced less than half that amount. In 2014 China became the largest importer of oil in the world.[13] More than half of China's oil imports come from the Middle East (mostly from Saudi Arabia), though 10 percent come from the Americas, with Venezuela and Brazil being the largest providers.[14] As we will see later in the chapter, this sector has also been a key area of foreign direct investment in Latin America, with Chinese firms flocking to get into Latin American oil markets. In the next chapter we will show how China's policy banks have been extending massive lines of credit to the region's oil producing countries to extract ever more oil for export.

South America's vast deposits of energy, raw materials, and food are uniquely suited for China's growing demand. Mexico and Central America, however, have fared less well in the China lottery and have not experienced as much of a China Boom. Mexico and Costa Rica have been exporting a significant and growing amount of transistors for radios and televisions and integrated circuits for computers to China. Yet these exports are relatively small, and those countries have significant trade deficits with China.[15] As we will see in chapter 5, these countries export similar manufacturing goods to the rest of the world as China does, and have had a hard time competing with China in world and home markets.

Some pioneering Latin American companies have followed the exports to directly invest and sell on Chinese soil. Grupo Bimbo is Mexico's largest baking and snack company and one of Latin America's biggest *trans-Latins*—home-grown Latin American companies that invest abroad. Bimbo started doing business in China in 2006, and now it is hard to go into a convenience store without seeing Bimbo's fast food snacks near the register. Bimbo's CEO, Daniel Servitije, says it's a no-brainer: "From my perspective, if you want to be in any business today, you have to be close to what's happening in China. If we have global aspirations, we have to be in China." Bimbo has two plants outside Beijing and employs 1500 Chinese workers. Servitije sees his business only growing as Chinese consumers continue to prosper. Bimbo did $35 million in sales in China in 2010, and has a presence in 17 Chinese cities. Bimbo hopes to capitalize on what is expected to be an $8 billion dollar bakery market in China.[16]

Bimbo is at the forefront of Latin American investment in China. According to the Inter-American Development Bank (IDB), between 2002 and 2012 Latin American firms invested $917 million in China—quite a small (0.25) percent of the total amount of foreign investment from Latin America's companies abroad. Food and beverage giants like Bimbo and Gruma from Mexico and Brazil Foods and Marfrig from Brazil have all set up production and distribution networks in China. Other firms in the food and beverage sector have set up shop in China in order to see to it that their exports to China get to market and compete by working with distributors and focusing on the marketing of their products in the Chinese market.[17]

Whereas food and beverage producers from Latin America invest in China in order to directly sell to Chinese consumers or manage their exports to China, some of Latin America's manufacturing companies go to China to get in on the robust value chains that have emerged there. Brazil's Randon manufactures goods and components in the highway, farm equipment, and auto industries, while Mexico's Nemak produces aluminum components for the auto industry. General Motors is one of their biggest clients and has been setting up operations across China for over a decade. Randon, Nemak, and other firms followed their long-time client to China's auto market supply chains.[18]

Of course there is more to trade than just exports. Imports from China have been just as remarkable as exports to China for Latin America. As in the case of exports, imports have grown by a factor of 20 since 2000, whereas imports from the rest of the world only grew by a factor of two. Whereas Latin Americans ship out primary commodities, they import in a wide variety of manufactured goods from China. Increasingly office equipment, electronics, batteries, clothing, and appliances come from China. As we will see in chapter 5, these imports are putting pressure on Latin American firms in home markets, and causing a political stir as well.

The Panda Cometh

China's presence in Latin America is no longer solely through export and import markets. Increasingly, Latin Americans engage with the rapidly growing stock of Chinese companies that have set up shop across the Americas. China's oil and gas giants can be found wherever one finds oil and gas in Latin America—Argentina, Brazil, Colombia, Ecuador, Peru. China's mining companies scatter down the coast of Peru and then East into Bolivia. Chinese manufacturers are also now based in Latin America. Anyone who uses a Lenovo Think Pad in the region likely purchased it from Lenovo plants in Mexico and Brazil; cars and trucks, too. Chinese auto companies use Uruguay and Mexico as export platforms to the large Mercosur and NAFTA markets nearby. Indeed, Latin America is a winner in the China lottery for foreign investment as well. In 2000 Latin America hardly registered Chinese investment; by 2012 China was the third largest investor in Latin America, behind the United States and the Netherlands.[19]

In the earlier stages of its reform period, China initially blocked overseas operations of its companies in order to preserve foreign exchange reserves and to prioritize the development of mainland China. That all changed in 2001 when Chinese Premier Zhu Rongji recommended that China embark on a "going out" strategy that would encourage its flagship firms to invest abroad and bid for global contracts as part of his country's Tenth Five-Year Plan. The premier said:

> We need to implement a "going outside" strategy, encouraging enterprises with comparative advantages to make investments abroad, to establish processing operations, to exploit foreign resources with local partners, to contract for international engineering projects, and to increase the export of labor. We need to provide a supportive policy framework to create favorable conditions for enterprises to establish overseas operations.[20]

Not surprisingly, many specific measures were included in the plan to encourage overseas investments by China's big companies that remain in place to this day. Importantly, the National Development and Reform Commission (NDRC) frequently publishes a list of permitted and encouraged investments overseas. China's Ministry of Foreign Commerce (MOFCOM) established a Department of Outward Investment and Economic Cooperation that conducts extensive research on the opportunities and risks associated with investing in various countries and sectors. MOFCOM also sets guidelines and regulations for the behavior of overseas companies.

The key engine of the go out strategy is financial support by the CDB and the China Export-Import Bank (CHEXIM), at least when it comes to the activities of large state-owned and state-supported firms that make up the bulk of China's overseas foreign direct investment (FDI). Chen Yuan, the pioneering head of CDB, has said that "We have become the principal source of finance of our country's overseas investments."[21]

China's banks do not make data on its overseas financing publicly available. Acting as economic journalists, my colleague Amos Irwin and I put together our own database that attempts to track the extent to which China's state-run policy banks provide financing for Chinese firms to go abroad. We did so by combing through English- and Chinese-language news articles in, for example, the *Wall Street Journal* and the *People's Daily*; through company filings with the US Securities and Exchange Commission (SEC); government reports from both China and the host countries; and bank reports from CDB and CHEXIM. We only included data if we could confirm it from multiple reliable sources. We estimate that between 2002 and 2012 Chinese firms were extended approximately $140 billion in loans and lines of credit specifically to go abroad. Sixty-four percent of the finance came from the CDB, 24 percent from CHEXIM, and the rest from China's big four banks. We compared our findings with those who studied Japan's lending to its firms during its industrialization period, when Japan too supported the globalization of its national champion companies. Financing as a percentage of total GDP in Japan during its heyday was 0.26 percent, compared to China's 0.31 percent. As a share of total FDI Japan was 16 percent, China 31 percent. China is supporting the globalization of its national champion companies like none other before.[22]

Between 2002 and 2013 China's overseas foreign direct investment flows grew from $2.7 billion to $90 billion and are predicted to outstrip inward foreign investment in 2015. In 2012 Chinese firms poured $9.2 billion into Latin American countries in the form of new plants or mergers and acquisitions. The stock of Chinese foreign investment in Latin America by 2012 was approximately $50 billion. Interestingly, the pattern of investment largely tracks the patterns of trade, with over 94 percent of all Chinese FDI into Latin America going into the energy, mining, and food sectors. This contrasts with tastes of other foreign investors operating in the Americas. Europeans, Americans, the Japanese, and others only put 42 percent of their total FDI into Latin America's energy, mining, and food companies, preferring to invest the majority into manufacturing and services. Like trade, then, Latin America's primary commodities are not only of great strategic interest to China's consumers and companies on the mainland, but also to China's new global champions.[23]

What also makes Chinese investment into Latin America distinct is that it is dominated by state-owned enterprises rather than by private-sector multinationals, as is the case with investment from the industrialized nations such as those from Europe, Japan, the United States, and even emerging markets such as South Korea. According to calculations by Enrique Dussel Peters, economist and director of the Center for China-Mexico Studies at the National Autonomous University of Mexico, 87 percent of all Chinese foreign investment in Latin America is from state-owned companies and 99 percent of all the state-owned company investments in Latin America were concentrated in the energy and raw materials sector. Private-sector actors represent just 13 percent of the total and concentrate largely in the manufacturing and services sectors.[24] Private-sector firms are largely not financed by the CDB and CHEXIM, with the exception of firms such as Huawei (telcom) and Geely (auto).[25] Rather, private-sector firms are financing their globalization through retained earnings. The private sector comprises the majority of the number of Chinese investments across the world and in Latin America. However, at present the private sector is dwarfed by the dollar amount of overseas investment represented by China's state-owned enterprises.[26]

Energy and Mining

By far and away the largest Chinese investments in Latin America are in the energy and mining sectors. With just a few exceptions these investments are dominated by China's "big three" large state-owned firms—China National Petroleum Corporation (CNPC), China National Offshore Oil Corporation (CNOOC), and the China Petroleum and Chemical Corporation (SINOPEC)—which are backed by finance from the CDB, their own in-house financing units, and the larger government apparatus enabling China's go out policy. Firms in this sector are more apt to merge with or acquire existing operations in order to learn about and adapt to new conditions as they globalize. What is more, China's overseas oil and gas companies are more likely to sell a newly acquired barrel of oil on world markets than ship it home.[27]

Argentina and Brazil are the recipients of the majority of Chinese investment in the oil and gas sectors, though Colombia, Ecuador, Peru, and Venezuela are also destinations for Chinese firms. The two largest acquisitions in Argentina are by the Chinese firms CNOOC and SINOPEC. CNOOC specializes in offshore exploration and production, with operations in the Caspian Sea, Australia, Canada, South Asia, and western Africa. In March of 2010 CNOOC acquired a 50 percent stake in the Argentine firm Bridas Company for a staggering $3.1 billion. CNOOC teamed with Bridas to mix its knowledge of offshore with onshore production, leaving the company to be largely managed by the founders of Bridas, the Bulgheroni family. Since Bridas has a 40 percent stake in PanAmerican Energy (PAE) corporation, this merger granted CNOOC access to Argentina's large Cerro Dragon petroleum reserve, operated by PAE. PAE's exports in 2011 were $4.6 billion.[28]

SINOPEC's activities, at home and abroad, are in what are called "downstream" operations—refining and sales. However, the firm has begun to rapidly expand into "upstream" operations—exploration and production of oil and gas, as well as a number of petroleum-based chemicals. SINOPEC is a truly global company, with operations in Iran, Saudi Arabia, Kazakhstan, Brazil, Canada, Nigeria, and beyond.[29] Also in 2010, SINOPEC acquired 23 fields operated by US-headquartered Occidental Petroleum in Santa Cruz, Chubut, and Mendoza, Argentina. At the time, Occidental's proven reserves had reached 393 million barrels and amounted to 6.4 percent of Argentina's total oil production. SINOPEC's exports from Argentina in 2012 were $1.2 billion.[30] SINOPEC's largest acquisition in Latin America was the purchase of a 40 percent stake in the Spanish firm Repsol's Brazilian operations for $7.1 billion in 2010. SINOPEC reportedly invested an additional $1 billion into the firm's operations in 2013.[31]

Related to energy investment is Chinese investment in the electricity sector. China's mammoth State Grid Corporation, the largest electricity company in the world, serves 1.1 billion people in China and has close to 2 million employees. State Grid has operations in the United States, Venezuela, Portugal, the Philippines, Australia, India, and more. In 2010 State Grid made two major acquisitions in Brazil totaling $2.2 billion. The first was the acquisition of seven national electricity transmission companies and twelve transmission lines, making State Grid the fourth largest energy transmission company in Brazil.[32]

Mining investments are also of an immense scale. The largest mergers and acquisitions (M&As) project in the mining sector was in 2011 when a group of five Chinese state-owned enterprises purchased a 15 percent stake in the Brazilian mining firm Companhia Brasileira de Metalurgie e Mineracao for $2 billion, granting the Chinese firm access to rare-earth elements in Brazil.[33] Perhaps the country where Chinese firms are most active, however, is Peru. Chinese mining firms are engaged in at least eight major mining projects in that country, including the Shougang iron mine, where Chinese presence dates as far back as 1992. The Aluminum Corporation of China (CHINALCO) acquired the Canadian firm Peru Copper, and has invested more than $3 billion into its new Peruvian copper operations to date. The project is named for Mount Toromocho (in Spanish, "bull with no horns"), the site for the copper mine, which will result in hollowing out an open pit larger than New York City's Central Park.[34]

Agriculture

China has been promoting foreign investment in Latin America's agricultural sector as well, especially into the planting of oil seeds, cotton, and vegetables; the harvesting and shipping of timber; and ocean fisheries. Indeed, China's Ministry of Commerce created a special fund for Chinese agricultural companies to go out in these same sectors. According to detailed research by Margaret Myers of the Washington-based Inter-American Dialogue, in 2005 Pengxin Group, a private Chinese company, purchased land for soybean production in Santa Cruz, Bolivia. Chinese firms Zhenjiang Fudi and Chongqing Grain Group form part of similar purchases in Brazil. Chinese companies are also getting in on Chile's world-class wineries, with the Chinese wine firm Great Wall purchasing Chilean land for such purposes.

Myers also documents that Chinese agricultural processing firms such as Chongqing Grain Group, Sanhe Hopefull, and China National Heavy Machinery Corporation have been investing in pressing plants, mills, and more across the Americas. In Caixin, a Chinese media source, Myers attributes China's agricultural expansion into Latin America as being a result of a "'two markets, two resources' approach to food security, wherein the country works to improve domestic production capacity in staple foods while seeking to control production, processing, and logistics for commodities, like soy, that cannot be supplied domestically in sufficient quantities."[35] Relative to energy and mining, however, and even manufacturing, Chinese agricultural investment in Latin America is still very small.

Manufacturing

While the majority of Chinese investment in Latin America is in energy, mining, and related infrastructure, there is a growing presence in Latin American manufacturing as well. China's investment in energy and raw material is resource-seeking, but China's overseas investments in manufacturing are geared toward getting better access to domestic markets in Latin America, to serve as an export platform to nearby markets, and to acquire technology and know-how.

The Chinese firm Lenovo made global headlines in 2005 when it purchased the Think Pad from IBM for $1.75 billion.[36] This move helped the company get instant brand recognition, market share, and technology. Lenovo is a private company that was fostered by the Chinese government in the 1980s. It is now one of the largest electronics companies in the world, making and selling laptops and desktops, and is the largest seller of smartphones in mainland China. Lenovo surpassed Hewlett-Packard as the leading seller of personal computers, with 17.3 percent of the world market (Hewlett-Packard had 17.1). Lenovo started in Brazil in 2005, shortly after acquiring the Think Pad. In 2012 Lenovo acquired Brazil's CCE and doubled its market share in Brazil, the third largest computer market in the world.[37] In 2009 Lenovo opened a manufacturing and distribution plant in industrial cluster of Monterrey, Mexico, where it produces and sells its products to three NAFTA countries.[38]

China's car companies are also going global and can be found in Brazil, Mexico, and Uruguay. Between 2006 and 2012, China announced a total of nearly 6 billion dollars of auto-related investments in Latin America.[39] To many Uruguay is a small beef- and wool-exporting country with a wonderful and cosmopolitan capital city, Montevideo, and a summer beach hotspot, Punta del Este. This is true. Uruguay is also becoming a hot spot and testing ground for China's fast-growing automotive companies. Uruguay is part of the Mercosur Agreement, a common market and free trade zone between Brazil, Argentina, Uruguay, Paraguay, and now Venezuela. With its skilled and reliable workforce, less volatile political environment, and close proximity to Argentina and Brazil, Uruguay is fast becoming a place to manufacture goods for reexport into other Mercosur countries. When measured relative to GDP, Uruguay receives the third largest amount of foreign investment in Latin America, to Chile and Panama. China has awakened to this trend, with textiles, telecom, chemicals, and auto companies flocking to Uruguay.[40]

Chery Automobile Company produced its first car in mainland China in 1999; by 2013 it had 20 different models and the capacity to produce 900,000 cars per year. In 2007 Chery joined forces with the Socma company from Argentina to form Chery Socma. The Uruguay plant makes a number of models for the regional and domestic market. Rather than source from local firms, Chery Socma assembles "complete knock-down" kits—kits that are fully imported from mainland China and assembled in the Uruguay plant—and can produce 32 to 36 cars per day. Chery also has auto plants in Brazil and Venezuela.[41]

Services: Telecom and Banking

China's two telecom giants, Huawei and ZTC, are the exceptions to the rule when it comes to financing from the CDB and CHEXIM. The majority of the firms that receive favorable financing from those banks are state-owned enterprises. These firms are private companies, and the government doesn't hold any shares. That said, Huawei has a $30 billion credit line from the CDB, and ZTC has $15 billion. Huawei has 19 offices in Latin America; ZTE has 16.[42]

Alex Zornig, chief financial officer for Tele Norte, Brazil's largest land-line telecom company, told Bloomberg the CDB extended his company an offer he couldn't refuse. In 2009, Tele Norte purchased network equipment from Huawei by taking advantage of Huawei's huge line of credit with the CDB. The CDB offered Tele Norte a two-year grace period on paying up, and the interest rate was only two percentage points above the London Interbank Offered Rate (LIBOR), or 4 percent. If Zornig had gone to the dollar markets in the United States, they would have paid closer to 5.99 percent. Mexico's giant America Movil also went to the CDB well in 2009 to purchase $1 billion to upgrade its mobile network.[43] It is deals like these that helped Huawei surpass Ericsson in 2012 to become the largest telecommunications provider in the world.

The next frontier may be banking, as China's loosens its remaining restrictions on the globalization of its financial sector. One of China's big four banks, ICBC, took an 80 percent stake of Standard Bank of Argentina in 2011 for $700 million.[44] According to research by Evan Ellis, one of the closest watchers of China in Latin America, ICBC now operates 99 branches with over one million clients and 3,200 employees in Argentina. The other big four banks are increasing their presence in Latin America as well, with CCB and BOC establishing a presence in Brazil, and CCB in Peru.

Latin America's China Boom

After decades of reform with lackluster result in the Americas, China came to the rescue. Latin America happened to have exactly what China needed as China turned the corner of the century. Most Latin American countries, at least those in from South America and the Caribbean with rich stocks of primary commodities, benefited from the China Boom in a variety of ways. The result was the best decade of economic growth in the Americas since the state-led industrialization period.

Chinese demand for Latin American primary commodities couldn't have come at a better time. At the turn of the century the region had been plagued by a half decade of financial crises, and Chinese demand was a big lift. Even more significant was the fact that Chinese demand for Latin American exports surged in the wake of the global financial crisis, allowing the region to be less hard hit. To recover from the crisis China put together a stimulus package of over 12 percent of its GDP. This stimulated ever more investment in new cities and factories, thus accelerating demand for Latin America's commodities. China came to the rescue, as Latin America's two other major trading partners, the United States and Europe, floundered for a half decade or more.

Exports to China came with a bonus. Because China was demanding so much iron ore, copper, soy, and other commodities, these commodities became more scarce. As the laws of supply and demand dictate, scarcity brings higher prices. Indeed, the commodities supercycle spurred by China's rise is also associated with one the largest and longest commodity price spikes in modern history.[45] Between 2003 and 2011 China accounted for 50 percent of the growth in key commodities that Latin America provides to world markets. Looking at the period after the financial crisis, from 2009 to 2013, China accounted for 83 percent of the growth. So not only did Latin American countries do better by selling to China, they also got higher prices when they sold their commodities the world over.

The economist Rhys Jenkins has attempted to estimate what the rise in Latin American export earnings were as a result of the rise in prices due to the rapid growth in demand from China. Looking at a basket of 15 commodities that comprise the vast majority of Latin American exports to China, Jenkins estimates that the effect of Chinese demand on Latin American export earnings between 2002 and 2007 was between $41 to $73 billion dollars. Given that the total value of exports to China from Latin America increased by $34 billion during the period, this indirect China effect was even higher than the direct effect of exports. In other words, direct Chinese demand was only half the benefit that accrued to Latin American economies due to China's rise.[46]

Indeed, the Latin American commodity boom brought windfall profits to the region. The high prices of commodities increased what economists call the "terms of trade" for Latin America. Measured as the ratio of export prices to import prices, the higher the terms of trade, the higher the gains from trade, as a nation will bring in more export revenue relative to import revenue. The International Monetary Fund (IMF) calculates that Latin America's commodity boom from 2002 to 2012 brought unprecedented income windfalls to Latin America relative to past booms since the 1970s—estimating that income has been 15 percent higher than what it would have been had no terms of trade shock occurred. Indeed, according to the IMF the average cumulative income windfall during the China Boom was equal to 100 percent of one year of GDP. In other words, thanks to the China Boom, Latin America got an extra year of economic growth.[47] The increasing terms of trade for Latin America helped the region accumulate more foreign exchange reserves, which help boost investor confidence and provide insurance in case of pressure on their exchange rates. Increasing export revenue can also bring in more tax revenue and reduce pressure on public budgets.

Part of the reason the terms of trade improved for the region was also a decline in prices due to the increase in competitive imports from China. Decreases in prices particularly benefit consumers; as the price of their overall consumption basket decreases they have more income to save or spend. Decreasing prices also benefited some manufacturers in Latin America, particularly in the export manufacturing sectors in Brazil and in Mexico. Decreasing prices for importing inputs may have led to more efficiency and competitive prices for their finished goods for export.[48]

Indeed by the mid-2000s, the Latin American economies started to become linked to the fate of the Chinese economy. Studies by the World Bank show that the comovement of economic activity—the tightness between an increase in growth in China and an increase in growth in Latin America—between China and Latin America began to intensify significantly by 2007, and then moved in lockstep after the financial crisis. Indeed, Latin America is now so linked to China that news of small changes in the Chinese economy have an impact on Latin American currency and capital markets. Good news in China's industrial output data mean good news for Latin American markets on the same day. Bad news, however, also causes shocks to Latin American markets.[49]

During Latin America's China Boom, from 2003 to 2013, the region grew at 3.6 percent per year, and 2.4 percent in per capita terms. That puts the China Boom as the era of the largest per capita growth rate in over 100 years, though in terms of absolute growth the state-led industrialization period saw 4.9 percent growth. In one of the more groundbreaking reports on China and Latin America, the World Bank notes:

> This suggests that the robust growth observed in Latin America and the Caribbean in the past decade is an important measure of its connections to China, both directly (via trade and increasingly also FDI channels) and indirectly (mainly via China's impact on international prices of commodities). In fact, it has led many, including ourselves in past reports, to suggest that the observed real de-coupling between emerging economies and the advanced world largely hinges on the rise of China (and India) in the global economic landscape. The question therefore is whether Latin America and the Caribbean can leverage on its deepening connections with China and turn it into an important (but not the only one) source of long-term growth.[50]

One area where many Latin American countries did leverage China's gift was in setting up and bolstering programs that reduced poverty and inequality. During the China Boom, Latin American inequality declined by as much as it had increased during the Washington Consensus. According to extensive research by a team led by noted Latin American economist Nora Lustig, the leading reason for reduction in inequality was an increase in worker incomes during the period. Income rises were in part driven by commodity exports to China and beyond, but also due to skill level rises in some countries and hikes in minimum wages, as in the case of Brazil. The second leading driver of reductions in inequality was an increase—in scale and strategy—in government antipoverty programs. The countries that decreased inequality the most were among the most unequal to begin with—and span the political spectrum. One innovative program pioneered by Brazil and Mexico that has swept across Latin America and the developing world is called conditional cash transfers, or CCTs. Under a CCT households are given funds on condition that they send their children to school and get regular check-ups. Not only does such an approach help the poor immediately, but it helps build a healthy and more skilled workforce for tomorrow. Antipoverty programs like these were bolstered by income windfalls from the China Boom, especially in South America. However, countries such as Mexico that did not greatly benefit from the China Boom also increased such programs.[51] As we will see in the next chapter, others benefited directly from large loans from China that gave countries fiscal space to fight poverty and more.

4

Yuan Diplomacy

In the late spring of 2013, shortly after being sworn in as China's new president, Xi Jinping made his first visit to the United States. Xi *paid* a visit to Latin America first, however. Like his predecessor Hu Jintao, Xi visited Latin America and provided upward of $5.3 billion in financing for energy and infrastructure projects. At the same time, Chinese businessmen started negotiations with Daniel Ortega of Nicaragua to build and finance an alternative to the Panama Canal through that country.

A startled United States quickly patched together a goodwill tour throughout the region for Vice President Joseph Biden. Biden made glowing speeches about a new future for US–Latin American relations, but had little more to offer. During the summer of 2014, Xi and his entourage were back in the Western Hemisphere. The Chinese set up camp in the region for seven days, visiting Brazil, Argentina, Venezuela, and Cuba, and provided another $21 billion for new projects. President Obama, by contrast, spent one day in Mexico in 2014. Since 2001 Chinese heads of state have made just as many visits to Latin American countries as the United States has, but have left upward of $119 billion in loans of credit behind in the process.

"Dollar diplomacy," the William Taft–era policy of providing finance to Latin American governments to promote US commercial and political interests, has been replaced by "Yuan diplomacy." As part of its go out strategy, China's development banks started financing foreign governments to help them support energy, mining, and infrastructure investment. By 2014 Chinese development banks were providing more finance to Latin American governments than the World Bank or the Inter-American Development Bank (IDB). In 2010 and in 2014 China provided Latin American governments more funds than the World Bank, the Inter-American Development Bank, and the US Export-Import Bank (US Ex-Im) combined.

China's are the new banks in town. Not only does China have deep pockets, Chinese finance tends to flow to countries that have a hard time gaining access to global capital markets. The largest recipients of Chinese finance are Argentina, Brazil, Ecuador, and Venezuela. China has also begun to finance Mexico to get in on the ground floor of new oil exploration, while more timid Western financial markets watch with more caution.

What is more, China's billions in finance are more in line with what Latin American nations want, rather than what Western development experts say they need. Whereas the US and International Financial Institutions (IFIs) such as the World Bank and IMF tend to finance in line with the latest development fads such as trade liberalization, health, and education, Chinese loans tend to go into energy, infrastructure, and industry projects in a region that has an infrastructure gap of $260 billion per year. Latin America's roads, ports, telecommunications networks, and energy systems are severely lacking.[1]

Chinese loans do not come with the harsh strings attached to IFI finance. The IFIs are notorious for their conditionalities that make borrowers sign on to austerity and structural adjustment programs that have had questionable outcomes on growth and equality in the region.

China has become more bold and has taken on more risk in part because of its innovative finance schemes. Half of Chinese finance is in the form of a unique lending instrument—the commodity-backed loan where Latin American governments ship hundreds of thousands of barrels of oil to China to partly repay the loans.

Not only has all the new financing helped Latin American governments meet their needs, it has improved the profile of Latin Americans in the eyes of the global investment community. Citing the fact that Ecuador has continuously paid China back in dollars and oil, the ratings giant Moody's upgraded that country's bond rating on two occasions. China has helped Ecuador secure access to global capital markets as well.

Yuan diplomacy is paying off in other ways. According to recent opinion polls in Latin America, China is now viewed as becoming very influential across the region. The United States is generally seen as more influential on the whole, but China is now seen to be having a more *positive* influence—close to 68 percent of those polled say China's influence was positive, only 62 percent say the same for the United States.[2]

The New Banks in Town

As early as 1998, then Chinese President Jiang Zemin championed the globalization of Chinese investment and lending. He argued that "regions like Africa, the Middle East, Central Asia, and South America with large developing countries [have] very big markets and abundant resources; we should take advantage of the opportunity to get in."[3]

Also in 1998, Chen Yuan was appointed Chairman of the China Development Bank (CDB). This act elevated the CDB into one of the most important institutions in China. Chen Yuan is the son of Chen Yun—seen as one of the "eight elders" of twentieth-century China who served under both Mao Zedong and Deng Xiaoping. Chen Yun oversaw the transformation of the Chinese economy during the CCP's first 40 years in power. By virtue of placing Chen Yuan to head the CDB, then, the institution was given special prominence.[4]

So "get in" they did. On January 17, 2011, *Financial Times* reporter Geoff Dyer and colleagues published a front-page story tallying that China's two major banks for overseas finance, the CDB and the China Export-Import Bank (CHEXIM), had provided $110 billion in development finance across the world in 2009 and 2010. To put that figure in perspective, the reporters noted that the World Bank group had provided $100 billion during the same period.[5] Further work by myself and colleagues found that during that period almost half of that finance went to Latin America.

At the turn of the century, the only games in town for external development finance were the World Bank and the Inter-American Development Bank.[6] Now there is a new bank in town, the China Development Bank (CDB). Between 2007 and 2014 the CDB provided more finance to Latin American governments than any other development bank operating in the region. Along with CHEXIM and the People's Bank of China (PBOC), China's state "policy banks" are increasingly where Latin American finance ministries go to first for project finance.

The CDB and CHEXIM are the centerpieces of China's go out policy. During a series of extensive 1994 reforms of the China's financial sector, the CDB and CHEXIM were created to serve as policy banks, whose loans would explicitly support the government's policy objectives.[7] Prior to 1994, policy lending had been the responsibility of the "big four" Chinese banks discussed in chapter 2. The CDB and CHEXIM were designed to free the big four to act as commercial banks. In separating policy from commercial lending, the government sought to reduce bank managers' moral hazard. If managers could blame all their losses on policy loans, they had an incentive to direct their commercial loans toward high-risk, high-return projects.[8]

CDB and CHEXIM follow slightly different mandates. CDB mainly supports China's macroeconomic policies—laid out in the Five-Year Plans—largely supporting energy and infrastructure projects. The CDB focuses on project finance, export credits, and, as we saw in the last chapter, loans to Chinese firms for their overseas investments. CHEXIM is China's export credit agency, providing letters of guarantee, export seller's credits (for Chinese exporters and investors), export buyer's credits, and concessional foreign loans.[9] The CDB has had high profits and a balance sheet that is even healthier than China's big commercial banks. CHEXIM also lends much of its capital at or near commercial rates, and boasts a low share of nonperforming loans.[10]

The PBOC is of course is China's central bank, and has played a relatively small role in providing direct project finance to Latin American governments. Instead, the PBOC has extended swap lines to two Latin American governments. A currency swap line is a mechanism whereby the central bank of one country extends a line of credit in its currency to the central bank of another country. The recipient country can use the funds to either pay for imports from the creditor country or use the funds to increase the foreign exchange reserves of the recipient country. Since 2010 the PBOC has provided upward of US$426 billion in currency swaps to 21 central banks across the world, more than the $333 billion signed by the US Federal Reserve during the same period.[11] Two of those countries are Argentina and Brazil, amounting to $41 billion. Argentina has been drawing on its swap for $11 billion. Brazil's swap arrangement is for $30 billion, but at this writing it does not appear that Brazil has drawn.[12]

Compiling data on the overseas activities of the CDB and CHEXIM is no easy task. At present China's policy banks lack transparency on such matters. In an attempt to get a picture of Chinese finance in Latin America, in 2011 Amos Irwin, Katherine Koleski, and I set out to put together an estimate. Putting on economic journalism hats, we consulted a wide variety of publicly accessible sources to gather details on each loan. We found loan agreements published by the Venezuelan and Bolivian governments in their official gazettes. Brazil's state-owned oil company, Petrobras, is a publicly traded corporation; we uncovered the interest rate on CDB's loan-for-oil deals with Petrobras by examining the company's filings with the US Securities and Exchange Commission (SEC). We also discovered Chinese loans in the Jamaican and Venezuelan government's annual filings with the SEC. We classified loans as commercial or concessional based on reports from Chinese embassies in the borrowing countries. We found details on Brazilian and Ecuadorian loans-for-oil in local newspaper interviews with the countries' finance ministries. We supplemented and double-checked all sources with newspaper articles or governments in both the borrowing countries and in China. We omitted loans that have not been confirmed by reliable sources on both sides of the Pacific. The Washington-based Inter-American Dialogue, an influential think tank that boasts numerous former Latin American heads of state on its board of directors, published our results. The report was cited on the cover of the *New York Times* and in newspapers across the world. Exhibited in Figure 4.1, we now update the data and publish it annually on an interactive web page at the *The Inter-American Dialogue*.[13]

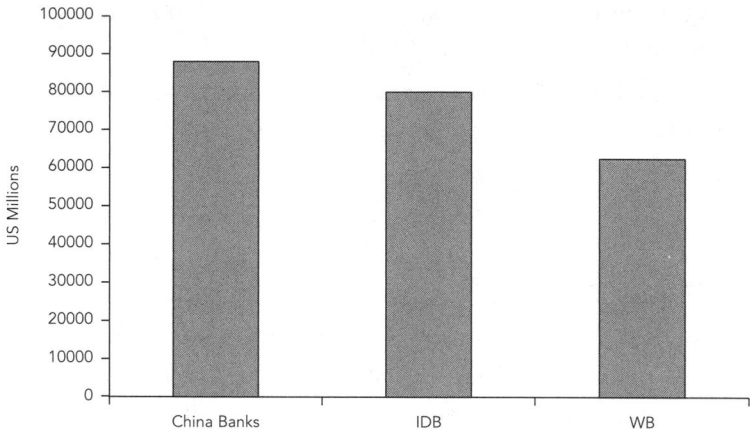

Figure 4.1 Development Finance to Latin America and Caribbean 2007 to 2014

According to our estimates, between 2005 and 2014 China's policy banks provided upward of $119 billion to 15 Latin American governments, with an average-sized loan approximately $1.7 billion. I always tell my students that whenever they see a number in the global economy they should ask "relative to what." One billion dollars for a new project is a monstrous amount of money relative to what myself or my students have in our pockets, but it is tiny relative to the size of the US economy ($17 trillion), or the size of the US budget (over $3 trillion). I decided to practice what I preach. When examining Chinese finance in Latin America, we compared our estimates to the record of other sources of development finance in the public and private sectors. The second largest lender during the period was the IDB at just $70 billion, followed by the World Bank at $67 billion.[14]

Latin America's share of China's global policy bank lending is thus likely the largest of all such lending by China. The global estimate of $110 billion performed by the *Financial Times* mentioned earlier only looked at the period 2009 to 2010. In 2013, I teamed with Deborah Brautigam of the Paul Nitze School of Advanced International Studies at Johns Hopkins University to compare Chinese finance in Latin America and in Africa. Professor Brautigam's landmark book *The Dragon's Gift: The True Story of China in Africa* is a classic that has established her as the leading scholar on China in Africa. If the *Financial Times* estimate of $110 billion was correct for 2009–2010, then Latin America and Africa combined were more than half for that period. For 2009–2010 we put Chinese finance in Latin America at $47 billion, and in Africa at $20 billion. Our full study covers 2003 to 2011, and we estimate that China provided $80 billion to Latin America and $53 billion to African countries.[15]

The majority of China's finance to Latin American governments is in the form of bilateral lines of credits or loans at commercial rates. In 2007, China and Venezuela set up the China-Venezuela Joint Fund (Fondo Conjunto Chino-Venezolano, FCCV). The FCCV is financed jointly with the Venezuelan National Development Fund (Fonden). The FCCV is managed by Venezuelan Economic and Social Development Bank (Bandes) and is designed to finance infrastructure projects in Venezuela. In 2013 China and the IDB established a $2 billion China Cofinancing Fund for Latin America and the Caribbean. The objective of the fund is to promote sustainable economic growth in the region. Specifically, it will complement the IDB's own resources to "alleviate poverty and reduce inequality, boost private-sector investment, improve competitiveness and social welfare, and support programs to mitigate the impacts of climate change and promote greater gender equality."[16]

Chinese and other big development banks do not overlap significantly in Latin America because they give different-size loans to different sectors in different countries. Not only is the scale of Chinese finance different in Latin America, so is the form of this finance. The vast majority of Chinese finance in the region goes into large infrastructure, energy, and mining projects. Finance from banks like the World Bank and IDB span a wider range of governmental, social, and environmental purposes. The Chinese banks channel 87 percent of their loans into the energy, mining, and infrastructure sectors. Only 29 percent of IDB loans and 34 percent of World Bank loans go to those sectors. Instead, the IDB and World Bank direct over a third of their loans toward the health, social, and environment sectors, which do not receive Chinese investment.

The CDB and CHEXIM say they provide financing in these sectors because they seek to directly support economic growth rather than social welfare. CHEXIM's website states that its projects must "be able to generate foreign exchange revenue and create jobs in the borrowing country. The [loans] focus on supporting infrastructure such as energy, transportation, telecommunication projects, and high-efficiency sectors such as manufacturing, processing, and agriculture in the borrowing country."[17]

In her book Brautigam argues that in Africa, China is filling an unmet need for energy and infrastructure lending, which was all but abandoned by the World Bank decades ago. She points out that from 1946 to 1961, three-quarters of World Bank lending funded transportation and electrification. Today, that share has plummeted because the Millennium Development Goals focus donors' attention on indicators of social welfare. Chinese banks, on the other hand, copy Japanese banks' focus on infrastructure and transportation, because they credit it with spurring Chinese development in the 1970s. Chinese finance thus complements World Bank and IDB loans rather than supplants them.

In addition to the largely commercial financing provided by the CDB, CHEXIM, and the swaps from the PBOC, China also provides upward of $5 billion in official aid to Latin America each year as well. China started providing Latin American governments with aid as early as 1996, when it granted $387 million to the region, and has now provided aid to 18 countries in the region.[18] Chinese aid played a key role in Haiti. China was the first country to send search and rescue teams to Haiti, and also helped with medicine, shelter, food, and water. According to forthcoming research by Brown University scholar Barbara Stallings, other examples have included emergency aid for the dengue fever epidemic in Ecuador, aid to recover from a mudslide in Bolivia, a hurricane in Uruguay, an earthquake in Peru, and a flu epidemic in Mexico.[19] Stallings points out that while Chinese aid to Latin America is fairly small, it is often part of the larger package of financing provided by CHEXIM and CDB to a country, and thus CHEXIM often has a seat at the table.

Why is China providing so much finance to Latin American governments relative to other parts of the world? Latin America provides a perfect match for China's go out strategy. Latin America is a source of key commodities that China needs at its present stage of development, and is a destination for many of China's foreign companies wishing to expand and become major global players in those same commodities. Thus, China's policy banks provide finance to the companies to go to Latin America to set up operations. Latin America has a major infrastructure gap, however, which is proving to cause bottlenecks in getting prized commodities to Asian markets. That leaves yet another match: the CDB and CHEXIM can provide finance for major infrastructure projects, and have many companies that are fit to do the job.

Risk Analysis with Chinese Characteristics

China's policy banks do their homework, and they had good teachers. According to Deborah Brautigam, in 1958 Japan provided India with a large loan to develop iron mining in Goa, a state on India's western coast. Japan provided finance; India paid back in iron ore. Japan mimicked this policy with China and financed a significant amount of China's industrialization projects in exchange for oil. By 1978 China had signed 74 such contracts with the Japanese.[20] Japan has continued this formula to this day, providing commodity-backed finance to Venezuela as recently as 2011.[21] As we saw in the last chapter, the CDB had a similar framework when financing China's domestic industrialization over the past three decades—providing loans to local governments that used land as collateral. As China's policy banks have gone abroad, commodity-backed finance has become the cornerstone of CDB and CHEXIM finance across the world, especially when debtor countries are considered to be risky bets. That's why we see China providing finance to countries and projects that most investors wouldn't touch.

About half of Latin America's contracts with Chinese policy banks are commodity-backed. All of China's commodity-backed loans to Latin America are secured in oil. The majority of these loans-for-oil deals go to Venezuela and Ecuador, and one to Brazil. Venezuela and Ecuador each have a very difficult time borrowing in conventional capital markets. In Venezuela's case this is due to political and economic uncertainty, in Ecuador's due to a 2008 default. Brazil has maintained a healthy credit rating, but its state-owned oil company Petrobras has had difficulty raising funds for a new oil discovery off the coast of Rio de Janeiro (referred to as the "Lula Field"). Petrobras has issued bonds and has received funding from the Brazilian National Development Bank (BNDES), but the project is seen as risky given that the oil is in ultra-deep waters and under the continental shelf—not to mention an explosive corruption scandal that came to light in 2015, which led to the downgrading of bond and credit ratings for Petrobras.

China's policy banks are willing to take on more risk for these countries and projects by securing the finance with oil. In general, the loans-for-oil deals in Latin America entail a package put together by the CDB, the debtor nation's Ministry of Finance, the national oil company exporting the oil, and the Chinese company that will be importing the oil. The Latin American Ministry of Finance signs the loan agreement with the CDB, and the Chinese importer signs a purchase agreement with the national oil company that is specified in barrels of oil per day. The proceeds are deposited into an escrow account at the CDB until the loan is repaid. It is thus not the export of oil that repays the loan, but the proceeds from the sale of the oil at spot market prices on the day of sale. CDB grants a billion-dollar loan to an oil-exporting government like that of Ecuador. Ecuador's state oil company, Petro Ecuador, signs a contract to sell Chinese oil companies hundreds of thousands of barrels of oil per day until the loan has been paid back, perhaps for 10 years. Chinese oil companies purchase the oil at market prices and deposit their payments into Petro Ecuador's CDB bank account. CDB withdraws the interest payments and principal repayment, a preagreed-upon amount that might reach 30 percent of the total oil revenue, directly from Petro Ecuador's account. The rest of the revenue returns to Ecuador. A $4 billion loan to Venezuela in 2011 was secured with sales of 230,000 barrels per day. Ecuador received a $1 billion line of credit from China in 2009 that is partially secured with 39,000 barrels of oil per day. Two Chinese loans to Latin America are supplier's credits from PetroChina to PetroEcuador. PetroChina is part of the large Chinese state-owned oil company Chinese National Petroleum Corporation. With the exception of some lines of credit to Venezuela that are cofinanced with Venezuela that go to infrastructure projects, the bulk of commodity-backed Chinese finance to these countries is for oil exploration and extraction.[22]

Chinese loans often come with a tacit understanding that Chinese companies will be doing a significant amount of the work related to the project or that the project will involve Chinese imports. In

China, these credits have been called different names: "hu hui dai kuan" (mutual benefit loan) and "shiyou, xindai, gongcheng yi lanzi hezuo xiangmu" (cooperation package of oil, credit, and construction projects).[23] In a $340 million loan to Jamaica for infrastructure in 2010, 60 percent went to a Chinese firm to do harbor construction, 40 percent to local firms. CDB's 2010 $1 billion loan-for-oil to Ecuador mandated 20 percent Chinese purchases. At the other extreme, CHEXIM gives 100 percent export credits, like a 2010 $1.7 billion loan to pay a Chinese company to build the Coca-Codo-Sinclair hydroelectric dam in Ecuador. In a 2011 loan to Ecuador to finance Ecuador's annual budget and to invest in hydroelectric energy projects, the hydro projects were awarded to Chinese firms.

Since Venezuela committed to spend the majority of its 2010 $20 billion loan on Chinese goods and services, CDB denominated half in Chinese yuan. Though this is the largest Chinese currency loan to date, CHEXIM has also issued yuan-denominated lines of credit to Jamaica and Bolivia for equipment and construction. Whether the loans are issued in yuan, dollars, or simply establish a line of credit with a given Chinese company, the purchase requirements allow Chinese banks to reduce their exposure to default risk. As Brautigam notes, it also reduces the recipient's room for corruption.

Latin America is not the only region where China engages in commodity-backed finance. China has signed loans-for-oil deals with Angola, Kazakhstan, and Russia as well.[24] Between 2003 and 2011 China's policy banks provided upward of $50 billion to African countries, half of which were secured by commodities. In addition to Angola, African nations with commodity-backed finance from China include Congo-Brazzaville, Democratic Republic of the Congo, Equatorial Guinea, Ethiopia, Gabon, Ghana, Nigeria, Sudan, and Zimbabwe. Interestingly, aside from Angola's loans, Africa's China finance is secured by a variety of commodities, including exports to China of oil, cocoa, platinum, and tobacco, and profits from copper and diamond mining.[25]

This innovative financing method fulfills multiple objectives on both ends of the transaction. They help China establish diverse, long-term oil supply chains; promote Chinese exports; put dollar reserves to a more productive use than low interest rate Treasuries from the United States; expand the international usage of the Chinese yuan; and win favor with borrowing governments. Erica Downs, formerly of the Brookings Institution, argues that as a hybrid of policy and commercial banking, CDB has designed the loans-for-oil to fulfill both policy and commercial objectives. In addition to securing oil supplies, helping Chinese companies expand abroad, and building relationships with South American governments, the oil-backed commercial loan terms lower risk and increase profits.[26]

Neither Sweetheart Nor Neocolonial

Chinese finance in Latin America is causing conflicting types of consternation in the global community. A few years back the *Washington Post* opined that "China is a master at low-ball financing, fashioning loans of billions of dollars at tiny interest rates that can stretch beyond 20 years . . . This has become a headache for Western competitors, especially members of the 32-nation Organization for Economic Cooperation and Development (OECD), which long ago agreed not to use financing as a competitive tool."[27] Others interpret China's finance to Latin America and beyond in quite the opposite manner, arguing that Chinese finance is exploitative and even neocolonial.[28]

My colleague Amos Irwin and I have been looking into these questions in Latin America very closely for the past five years. I have also worked with Deborah Brautigam to compare our results with the African case. We come to the conclusion that by and large, Chinese finance is neither "sweetheart" nor neocolonial. Rather, China's policy banks behave in a fairly similar manner to other development finance institutions operating in the region such as the World Bank, the Inter-American Development Bank, and the Development Bank of Latin America (CAF), as well as other export-import banks. The majority of Chinese finance in Latin America is offered at commercial rates of interest. When rates are slightly higher than those offered by China's counterparts, it is usually a function of the higher risk that is being taken on for the project. When rates are slightly lower or concessional, that is due to the fact that they are earmarked as being in part aid, and are thus by definition more favorable. If you want to take the work of myself and my colleagues on our word you can skip to the next section of the chapter, "Good Neighbor Policy." If you care to read a detailed discussion of interest rates on Chinese loans in Latin America, follow me.

Despite CDB's "development bank" label, the Chinese bank generally charges borrowers the full cost of finance. This is why Deborah Brautigam has referred to the CDB as "the development bank that doesn't give aid."[29] The World Bank group effectively offers concessional rates because its credit rating is so strong that it often does not add a risk premium to its loans. The CDB does add that premium. It is not surprising, therefore, that CDB's interest rates are higher. Instead of giving development aid through its development bank, China channels it through CHEXIM.

The CDB offers mostly commercial interest rates that are fairly analogous to the World Bank, IDB, and the CAF, and sometimes slightly higher. In 2010, CDB offered Argentina a $10 billion loan at 600 basis points above LIBOR.[30] The same year, CAF's rates on loans to Argentina ranged from 155 to 235 basis points above LIBOR. The World Bank's International Bank for Reconstruction and Development (IBRD) charged Argentina a spread of roughly 85 basis points.[31] The Chinese interest rate is hundreds of basis points larger than both CAF and IBRD rates. In 2009, CDB gave Brazil a $10 billion loan at 280 basis points over LIBOR. The IBRD gave Brazil a $43.4 million loan in 2000 at a variable spread of 30 to 55 basis points. These differences certainly debunk the idea that the mainstream development banks are being outcompeted by the CDB, but are also not significantly large enough to be called neocolonial either.

CHEXIM by definition subsidizes its smaller loans on the grounds that they constitute development aid for low-income countries, although these loans constitute only a fraction of total Chinese lending. The subsidized rates on small loans are somewhat lower than those of the US Ex-Im Bank. CHEXIM's lowest interest loans were its 2 percent loans to Jamaica and Bolivia in 2010. In order to offer these loans, CHEXIM receives subsidies directly from the Ministry of Finance.[32] China budgets these subsidies as official development aid, although OECD countries prohibit mixing export credits with development aid. To compare China and US Ex-Im interest rates on loans to different countries, Amos and I used the OECD's country risk premiums to compensate for the fact that some countries are riskier than others. While the US Ex-Im Bank charged 1.5 percent to 2.5 percent above the OECD risk premium, CHEXIM's interest rates on small loans ranged from 0.31 percent below the premium to 0.69 percent above it.

From the US Ex-Im Bank's perspective, CHEXIM's rates undercut US Ex-Im rates and make Chinese deals more competitive. From CHEXIM's perspective, it is blending export promotion with development aid to offer lower-cost options to countries in need. In any case, these loans constitute only 1.2 percent of total Chinese finance to Latin America.

According to our research, the bulk of CHEXIM's funding, like that of CDB, comes at slightly higher interest rates. Eighty-two percent of CHEXIM funding to Latin American borrowers carried commercial interest rates.[33] These commercial-rate loans include a $2.4 billion loan for the Baha Mar resort in the Bahamas and two loans to finance dams in Ecuador totaling $2.2 billion.[34] CHEXIM is not undercutting US Ex-Im Bank on these loans; it charged 6.9 and 6.35 percent interest on the Ecuador loans—about 2 percent higher than US Ex-Im rates, even adjusting for Ecuador's higher risk premium.[35] We further confirmed this by looking at Ecuador's *Foreign Debt Bulletin*, bearing out the finding that China's interest rates are closer to commercial rates. In 2011, rates on CDB and CHEXIM loans exceeded those from all banks other than Russia's Export-Import bank to Ecuador, including private banks. In 2013, CHEXIM's $312 million loan was Ecuador's most expensive loan of the year. The same year CHEXIM also gave a small, concessional 2 percent loan of the type discussed above.

Amos and I have also compared China's finance to Latin America with what Latin American countries are getting through private markets. In a paper published in the academic journal *Pacific Affairs* we looked at Bloomberg data on rates for debt issuance by Latin American governments. If the governments had not issued sovereign bonds in approximately the same year with similar maturities to Chinese loans, we looked at rates for sovereign debt issuance by other governments with similar debt ratings. Second, we referred to J. P. Morgan's Emerging Markets Bond Index Plus (EMBI+). The EMBI+spread represents the interest rate spread (difference) above US Treasuries of a government's previously issued dollar-denominated sovereign debt traded in secondary markets.

Again, our analysis found that Chinese interest rates are closer to market rates. For example, Ecuador is paying 6.9 percent and 6.35 percent interest on two 2010 dam loans from CHEXIM. CDB is charging Ecuador 7.25 percent for the first loan-for-oil, 6 percent for the second, and 6.9 percent for the third. There is no easy private-market equivalent, since Ecuador has not issued sovereign bonds since 2005, when its 10-year bonds paid 9.375 percent. The average rate for governments with B- Bloomberg Composite Ratings for seven- to 23-year maturity in 2009–2011 was 7.8 percent. The EMBI+spread on Ecuador's 2005 bonds in the secondary market in 2010–2011 ranged from 7.5 percent to 10 percent. The Chinese rates are thus in the same ballpark, but slightly lower.

In Argentina's case, the Chinese rates also appear similar. Argentina paid 600 basis points above LIBOR on a 2010 CDB loan, or roughly 6.5 percent. The same year, Argentina offered sovereign debt with similar maturity at rates ranging from 7.82 percent to 8.75 percent. As with Ecuador, the average coupon rate for governments with B- Bloomberg Composite Ratings for seven- to 23-year maturity in 2009–2011 was 7.8 percent. J. P. Morgan's EMBI+spread for Argentina from 2009–2011 ranged from 8 to 10 percent.[36] Thus the Chinese rate clearly falls below the private market rates, but not by orders of magnitude.

Brazil's state-owned oil company, Petrobras, also received China's financing at lower rates than it can access on the private market. Its $10 billion loan from CDB in 2009 carried an interest rate of 2.8 percent over LIBOR. Also in 2009, Petrobras issued corporate bonds worth $1.5 and $2.5 billion at 6.875 and 5.75 percent, respectively.

In Venezuela's case, the Chinese banks charged rates well below those of the private market. CDB gave the $20 billion loan at a floating rate of 50 to 285 basis points over LIBOR, or roughly between 1 percent and 4 percent. Meanwhile, Venezuela has issued sovereign debt at rates more than twice as high—between 7.75 percent and 12.75 percent from 2009 to 2012. Its EMBI+spread for the same period has ranged from 10 to 12 percent. Compared to the cases of Ecuador and Argentina, this interest rate differential is much larger for Venezuela.[37]

Good Neighbor Policy

Chinese finance in Latin America is also becoming very popular in the region because it operates under a different set of enforcement standards when compared to conventional finance. In today's capital markets and development banks, finance is usually offered on condition that a set of policy reforms be undertaken. Second, if a nation does not meet the terms and conditions of the financing agreement, that nation is shut out of capital markets altogether until the nation can show that it can repay.

This set of policies, associated with the Washington Consensus, has made it quite difficult for nations like Argentina, Ecuador, Venezuela, and others to obtain finance in the twentieth century. These countries have a long history of default and have been deemed at higher risk by most capital market indices. It was noted earlier in the chapter that China's policy banks are more apt to invest in these countries because of the innovative finance schemes and the strategic need for resources that such countries offer China.

When Chinese banks do come, they do not impose policy conditionalities of any kind, in keeping with general foreign policy of nonintervention. Chinese lending follows the nation's Five Principles of Peaceful Coexistence, which prohibit meddling in other countries' domestic affairs. Brautigam has argued, in the African case, that Chinese loans actually constitute a different philosophy of development assistance. Rather than forcing the borrowers to comply with Western norms, Chinese partners treat them as equals and simply seek to do business with them. If Chinese lending appears to generate economic growth, developing countries may reject the World Bank's "big brother" philosophy and demand Chinese-style equal treatment from Western powers.

By contrast, the International Monetary Fund (IMF) and World Bank impose stringent conditions on its borrowers. The IMF is notorious for imposing strict budgetary conditions on recipient nations and for requiring nations to slash social spending in order to meet those conditions.[38] Indeed, when Lula took office in Brazil he walked into an IMF program that required he run a budget surplus of over 3 percent of GDP. Conditionality comes in other forms as well, however. The World Bank loaned $485 million to the Brazilian state of Rio de Janeiro in January 2011 as "budget support" or discretionary funding. Although the World Bank did not tell Rio how to use the loan, it would not transfer the loan until Rio fulfilled a two-page list of conditions. To receive the first half of the loan, Rio had to integrate tariffs for intercity transportation, expand the environmental department's human resources and financing, levy a fee on water users for watershed management, implement disaster risk mitigation policy, broker an agreement on housing plans with the municipal governments, increase land titling programs, establish social programs in the slums, and set up a directive committee led by the vice-governor. To receive the second half of the loan, Rio had to restructure the Secretariat of Social Assistance and Human Rights, double land tenure regularization capacity, change the State Housing Fund's operating rules with respect to low-income families, create an integrated plan for metropolitan governance, and execute a monitoring and evaluation program.[39]

The policies that the international financial institutions impose on their borrowers are not necessarily bad policies. That said, *any* imposition of policies by foreign creditors has become stigmatized in the region due to a long and troubled history of World Bank and especially the IMF programs in the Americas. During the crisis-ridden 1980s these institutions conditioned loans on fundamental policy reforms such as privatization, trade liberalization, and the general decline of the state in economic affairs. As shown in chapter 2, these policies brought some improvements, but the overall record was economically dismal and politically abhorrent—especially for the left-of-center champions of equity and social justice that have come to power in many countries since the 2000s.

Countries in Latin America have formed coalitions with other developing countries against the IMF and World Bank in recent years as well. In addition to getting the policies wrong, these countries argue that the institutions do not represent the interests of their clients. There is quiet agreement that the head of the World Bank will always be someone from the United States, and that the head of the IMF will always be a European. Moreover, the United States always has veto power in both institutions over the final policy. Latin American countries were very instrumental in the 2000s to introduce quota-voting reform in these institutions, but such reforms have been held up by the US Congress.

Ambassador to Bolivia Shen Zhiliang proudly relates that it is China's "principle" not to "impose political conditions." A Ugandan government spokesman stated that Western lenders' "conditions are probably well intentioned, but they are humiliating." By contrast, the Heritage Foundation points out that "Many African governments like the Chinese policy of 'non-interference' in their internal affairs." Hugo Chávez declared that the Chinese aid "differs from other multilateral loans because it comes without strings attached."[40]

Chinese finance to Ecuador, and Ecuador's willingness and ability to pay China back, has triggered Western capital markets to improve their outlook for the country. As noted earlier, Ecuador defaulted on many of its debts in 2008 and has been shunned from conventional capital markets. The CDB and CHEXIM, however, have stepped in with $10 billion in loans and lines of credit to Ecuador. Some of those loans have been for discretionary budget spending in Ecuador. Some of them have also been secured with oil. Ecuador's ability to raise funds from China, and the fact that

Ecuador has been paying China back, led the credit rating agency Moody's to upgrade Ecuador's credit in 2012. "In spite of its lack of access to international capital markets since 2008, after the government defaulted on its 2012 and 2030 Global Bonds, Ecuador has managed to secure significant amounts of external financing from China," Moody's analyst Sarah Glendon told Bloomberg news.[41]

China has also showed willingness to help Venezuela to prevent a full-on default. Since the turn of the century Venezuela has been actively spending public funds to expand social inclusion to the country's poor. The country, first under the direction of Hugo Chávez and then under Nicolas Maduro, was able to fund such expenditures given the high price of oil in the 2000s—and due to the joint fund with China. Without these sources Venezuela would have had very little luck raising such funds in international capital markets.

In 2014 the price of oil began to slide significantly, and Venezuela's cash flow narrowed. According to official reports, Venezuela was able to renegotiate some of the details of their loans-for-oil with China in order to meet anticipated cash-flow problems in 2014. One of Venezuela's loans-for-oil required a minimum shipment of 300,000 barrels of oil per day to make sure the loan would be repaid back at a rate between $40 and $70 per barrel. When the deal was struck, oil was trading at approximately $50 per barrel. Given that prices soared to over $100 in early 2014, Venezuela was overpaying for its loan and the Chinese were reimbursing China for those windfalls. The new arrangement allows for Venezuela to only sell enough oil as is necessary for the loan, and avoid delayed reimbursements, and extends the three-year repayment period deadline.[42] Later in 2014 conditions worsened in Venezuela. The price of a barrel of oil continued to plummet, as did the value of the country's currency. Apparently with Chinese approval, Venezuela moved $4 billion in loans from China that were earmarked as infrastructure and development loans into their foreign exchange reserves account.

China has also thrown a lifeline to Argentina. As noted earlier, the PBOC has extended swap lines to Argentina and Brazil. In 2013 the central banks of China and Argentina agreed to an $11 billion currency swap. Argentina experienced a grave financial crisis in 2001 and 2002. In the aftermath of the crisis, Argentina renegotiated its debts with the majority of its bondholders. However, a number of hold-out investors took Argentina to New York courts and sued Argentina for not paying them the full value of their investments. This highly unusual case caused a great deal of controversy among the world's economic policymakers—with the United States and the IMF arguing that the New York judge's interpretation of the case that Argentina had to pay the full value of bonds to those who decided to hold out from their bond restructuring was both suspect and a threat to the stability of the sovereign debt regime in the world economy.[43] This case, as well as reduced demand for Argentine soy products due to a slowdown in Chinese demand, accentuated an already grave situation in Argentina. Export earnings nosedived, as did the value of the Argentine peso. Argentina's three-year currency swap with China allows each country to lend the equivalent of $11 billion in yuan or pesos over a three-year period. By mid-2015 Argentina drew on the swap and converted over $1 billion from yuan to dollars in order to bolster its dollar foreign reserves as well.[44]

Currency swaps aren't only going to nations considered as inherently fragile. Indeed, Latin America's most stable economy from a macroeconomic perspective, Chile, signed a three-year currency deal with China in 2015 for $3.6 billion.[45]

These lifelines may only be the beginning. On the sidelines of the 2014 World Cup in Brazil, the BRICS (Brazil, Russia, India, China, and South Africa) countries established a New Development Bank and a Contingency Reserve Arrangement to provide more development finance and financial safeguards across the developing world while also presenting an alternative decision-making model to the World Bank and the IMF. Unlike the World Bank, the $100 billion New Development Bank will have a one-country, one-vote system and no country will have veto power. Unlike the International Monetary Fund, the $100 billion Contingent Reserve Arrangement will allow countries to draw on the fund for balance of payments difficulties (similar to those experienced by Argentina and Venezuela) and make decisions on a consensus basis.[46] These new arrangements help China spread risk better as well. Rather than being exposed to the shaky borrowing histories of nations such as Venezuela on a bilateral basis, China can share that risk with the BRICS.

In January of 2015 China hosted the first ever China–CELAC cooperation summit. At that venue, China commited $20 billion in special loans for Latin American infrastructure cooperation, $10 billion in preferential loans for Latin American countries, founded a $5 billion China–CELAC Cooperation Fund, and a $50 million China–Latin America Infrastructure Cooperation Special Fund—this on top of a $50 million China–Latin America fund for agricultural research and development centers and a 500,000-ton food reserve.[47]

It seems that every time a Chinese leader goes to Latin America, he puts his money where his mouth is. In mid-2015 Chinese premier Li Keqiang spent just over a week in South America, visiting Brazil, Peru, Colombia, and Chile. That was long enough to provide a $10 billion loan to Brazil's embattled state-owned oil company Petrobras, facilitate a $27 billion fund for infrastructure development in Brazil, and a $30 billion dollar China–Latin America cooperation fund for promoting infrastructure and industrial capacity.[48]

What a difference a decade makes. At the turn of the century Latin America seemed like a fragile continent dependent on

Washington for trade, finance, and ideas. By 2013 Latin American countries had a new trading partner that also provided no-strings-attached finance for its energy and infrastructure projects. Contrary to opinions that China may thus circumvent Western efforts in the region, China complemented them. Chinese finance largely flowed to countries and projects that Western-backed financial institutions did not partake in. When China did provide financing in similar areas, such finance was most often at commercial levels, not sweetheart deals that would undercut the West. Instead, China adapted new financing techniques to take on more risk to go where the West would not. This new trade, investment, and finance that surged due to China's rise from 2003 to 2013 in Latin America can be seen as nothing less than the region's China Boom. As we will now see, however, many governments in the region became too complacent with their burgeoning relationship and may not be equipped to benefit from the next stages of China's rise.

5

Back to the Nineteenth Century?

Colombians almost lost their hats to the China Boom. The *Vueltiao*, a cowboy-like hat that is handcrafted by artisans from the Zenu tribe, is a symbol of Colombian culture. With the same secret technique that they have practiced for over 1,000 years, the Zenu weave together natural fibers from palm trees to make hats that are resistant to sun and water. When then US President Bill Clinton traveled to Colombia in 2000, he was presented with a Vueltiao by then Colombian President Andres Pastrana. The hat was declared a Colombian national symbol in 2004.

A secret no more. According to Eder Suarez, a Vueltiao hat seller interviewed by *El Tiempo* newspaper, Chinese businessmen descended on the indigenous area of San Andres de Sotavento and began watching how the Vueltiao was made. Shortly afterward Chinese versions of the Vultiao began to appear in Cartagena. The Chinese version was synthetic and mass-produced, but similar enough in appearance to an authentic Vueltiao that it easily fooled tourists looking to bring home a symbol of Colombia—especially given that the Chinese knockoffs sold for half the price.

The Zena artisans were walloped by the entrance of China into the domestic Vueltiao market. Over 50,000 families depend on making Vueltiao hats for their livelihood, and of those there are at least 6,200 women who are the primary breadwinners for their families.[1] Eder Suarez spent his entire life making Vueltiao and selling the hat at a stand in Cartagena; he said, "I have to feed my children and they have forced me to betray my principles by selling both types of hat, and unfortunately I have to admit that the Chinese hat sells out faster than our hat." According to Suarez, at their high point in 2013 the Chinese hats sold at three times the rate of Colombian hats; in a typical month Suarez sold 180 Chinese copies, and only 60 authentic hats.[2] While a Chinese hat sells for 20,000 Colombian Pesos ($10), the cheapest authentic Vueltiao sell for 40,000 Pesos ($20).

In the Colombian town of Tuchin people called on then-President Juan Manuel Santos to act to defend their cultural symbol and source of income. "We are asking President Santos to help us, to do something for us, and if we do not accomplish anything with that we will have to act the way our traditions mandate," said the mayor of Tuchin, Eligio Antonio Pestana. "The way our traditions mandate," in this case, means a group of people going to Monteria to as a symbol of protest.[3] The Colombian government was quick to act. The Vueltiao had been marked as "intellectual property" in 2011, and in 2013, when the Colombian national press began to cover the sales of Chinese Vueltiaos, the government ordered the suspension of "production, commercialization or sale of all hats that try to imitate or replicate the hats protected as 'Tejeduria Zenu,' or the hats protected by the 'Sombrero Vueltiao' brand, with the goal of substituting it."[4] Then–Trade Minister Sergio Diaz-Granados told Bloomberg that the sombrero "is entitled to the same protected status as dry-cured ham from Parma, Italy, or sparkling wine from France's Champagne region." Colombia also slapped a $4 per kilogram tariff on imported apparel and footwear.[5]

In a press interview, Colombian Finance Minister Mauricio Cardenas summed up one of the dark sides of the China-led commodity boom in Latin America: "While we're all happy with one side of the story, enjoying the high price for our commodity exports, the economic impact on the currency and manufacturers can be very negative."[6] What happened with the Colombian Vueltiao is symbolic of a trend that became associated with the China Boom across the Americas. Argentina and Brazil lost toys and shoes; Mexico and Guatemala lost their shirts and computer exports. What Cardenas was alluding to was the fact that the China Boom was associated with the appreciation of national currencies in the region, and a subsequent reduction in the competitiveness of manufacturing and other noncommodity export sectors in Latin America. The appreciation of a currency is another way of saying that a domestic currency is more expensive. If it is more expensive vis-à-vis another country's currency, the competitiveness of the goods and services from the country with the higher value will suffer. Stories like the Vueltiao were a hindrance during the China Boom. Now that the boom is slowing or plateauing, these failures may come back to haunt the Americas for decades. In fact, if the region doesn't start getting the right policies in place, many fear that they will go back to the nineteenth-century economic structure described in chapter 2.

The Curse

Economists have a term for those economies that are well endowed with natural resources but never seem to accelerate into modernity. Latin Americans know the term all too well, as they spent the better half of the twentieth century trying to dispel it. You might think that countries richly endowed with oil, iron ore, soybeans, copper, and other scarce natural resources would hold the key to wealth creation in the global economy. Unless, that is, such a country falls victim to the "resource curse."[7]

The truth is, countries well endowed with natural resources often perform worse than countries without such riches, especially when they have weak institutions that cannot capture some of the benefits of commodity-led growth and invest them into activities that foster long-run development. When demand and prices for primary commodities rise, so does the value of a nation's currency. Currency appreciation makes consumers favor imports over domestic production while at the same time making noncommodity export sectors less competitive. When demand and prices of primary commodities stop growing, currencies depreciate. If a nation's currency is determined by the market, export competitiveness can recover when a currency depreciates—as long as there has been adequate investment in productivity-enhancing activity and as long as the private sector has not accumulated a lot of dollar-denominated debts.

Let's start by looking at what can happen on the way up. Currency appreciation from rising prices, demand, and speculation can cause companies and governments to take on too much debt. When dollars are cheap relative to local currencies, countries can take on a lot of dollar-denominated debt without it being a lot in comparison to the size of their (local currency) economy. Currency appreciation can also make a country's exports too expensive relative to their competitors in the global marketplace. Moreover, currency appreciation empowers local consumers to purchase imported goods rather than domestically produced goods. If nations aren't careful, these forces can combine to hollow out the industrial and employment base of an economy, and then there is little to turn to but increased debt when demand and prices decline.

It gets worse on the way down. If demand or prices plateau for commodities, the value of a nation's currency can slide downward too. This can be a major source of financial instability if most of the borrowing on the way up was done in US dollars or other foreign currencies. If the value of a currency falls by half, then companies and governments have to come up with twice as much in local currency in order to pay back dollar-denominated debt. That is a tall task given that the source of growth in the economy— the commodities exports—are experiencing a downturn and when industry has been hard-hit from lagging competitiveness due to the high prices of exports and domestic consumers purchasing more imports. If the country has a floating exchange rate—an exchange rate that adjusts according to supply and demand—exchange rate depreciation can sometimes trigger a boost in exports given that they are price-competitive again. The problem is, if a country hasn't invested in the noncommodity industries they often lag in productivity, and global consumers may not want enough of their products no matter how cheap they become.

The resource curse has a cure. Governments may tax commodity-exporting sectors during upswings and invest the windfalls into industry, innovation, and education. Windfall reinvestments can keep industry competitive and build out new industries and workers as an economy expands. If these investments are coupled with exchange rate management, being endowed with resources can be a blessing rather than a curse. But what seems easy for policy is very hard in a world of politics. Big commodities exporters and international financial interests don't see it in their interests to be regulated, and push back on governments trying to strike the right balance. At the same time, the beneficiaries of innovation, industrialization, and education policies are at their weakest, or by definition (in the case of industries and skilled workers that do not exist yet) they have no standing in the political process. It thus takes strong leadership and long-term insight for governments to manage the resource curse—leadership that is waning when politicians are reliant on the big commodity exporters for political and financial support.[8]

With a few notable exceptions, Latin American countries did not manage the financial instability associated with the China Boom and the global financial crisis; they watched idly as Latin American manufacturing exports lost competitiveness to China, and fell far short of capturing and reinvesting some of the windfall profits attributed to the China Boom. This is very concerning. As growth slows in the region, there are fewer other options for Latin American economies to fall back on.

The Primarization of Latin American Exports

I started thinking about the China–Latin America economic relationship while working in Mexico's so-called Silicon Valley in 2005. The city of Guadalajara is in the Mexican state of Jalisco and had long been home to a cluster of electronics companies. My colleague Lyuba Zarsky and I were writing a book about the extent to which the North American Free Trade Agreement (NAFTA) had bolstered the electronics cluster. It turned out that NAFTA had taken a bite out of the sector—but the deeper into the century we got, the less the plant managers of electronics plants wanted to talk about NAFTA. They wanted to talk about China instead. In the year 2000, China and Mexico each had around 5 percent of the global computer market. By 2012, Mexico's share had fallen to 4.3 percent and more than half (55 percent) of the computers in the world came from China.[9] Ever since I finished the book with Lyuba, I have been researching China in Latin America. The lack of competitiveness in the Mexican computer market was replicated across the hemisphere during the China Boom—from machine parts in Brazil, hats in Colombia, textiles in Central America, and electronics in Mexico.

Exchange rate volatility and a lack of investment into innovation and industrialization in Latin America met exchange rate management and a mammoth Chinese industrial policy aimed at exporting manufacturing to the world. Latin America lost.

With the exception of Mexico, Latin American manufacturing has been losing its export competitiveness since the beginning of the Washington Consensus period. The manufacturing powerhouses of the 1950s, Argentina and Brazil, still maintain a significant domestic manufacturing base at home and have a hold on some regional markets. However, nations like these have been losing competitiveness globally for some time. In the 1960s Mexico created a number of export processing zones called "maquiladoras." Maquiladoras aim to attract foreign companies who can import their inputs duty free from abroad into the zone. Mexican workers then assemble the inputs into final products, which are then exported to the United States. Under NAFTA, Mexico had been gaining ground in the US market. All that changed during the China Boom. Mexican, Brazilian, Argentine, and other Latin American exporters had trouble competing with their Chinese counterparts in the US, world, and regional markets.

Losing export competitiveness is a deep concern for policymakers and economists. Export manufacturing helps put companies at the global technological frontier, and the interlocking global supply chains are where the most opportunities are for sales and expansion. Export manufacturing is also very employment-intensive and provides badly needed foreign exchange to pay for imports and pay back international debt. Losing export competitiveness can lead to higher levels of unemployment and make a country more vulnerable to price swings in commodity markets. It was Albert O. Hirschman who termed the commodity sector as an "enclave" that supports fewer jobs and has fewer linkages to the more dynamic manufacturing and services sectors in an economy.[10]

Before the turn of the twenty-first century, manufacturing as a percentage of total exports was above 60 percent but had fallen to almost 35 percent by 2015. As exports to China started to rise, primary commodities were over half of all Latin American exports. This has triggered a debate about the "reprimarization" of Latin American exports. As we saw in chapter 2, Latin America spent the better part of the twentieth century trying to diversify from primary commodity exports, only to see shares of commodity exports mimicking the nineteenth century in the 2000s.

The loss of export competiveness has been well documented by a number of scholars and policy analysts. With the Uruguayan political economist Roberto Porzecanski, I calculated the extent to which Chinese exports were outcompeting their Latin American counterparts in hundreds of product lines from automobiles to yarns. Borrowing from methodologies developed at the Asian Development Bank, we determined that a particular Latin American export sector was being outcompeted by its Chinese counterparts if Chinese exports were gaining market share in the product while Latin American exporters were losing market share or gaining at a slower rate. Looking at the period from 2000 to 2006, we found that 92 percent of all Latin American manufacturing exports were losing competitiveness to China in this manner, representing 39 percent of all the region's exports. The case was even worse for Mexico, because China's export processing zones specialized in similar products but were far superior in sophistication. During the same period, we found that 97 percent of Mexico's exports were threatened by China, representing 71 percent of that country's total exports. The only manufacturing sectors in Mexico weathering the storm were the automotive and trucking industries. China's big auto companies will soon find their way into Western markets, but have been slower to get off the ground. Cargo of cars and trucks is also very heavy, and thus expensive to ship overseas.

Mexico's proximity to the lucrative US market is therefore a real plus. Finally, the NAFTA has a little secret in it that requires that 62.5 percent of all cars sold in North America have to be produced in North America—giving Mexico an (unnatural) comparative advantage in exporting finished cars and trucks.[11]

Using the same methodology, Rebecca Ray and I calculated the extent to which Latin American manufacturers were losing competitiveness with China during the entire China Boom, 2003 to 2013. We found that 78 percent of Latin American manufacturers were losing out to China. Decomposing the threat by region, in the Caribbean 96 percent of manufacturers were losing export competiveness to China, 86 percent from Central America and Mexico, and 79 percent from South America.[12]

These findings have been replicated throughout the academic literature and by the work of those working at the World Bank and Inter-American Development Bank. Almost every study has found that Mexico and Central American countries have lost the most in terms of market share in the global economy to China. This is largely due to the fact that the "export basket" of Mexico, Honduras, Guatemala, and other countries are most similar to China's. Many Central American countries copied Mexico's maquila model, specializing in textiles and clothing for the US market. Between 2000 and 2010 Mexico lost over 1 million jobs in the manufacturing sector, with the yarn, textiles, and garment chains being among the most hard hit due to competition from China.[13] Maquiladoras in Central America and Mexico offered wages slightly higher than what was on offer for rural agriculture, and thus drew in a large low-skilled workforce to sew clothes or snap keyboards onto computers. China leapfrogged over these countries with its lower wages, a massive reserve army of workers from the countryside, and exchange rate policies.[14]

As the China Boom marched on, with Latin American exchange rates rising alongside it, South American countries started feeling the pinch as well. A 2011 survey of its membership by the Brazilian National Confederation of Industries found that two-thirds of the membership had lost customers to Chinese exporters. This has been confirmed by academic economists as well. Rhys Jenkins of the University of East Anglia teamed with Alexandre de Freitas Barbosa of the University of Sao Paulo in Brazil and found that the Brazilian footwear, mobile phone, motorcycle, steel tube, and furniture industries were the hardest hit from Chinese competition during the first decade of the 2000s.[15] In a follow-up study, Jenkins found that the value of Brazilian exports threatened by China was expanding—finding that 70 percent of the value of Brazilian exports were facing Chinese competition. China was competing with 80 percent of Brazil's exports to the United States, and 92 percent of Brazil's exports to the European Union. Perhaps most alarming was that Jenkins found that Brazil was facing stiff competition from China in regional South American markets, which have long been a stronghold for Brazilian exports. What is more, Jenkins found that Brazil's loss of competition was not confined to light manufacturing, but also to more high technology manufacturing sectors.[16]

Circling back to Hirschman's concern about the enclave economy associated with commodities exports, it appears that Latin American exports to China followed an enclave pattern. Examining the period 2000 to 2012, Rebecca Ray from our team at Boston University found that Latin America's exports to China support about 20 percent fewer jobs per US$1 million than the region's exports overall. As China continues to grow as a share of Latin American exports, this will necessarily drive down the employment benefits of exports overall. This is due to the fact that in Latin America, exports support 11.6 jobs in extractive commodities and

71.8 jobs in manufacturing for every US$1 million output in each sector. Of course, primary commodities production also creates indirect jobs such as infrastructure for roads and so forth, but that only increases the jobs intensity of extractive industries by a factor of two, still dwarfing the contribution of manufacturing.

Premature Deindustrialization?

Declining industrial competitiveness is a canary in a coal mine for what could become a broader trend of declining shares of industry in Latin America's economies. The diversification of both exports and the basic production structure of an economy are among the most key ingredients of economic growth. The more products that are competitive in the marketplace, the more opportunities there are for growth. Industry is the most technologically sophisticated and is the main driver of the kind of economic growth that can help countries move from rags to riches. Countries that have a broader set of economic activities are also more apt to withstand shocks. If there is a sudden decline in commodities prices, the economy can still rely on services or manufacturing, and so forth. Industrialization has brought more than just economic benefit. The economist Dani Rodrik from the Institute for Advanced Study in Princeton reminds us that:

> A progression of manufacturing industries—textiles, steel, automobiles—emerged from the ashes of the traditional craft and guild systems, transforming agrarian societies into urban ones. Peasants became factory workers, a process that underpinned not only an unprecedented rise in economic productivity, but also a wholesale revolution in social and political organization. The labor movement led to mass politics, and ultimately to political democracy.[17]

Rodrik, who coined the term "pre-mature de-industrialization," has demonstrated how Latin America's share of industry has deteriorated the most among developing countries in recent decades. Deindustrialization in the industrialized world is a well-known phenomenon, and the industrialized world occurred after rich countries had reached a certain level of income. The problem is that developing countries—and Latin America in particular—have begun to deindustrialize before the region has reached the living standards of the industrialized countries (before the level of industrialization began to decline in wealthier countries). Rodrik observes that Latin America has been deindustrializating since the 1980s (see Figure 5.1). Latin American countries "imported deindustrialization" during the Washington Consensus period by opening up their markets prematurely—before they were able to reach a healthier mix of industry in the economy.[18]

The question that is hotly debated in the hemisphere is whether the rise of China is accelerating the deindustrialization of Latin

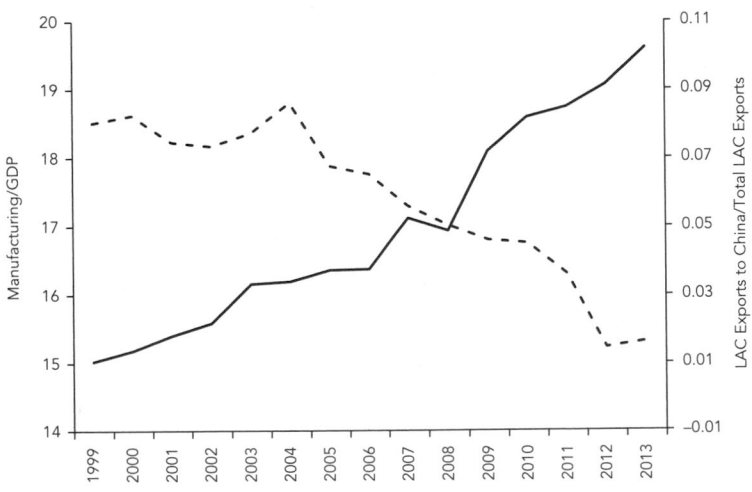

Figure 5.1 Premature Deindustrialization in Latin America?

America. Of course, declining export competitiveness in manufacturing will eventually trickle into the domestic economy. This is especially true in countries like Mexico and Central America where manufacturing is largely export-oriented. But manufacturing in commodity-rich South America is different. In Brazil, exports are only one-fifth of manufacturing production and employment (in Mexico it is closer to four-fifths).

Manufacturing as a share of the total economy was close to 30 percent in Brazil and Argentina by 1980, and over 20 percent in Mexico and Colombia. By 2013, industry declined to less than 15 percent in Brazil and Argentina, 17.8 percent in Mexico, and 12 percent in Colombia. The period of the most dramatic declines in Latin America was from 1990 to 2002. This was the period when the region took part in extensive trade liberalization efforts, and would thus support Rodrik's observation that the region's deindustrialization was imported. The China Boom, however, comes in second. In Latin America as a whole and in Argentina, Brazil, Mexico, and Colombia, manufacturing declined more than in the crisis-wracked "lost decade" of the 1980s.

In their study of Brazil during the China Boom, Jenkins and de Freitas Barbosa argue that China's impact on Brazil is small but growing fast. They estimate that imports as a share of Brazilian consumption have been growing in general, from 14 percent in 1996 to 20 percent in 2010. Chinese import penetration of Brazilian industrial consumption was small but growing faster than the average—starting at less than 1 percent in 1996 and reaching 5 percent in 2010. According to their estimates China appears to be taking exports away from other exporters to Brazil, rather than domestic markets away from local producers, with the exception of parts of the textiles and electronics industries, which were facing real pressure. The authors conclude that "the competitive pressure on the Brazilian industrial system from China, albeit small, is growing fast and at different speeds across sectors. The continuation of these trends would make the hollowing out of Brazilian manufacturing a real possibility."[19]

Another sign that domestic manufacturing is suffering damage from Chinese competition in their home markets is the increased frequency in antidumping cases against China at the World Trade Organization (WTO). Companies can appeal to their governments to put in place temporary protections if they can prove that they are suffering damage from a foreign exporter. Since 1995 Latin Americans have initiated close to 18 antidumping cases per year. Since China entered the WTO in 2001, more than half those cases have been filed against China and form the majority of all cases filed by Argentina, Mexico, Brazil, and Peru.

Argentina launched a 2009 case against China on behalf of unions and local manufacturers in the Argentine footwear industry. The case escalated, with China kicking Argentina back where it hurt most. Citing a 50 percent surge in Chinese imports from 2006 to 2007, and a 43 percent decline in the price of Chinese shoe imports from 2002 to 2007, Argentina took China to the World Trade Organization. Argentina registered an antidumping investigation against Chinese footwear, starting a four-month period of temporary antidumping measures.[20] After further grievance from industry and workers, in March 2010 Argentina imposed antidumping duties in the form of tariffs on Chinese shoes, to be in effect for five years.[21] These actions angered China's Vice Minister of Commerce Jiang Yaoping, who responded by saying that Argentina's measures were "totally anomalous and discriminatory."[22] Argentine Production Minister Debora Giorgi responded to Yaoping's comments by stating that Argentina took the measures "to protect the national industry and the work of 600,000 Argentine workers," and emphasized that "China is one of our largest trade partners. All we want is to hold a healthy and respectful relation of healthy competition."[23]

In April of the same year China struck back at Argentina. In retaliation for the increased protectionist measures, a Chinese trade body told traders to stop buying Argentine soya oil, claiming that the oil contained an excessive level of solvent, and therefore did not meet quality standards.[24] Before the dispute, Argentina accounted for 77 percent of China's soy oil imports, but afterward its share of the market fell to 12 percent.[25] While the countries tried to reach a solution to their dispute, many shipments of soy oil scheduled for April from Argentina to China were delayed. An Argentine oil trader commented to Mercopress: "It's odd that with Argentine soy-oil 40 to 50 USD cheaper than other countries, not a single Chinese importer is asking us to load the contracts that we had already agreed upon."[26] In July 2010, Argentina's president, Cristina Kirchner, visited China. China agreed to accept Argentine oil again, in exchange for allowing China to play the central role in the modernization of Argentina's ailing railroad system. As a result of this meeting, China resumed accepting oil and Argentina made China the central part of its railroad modernization program.[27] Speaking to Bloomberg, Li Qiang, managing director at Shanghai JC Intelligence Co., said, "China and Argentina seem to have improved relations recently and the two countries want to put the soybean oil row behind them to form a more extensive trading partnership in areas including energy and railroads."[28]

Brazil was also involved in a highly publicized footwear case. The Brazilian footwear industry is the third largest in the world after China and India. Production takes place in many areas of the country, especially the Vale dos Sinos in Rio Grande do Sul, and Franca in Sao Paolo. The sector is strongest in Franca especially, supporting a large part of the employment in the region. Producing shoes is strategic for Brazil, as it has the technology, raw materials (cattle to produce bovine leather), and the labor, which includes people who are specialized in shoe design and production.

Brazil's main advantage had been, however, a low production price due to cheap labor.[29] Currency appreciation that had been persistent in Brazil since its crisis in the 1990s led many international footwear producers to look for cheaper shoes, which they found in China. There was simultaneously an increased supply of Chinese shoes as China developed capital to produce better shoes, and even recruited Brazilians to consult on designing footwear.[30] The major Brazilian newspaper *Folha de Sao Paulo* published a story in October 2003 about Aethelwald Zilli, a Brazilian who moved to Dongguan in China. Zilli told reporters that "China pays those in the footwear industry very well, they want to get all the technology they can in order to become a presence in the footwear industry." While unemployed after the Brazilian financial crisis, Mauro Willrich saw an ad in a local Brazilian newspaper recruiting people knowledgable of the footwear industry. He promptly moved to China where he was given an apartment, food, and airfare to be employed by Paramount shoe manufacturer, along with 150 other Brazilians. (Paramount manufactures American brands such as Nine West.) Fabiana Ebert, who moved to China in 2002 to work in the footwear industry, summed up the feelings of many Brazilian immigrants to China, and said, "In [Brazil] many companies are struggling, and it is difficult to get a good job."[31]

As in Argentina, by 2008–2009 Chinese shoes were significantly penetrating the Brazilian market. In October of 2008 the Brazilian Association of Footwear Industries (Abicalcados) lodged a complaint against Chinese shoe imports, and in 2010 the Brazilian authorities imposed a definitive anti-dumping duty on some types of Chinese shoes, amounting to $13.85 per pair of shoe. This was to be applicable for five years.[32]

In response to the tariffs Bai Ming, a researcher at the Chinese Academy of International Trade and Economic Cooperation, told the *Global Times*: "Under the current global economic slowdown, many countries are resorting to protectionism . . . The protectionist practices will not only impact the bilateral trade but also China's interest in investing overseas."[33]

That was just fine by Abicalcados, who announced that by 2010 at least four national manufacturers of shoes signed contracts to produce shoe parts that would have previously been made in China, after the antidumping measures imposed by the government.[34] In July of 2012, Brazil went further and voted to add an additional 182 antidumping duties to unfinished footwear products from China.[35]

The China Boom and Financial Instability in the Americas

Back in 2010 the future never looked brighter for Brazil. It had been singled out by Goldman Sachs as one of the engines of global growth, hit the cover of *The Economist*, and won bids for the World Cup and the Olympics. Underneath the record growth figures that Brazil had experienced until then was booming demand and prices for Brazil's iron ore, soybeans, and petroleum from China. Brazil mirrored heightened expectations for most of Latin America, especially the resource-rich nations in South America.

The story of Banco Pine, a midsize Brazilian bank, is a telling example of how the commodity boom had a dark side in terms of financial instability. In 2010 Banco Pine issued $125 million in corporate bonds for international investors in the booming corporate bond market. Banco Pine's offering was a smash success. Brazilian interest rates were over 10 percent in 2010, at the same time the Federal Funds rate for US Treasuries was close to zero. Investors thus borrowed dollars on the cheap in the United States and parked them in places like Banco Pine. As late as 2014 Banco

Pino's bonds were trading at $1.06 on the dollar, but by 2015 they had begun sliding at 94 cents. The *Financial Times* called Banco Pine a "bond in distress" and emblematic of emerging market corporate debt concerns after 2014.[36]

Banco Pine's issuance occurred when the Brazilian real had appreciated by almost 50 percent in 2010, and when the bank's prospects for lucrative projects looked boundless. What Banco Pine didn't see was that many of its investments were not going to pan out due to a change in Brazil's macroeconomic (and political) headwinds. Brazil's companies had become less competitive due to exchange rate appreciation and a lack of investment. Banco Pine's bond comes due in 2017, and if the Brazilian real continues to plummet as it has since 2014, the bank could face a crisis. Even if the worst doesn't happen, however, Banco Pine went into contraction mode—offering fewer loans—at exactly the time when the economy needed to be in expansion mode.

Modest-sized Banco Pine is emblematic of the financial instability that rumbled under the Americas during the China Boom. As we discussed in chapter 3, Chinese demand for Latin American commodities surged after 2003, as did the region's growth prospects. Chinese demand for commodities made them more scarce and further boosted the prices for commodities. This improved Latin America's terms of trade—the ratio of export to import prices for an economy. Getting higher prices for exports over imports can be not only helpful for growth, but also for maintaining macroeconomic stability. When a country has poor terms of trade—high import prices versus export prices—the country often has large external deficits that have to be covered by foreign borrowing. Because of the terms of trade, Latin America experienced a current account surplus from 2003 to 2007—meaning that on average the total value of exports exceeded the total value of imports. These surpluses allowed Latin American governments to pay down external debts. Whereas external debt amounted to more than 25 percent of GDP from 1998 to 2002, those levels were brought down to 5.5 percent from 2008 to 2013.[37]

Governments became more prudent, but the corporate and financial sectors in Latin America did not. In the bond market, for example, Latin American governments and corporations (including banks) issued $16 billion in bonds in 2003, but by 2014 they had issued over $100 billion. Of all Latin American issuances between 2003 and 2014, 83 percent were in the corporate sector, with 75 percent of the bonds denominated in dollars.[38] Forty-two percent of the bonds issued by Latin American entities were issued in Brazil.

What did the China Boom have to do with the Latin American borrowing spree, and to what extent should the region be concerned about financial fragility? For the first part of the question, pretend for a moment that you are a New York hedge fund or pension fund investor in New York in 2010. In the wake of the global financial crisis of 2008–2009, China puts in place a massive stimulus package of 12 percent of GDP. The bulk of this stimulus is in the form of credit to local governments for boundless urbanization and infrastructure projects.[39] Subsequently, demand for Latin American commodities and economic growth in Latin America are projected to increase because Latin America will be key in supplying copper, iron ore, and petroleum for China's investment surge. Meanwhile, the US economy in 2010 is slow to recover from the crisis, the Eurozone is in the midst of its own crisis, and Japan is still stuck in the doldrums. Latin America looks like a good bet.

But there is more. The Federal Reserve of the United States has deployed a mix of methods to bring US interest rates near zero, so borrowing large sums of money is cheaper than at any time in your career. You decide to borrow at near-zero interest rates in the United States and invest in bonds, currencies, stocks, and derivatives in Latin America, where growth projections interest rates can be over 10 percent and growth rates are projected to be high as well. You buy bonds issued by Banco Pine, stock in the Brazilian iron giant Vale, and foreign exchange derivatives in Brazil, Chile, Colombia, Peru, and beyond. You do very very well.

As Figure 5.2 makes vivid, capital flows surged into Brazil during the China Boom. After a sudden stop in capital flows during the global financial crisis in 2008, the forces just described triggered a quick surge back into Brazil's markets. The figure also shows how Brazil's exchange rate skyrocketed alongside the capital flows—appreciating by 40 percent in real terms from 2003 to 2011.

But individual investors and individual debtors seldom lack enough information to determine whether their investments tip the scales such that they bring risk to a country or region's financial system. That's where the International Monetary Fund (IMF) came in. In 2011 and 2012 the IMF raised concern and eyebrows when it told Latin America and other emerging markets that they might need to cool off the capital flows that were surging into their

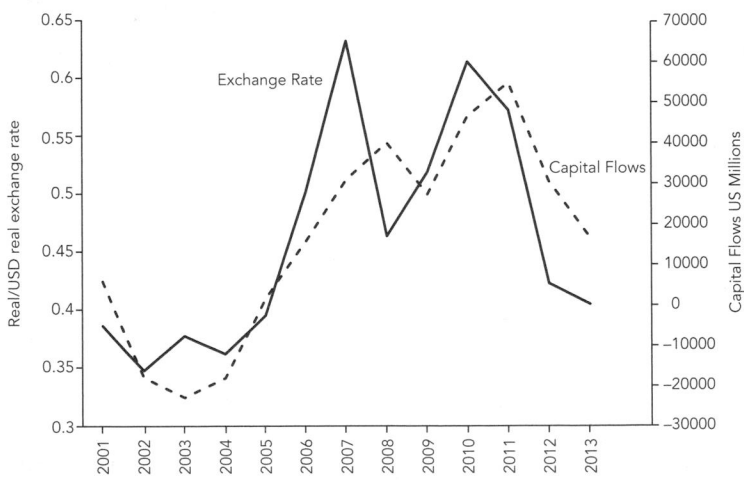

Figure 5.2 Exchange Rates and Capital Flows in Brazil

economies. Exchange rates in the region had appreciated almost 50 percent on the decade for many countries, and credit expansion in the private sector was approaching bubbling proportions. In the short term, the IMF warned, exchange rate appreciation and credit bubbles could hurt the competitiveness of firms and bloat the balance sheets of the private sector. In the medium to long term, the IMF feared, a slowdown in China or an increase in interest rates in the United States could trigger an unwinding of capital flows to Latin America that could cause exchange rates to depreciate and debt to balloon in proportion.[40]

The IMF recommended that countries put in place stiffer bank supervision so that Banco Pines did not borrow too much, and urged governments not to excessively borrow (while acknowledging that governments had manageable debt loads and that the bulk of the problem was in the corporate sector). The IMF also stressed the importance of having a flexible exchange rate and storing foreign exchange reserves in case an exchange rate plummeted to an unsustainable ratio. As a signal that the IMF was really serious about their diagnosis, they even recommended that countries might need to put in place capital controls on the inflow of capital—taxes or limits on investments in currency, bond, and stock markets—to stem exchange rate appreciation and asset bubbles. Capital controls had been shunned by the IMF for over a decade as unconventional methods that prevented much needed investments from reaching emerging markets. Capital controls had also fallen out of favor among mainstream finance ministers. The environment had become such a concern, however, that the IMF changed its tune by stating that nations may need to resort to such instruments alongside more traditional measures.[41] Even the more reluctant finance ministries also wouldn't rule them out. "We do not like capital controls," said Colombian finance minister Mauricio Cardenas in a press interview, "but we have not scrapped the idea altogether—it is always a handy option. I even have one plan in my desk drawer."[42]

Indeed, some Latin American countries were already practicing what the IMF was preaching, but perhaps not enough to fully stem the instability underlying the global economic environment of the China Boom and the slowdown in the West. Former governor of the Central Bank of Chile, Jose De Gregorio, argues that most countries weathered major financial turbulence through 2013 because most countries had good macroeconomic policies in place, had flexible exchange rates and used capital controls and foreign exchange interventions at crucial times, had good regulations for banks in place, and, crucially, had the "good luck" of high Chinese demand and commodities.[43]

By 2014 that good luck was running out. The luck of Chinese demand, high commodities prices, and cheap money from the United States started to turn in 2014. Without that luck, all of the other promising measures will be under significant stress. The combined slowdown in Chinese demand and lower commodities prices really hurt the Latin American economies. The IMF put Latin American growth at 1.4 percent in 2014, and projects just over 2 percent per annum for the next few years—way down from the 3.6 percent growth from 2003 to 2013. Commodity prices also hit a plateau in 2014, with some commodities such as petroleum sliding significantly. Even though the overall level of commodity prices still remained significantly higher in 2015 than at the turn of the century, what may be the biggest concern for the region is that prices no longer seem to be growing. The IMF reckons that even if commodity prices stayed at 2013 levels, GDP growth in Latin America to 2019 would be 1½ percentage points lower than during the China Boom.[44]

If prices do go down to historical levels the region could experience significant financial turbulence, according to calculations by Jose Antonio Ocampo, former finance minister of Colombia and now a professor at Columbia University in the United States. Ocampo recalculates the current account deficit in Latin America if commodity prices and the terms of trade returned to their 2003 levels. Under this scenario, Latin America would have faced a current account deficit of 7 percent in 2013—the same level that triggered Latin America's financial crises of the past.[45]

Exchange rate flexibility can certainly help as a shock absorber, but also comes with great risk. Given that three-quarters of Latin American debt in 2014 was denominated in dollars, depreciating currencies means ballooning corporate debt. Indeed, currency depreciation is now strongly linked to Chinese growth forecasts. Warnings abound across the financial press: "The Brazilian real dropped to its weakest level since late 2004 on Tuesday on disappointing economic data from top trade partner China and concerns over the health of Latin America's largest economy."[46] It is not just Brazil. The IMF analyzed the impact of bad news on China's industrial output on Latin American currency markets and found that bad news was associated with about a half percent decline in the value of the exchange rate for Latin America's main commodity exporters.[47] More bad news spells less demand and lower prices, plummeting Latin American currencies and ballooning corporate debt. If the private sector cannot handle the debt levels, countries may need to rescue the private sector. Corporate debt problems can quickly become sovereign debt crises even for the most prudent countries—as was the case with Ireland and Spain in the Eurozone.[48]

Of course, exchange rate flexibility may have a benefit as well. Falling currencies in Latin America could make Latin American manufacturing goods competitive again. What is more, currency depreciation can make imports too expensive and lure consumers to purchase more domestic goods and services. This benefit will only come if Latin American manufacturers are able to increase their productivity, as well as lower their prices.

While it is clear that China has significantly impacted the competitiveness of Latin American exports, by 2013 it was also clear that China was making modest inroads into domestic Latin American industry as well. The China Boom was also associated with more exchange rate volatility. If these trends continue we will witness a real hollowing out of Latin American industry, as the resource curse would predict. Rhys Jenkins also says that "on the other hand, the size and coherence of the internal market and the public policy options and institutions available mean that a different pattern of development is possible."[49]

Squandering the China Boom?

How well did Latin America do during the China Boom in terms of preventing the resource curse? Many countries in Latin America deserve praise for capturing some of the windfall profits of the China Boom and using those resources for social development— especially to reduce poverty and inequality. Without belittling the need for poverty reduction, however, the region's governments fell far short in capturing the rents from the China Boom and investing in upgrading technology, innovation, and industry so that those who are lifted from poverty can find a place for meaningful work.

From 2006 to 2009, the World Bank convened the Commission on Growth and Development that brought together Nobel economists with leaders from governments and the private sector across the world. The commission's final report stressed the need for nations to make capital investments into their economies to the tune of 25 percent of GDP or more. With such investment, the poorer countries of the world would finally be able to achieve growth rates that would allow them to catch up to the more well-off nations of the world and truly achieve higher living standards for their people. This was not the first articulation of the need to invest 25 percent or more to achieve growth; such a recommendation has long been touted by economists and international institutions. But coming from such an established group of contemporaries, the message permeated more world capitals than ever before.

Except those in Latin America. The IMF looked at commodity booms in Latin America since 1970 and confirmed that the income windfall from the China Boom in Latin America was "unprecedented in terms in magnitude." However, they also concluded that Latin America's effort to save the proceeds from the China Boom was significantly lower than past episodes. The IMF economists calculate that incomes due to the China Boom were 15 percent higher than they were in Latin America during the boom of the 1970s, accounting for a 1.5 percent of GDP on average during the period. At the margin, however, the IMF found that Latin Americans were not increasing their saving in proportion to the windfall. Not only were Latin Americans saving less on the margin relative to the past, but they also saved less of the China Boom than did other regions in the world.[50]

One of the reasons that Latin American countries had a relatively weak growth performance even during the China Boom was that there was a lack of capital investment into the region's economies. This is nothing less than a travesty, given that the windfalls experienced during the China Boom were among the largest in Latin American history. According to data from the World Bank, gross fixed capital formation as a percentage of GDP in Latin America was barely higher than during the crisis-plagued years of the Washington Consensus period. During the China Boom investment amounted to 19.6 percent of GDP, whereas from 1980 to 2002 investment averaged 18.8 percent. These poor investment levels were far shorter than the 25 percent seen as a rule of thumb for catch-up growth, and were dwarfed by China's staggering 45 percent of GDP of capital investments during the boom (up from 35 percent from 1980 to 2002). Even Africa, long plagued by slow growth and weak investment, was able to invest 25 percent of GDP during the China Boom years. Chile, Colombia, Mexico, and Peru did manage to invest at above average rates for Latin America during the China Boom, with Ecuador investing the most at 22.9 percent of GDP. In Brazil, despite its having one of the strongest national development banks in the world, investment was far below the average at a mere 18 percent of GDP.[51] It thus may come as no surprise then that Latin America had one of the lesser China Booms in the world—the sub-Saharan region grew by 5.2 percent during the China Boom (compared to Latin America's 3.6 percent), and South Asia by 7.1 percent.

The Economic Commission for Latin America and the Caribbean (ECLAC) came to similar findings when examining the fiscal revenues that Latin American governments were able to capture during the China Boom. ECLAC found that Latin America did not capture tax and royalty revenues from commodities production in proportion with the rise in the windfalls. What is more, ECLAC found that nations were more apt to quickly spend the newfound revenues than to invest them into innovation and industrialization or to put them into funds for stabilitization or intergenerational equity. To the credit of many nations, particularly Bolivia, Peru, and others, this expenditure went toward cash-transfer and other poverty programs that have helped reduce poverty and inequality in the region. Second, ECLAC found that windfalls were used to help accumulate foreign exchange reserves that have proved useful during periods of financial instability and may be essential going forward into the future.[52]

In terms of industrialization and long-run growth, Latin American governments and firms also failed to invest in innovation and technological change. Just look at Table 5.1. Whereas industrialized countries spend over 2 percent of GDP on research and development, Latin America put only 0.66 percent of GDP into research and development during the China Boom. Close to 500,000 patents were registered in Latin America during the period, but only 12 percent of those were by Latin Americans, meaning that most of the patents being registered were by multinational companies placing their patents in Latin America. By contrast, China invested 1.52 percent of GDP into innovation and technological upgrading and registered a mammoth 3 million patents. Seventy-one percent of patents registered in China were by Chinese, signaling new innovations.

Finally, while the region was able to stem the worst financial turbulence during the financial crisis, there has been a significant build-up of financial instability in the region. As noted earlier, the massive inflows of speculative capital accentuated exchange rate appreciation in the region and expanded credit to unsustainable levels. As China demand slows and interest rates rise in the

Table 5.1 Technological Innovation in China and Latin America, 2003–2013

	R&D	Patent Applications	
	(%GDP)	Total	Resident share (%)
China	1.5	3,039,498	71
LAC (ave)	0.7	491,744	12
Argentina	0.5	36,183	17
Brazil	1.1	222,467	19
Colombia	0.2	17,913	7
Mexico	0.4	146,751	5

United States, exchange rates will depreciate and the size of corporate sector debt could balloon to levels that could require states to intervene—which could then put them in financial jeopardy as well. Exchange rate flexibility may help regain some export competitiveness, but not without technological upgrading and manageable debt levels.

Perhaps the Achilles heel of the China Boom in Latin America is an aspect of the resource curse that has only recently begun to attract attention—the environmental and social aspects of commodity-led growth. To that subject we now turn.

6

The Dragon's Footprint

In September of 2014, over 400,000 people gathered on the streets of New York City to send a signal to the world leaders attending a United Nations summit on global climate change. People came from all over the world to be heard, including celebrities Sting and Leonardo Dicaprio, and politicians such as the French foreign minister, Laurent Fabius. UN Secretary General Ban Ki-moon was there, marching alongside former vice president of the United States Al Gore, Mayor of New York City Bill de Blasio, and naturalist Jane Goodall. For over six hours the marchers led chants, sang songs, and waved thousands of colorful placards making statements like "United for Climate Action," "Don't Mess with Our Mama!," and "Hands Off Our Future!" These voices were heard. The over 120 world leaders who showed up for the conference renewed pledges to reduce the impact of economic activity that threatens the earth's climate.[1] Indeed, months after the summit the world's two largest climate polluters, the United States and China, reached a landmark agreement to cap their emissions of pollutants that cause global climate change.

Leonardo Cerda and Gloria Ushigua came all the way from the Andean rainforests of Ecuador to participate in the march.

Ushingua's placard read "Andes Petroleum *out* of Sapara territory!" Cerda is a leader of the Kichwa people in Ecuador; Ushigua is from the Sápara people, where she is president of the Association of Sápara Women. Both the Kichwa and Sápara languages have been characterized as critically endangered by the United Nations. Their peoples live in the jungles of the Amazon in the eastern part of Ecuador and border Yasuni National Park, a UNESCO Biosphere Reserve singled out as being one of the most biologically diverse locations on earth. Andes Petroleum was formed by the Chinese oil giants CNPC and SINOPEC and has recently been awarded two concessions in Kichwa and Sápara territory—home to some of the most endangered peoples and most biodiverse areas in the world. A growing coalition of local and global activists are organizing to use the Andes story to epitomize the growing destruction of local and indigenous communities, biodiversity, and climate by oil companies in general and Chinese companies in particular.[2]

This story captures one of the most central challenges of the China–Latin America economic relationship. China's demand for energy and natural resources is what makes Latin America such a strategic partner as China continues to rise. Trade and investment in these sectors are key drivers of economic growth in the region. However, energy and natural resource extraction has long been endemic to environmental degradation and social conflict across the Americas. In the rainforests of Brazil, Ecuador, and Peru; in the mines of Peru and Bolivia; and beyond, the China-led commodity boom has ignited a new round of environmental struggle in the region. If Latin American governments do not manage these resources properly it will not only trigger environmental and social crises, but it will also threaten the region's economic prosperity. Indeed, according to estimates by the World Bank, the economic costs of natural resource degradation in Latin America already increased significantly during the China Boom.

Rightly or wrongly, Chinese companies are increasingly seen as the face of this new environmental destruction. Interestingly, while Chinese demand is certainly the key driver of commodity growth in the region, when Chinese companies locate in Latin America they do not tend to perform uniformly worse than their domestic or other foreign counterparts that invest in natural resource sectors. China has weaker environmental regulations at home and a fledgling set of environmental guidelines for its multinational companies. Despite that fact there are some cases where Chinese companies are capable of complying with national and international standards, and they are sometimes setting best practices. Nevertheless, China too will need to improve its social and environmental footprint as it continues to invest in Latin America. This will be important in order for China to maintain its image with other developing countries as a Southern partner that acts differently than Western companies and financial institutions. It will also be important in order for China to maintain and expand market share in a region that is an increasingly strategic one in terms of securing natural resources for China's prosperity.

The Dark Side of Commodity-Led Growth

Energy, food, and natural resources are the cornerstone of Latin America's comparative advantage. Thus the exploitation of primary commodities is key for trade and economic growth in just about every country in the region. As we saw in chapter 3, Chinese demand boosted prices for primary commodities worldwide until about 2013 and granted Latin America one of its better growth spurts in decades. The geography and demographics of Latin America happen to place much of the region's natural resources in pristine or ecologically sensitive areas inhabited by local communities (often indigenous) who earn their livelihoods in the same areas that are sought for exploitation by international firms and Latin American governments.

Remember that the bulk of Chinese trade with and investment in Latin America is in iron and copper mining, petroleum extraction, soybean farming and processing, and beef exports, as well as in new infrastructure projects to facilitate that trade and investment. Whereas creating new software packages or even sewing millions of tons of clothing in large factories is relatively benign from an environmental perspective, environmental degradation is endemic in the extractive industries. Take mining, for instance, where almost every step of the production process can have a significant environmental footprint. The initial clearing of land for a mine often degrades topsoil and reduces forest cover, and waste rock from the mining process can impact nearby habitats when dumped. Explosives are often used to extract minerals. That can stress wildlife and farm animals, while the subsequent dust can cause respiratory problems in people and wildlife alike. After an initial hole is made, chemicals such as cyanide and large amounts of water are used to leach the minerals from rock. This can trigger water shortages, and the cyanide can cause pollution in water supplies and irrigation systems, killing fish and jeopardizing human health. Modern mines often have holding ponds of the polluted water, but heavy rains and earthquakes can disrupt these ponds. The mining process produces "tailings"—large amounts of finely crushed and processed ore rock—which have to be disposed of safely once they have been exposed to cyanide, or they too can be harmful. Mining causes what is called "acid mine drainage," which drains from the waste rock when it rains—carrying heavy metals such as aluminum, arsenic, cadmium, lead, nickel, and zinc into waterways, irrigation systems, and blood streams as well.[3]

Inland oil extraction follows a similar path. Oil experts refer to oil exploration, drilling, and extraction as the "upstream" phase of the oil production cycle. Among the upstream environmental and social impacts are deforestation due to the clearing of areas in remote ecosystems and the moving of very heavy equipment into those areas. As in the mining industry, large quantities of water are needed to extract petroleum, and that process produces a significant amount of contaminated waste. This waste can be highly toxic and is often stored in waste pits. Like holding ponds in the mining sector, waste pits in the oil sector are highly susceptible to spills. Emissions from the process impact the climate, and workers and local communities suffer from being exposed to the waste and air pollution. In Latin America, inland oil exploration and extraction happens to be located in areas where many indigenous communities like the Sápara reside. One estimate says that there are 50 indigenous communities living within oil and gas exploration in the Western Amazon alone. In addition to the Sápara, other indigenous groups within oil and gas concessions in the Amazon are the Tagaeri in Ecuador, the Nahua in Peru, the Uwa in Colombia, the Ayoreo in Bolivia, and the Juma in Brazil.[4]

Soy farming and cattle ranching have similar environmental and social impacts, and have distinct issues as well. Land conversion for soy and cattle threatens biodiversity in places like Brazil, Bolivia, and Paraguay. When such conversion entails clearing forests, the carbon stored in trees is released into the atmosphere, accelerating global climate change. Clearing also puts pressure on indigenous communities. In the soy sector pesticides also impact water and irrigation capabilities. In the Amazon the two often go together. First, cattle ranching deforests an area and puts pressure on native peoples. Then, once the land is cleared, soy farmers move in.[5]

One aspect that cuts across the production of all these activities and significantly accentuates environmental damage is the expansion of access roads and other infrastructure projects to facilitate extraction and cultivation in remote areas. The act of building roads requires more land clearing and heavy equipment, and generates more waste. Infrastructure projects also facilitate the movement of other people and settlers, putting further pressure on water supplies, land, biodiversity, local communities, and native peoples.[6] For the Amazon, some estimates reveal that each kilometer of legal roads brings three kilometers of illegal roadways that trigger illegal logging, poaching, illegal mining, and more. Damming rivers causes significant disruption of river ecologies, including impacting fish migration, spawning habitats, and people who thrive from such ecologies.[7]

This is a glimpse at the darker side of commodity-led growth that has been the Achilles heel of Latin America and that has shaded development for at least a century. Noted environmental economist Edward Barbier has shown how Latin American economic development is dependent on converting land for natural resource exploitation as a source of economic growth. If Latin American governments were saving the windfalls from commodity booms and investing them in alternative uses that could generate economic growth and employment, then natural resource exploitation would not be as much of a grave concern.[8] Unfortunately, Barbier further confirms that the region has not historically done so. He finds that during booms there are surges of investment into resource-intensive sectors and a drain away from more employment-based sectors. Each boom puts more pressure on the environment and pushes poorer people into even more environmentally sensitive lands, and thus accentuates the environmental degradation associated with a boom.[9]

According to the United Nations, during the China Boom the annual rate of forest loss in Latin America was 0.46 percent—more than three times the global rate per annum. This is alarming given that Latin America is among the world's most biodiverse regions in the world, housing 21 percent of the world's land, 22 percent of the world's marine ecosystems, and 16 percent of the world's freshwater ecosystems. Indeed, the United Nations also estimates that Latin America contains somewhere between 30 and 50 percent of all species of mammals, birds, reptiles and amphibians, and plants and insects on earth.[10]

From this perspective, the recent commodity boom has come at great economic cost. Each year the World Bank calculates the economic costs of natural resource depletion for the majority of countries in the world—from an algorithm based on rates of depletion, the amount of windfall captured, and so forth. Between 2003 and 2013—the China Boom—the economic costs of natural resource depletion in Latin America amounted to 8.6 percent of annual GDP on an annual basis.[11] That is more than double the 3.6 percent annual economic growth the region experienced during the period, implying that the recent boom was in many ways an illusion that will come home to roost in the future through natural resource scarcity and the inability of the region to absorb the wastes from environmental degradation.

Enter the Dragon

Given that China's trade and investment in Latin America has been a key driver of economic activity since the turn of the century, Chinese demand is also partly responsible for environmental degradation and social conflict in the Americas. Eighty-seven percent of Latin American exports to China are in energy, mining, or agriculture—whereas only 55 percent of Latin American exports to the rest of the world are in such sectors. Ninety percent of Chinese private investment is in these sectors, and over 80 percent of China's loans to Latin American governments are in natural-resource-based or infrastructure projects as well.

It should come as no surprise, then, that the environmental impact of Latin America's trade and investment with China is more harmful than the economic activity in the region that is not directly linked to China. With data provided by climate scientist Glen Peters (as part of a broader project led by me), Rebecca Ray examined the extent to which China–Latin America trade contributes more to global climate change than does Latin America's non-China-related economic activity.[12] Climate change is caused by many factors, such as emissions from power plants and cars, the clearing of forests, methane released from cattle, and more. Each of these impacts is measured in different ways, and scientists have created a metric called "carbon equivalent" that scales these measures together into one composite. Measured in this way, we found that each dollar of economic activity in Latin America generates about 1.1 kilograms of carbon pollution. Latin American exports are more carbon-intensive, given the region's reliance on natural resources and primary commodities associated with the clearing of forests and methane emissions. Thus we were not surprised to find that the carbon intensity of Latin American exports were 1.7 kilograms per dollar. We were even less surprised to find that Latin America's China trade is the most carbon intensive, at nearly 2 kilograms per dollar—given that China trade is much more concentrated in natural-resource-based sectors than is the rest of Latin America's trade. Because China–Latin America trade is the fastest growing area of export activity for Latin America, the implications for climate change are considerable.

Ray found similar results when looking at water scarcity in the Americas. As noted above, water is essential for natural resource exploitation. Water is needed in the extraction process and is needed to absorb the waste products from extraction. In farming, of course, water is needed to grow crops. We found that the water intensity—the number of cubic meters of water needed to produce one dollar of economic activity—of Latin American GDP is 0.3 cubic meters. However, the water intensity of Latin American economic activity destined for China is 10 times as large, at 3.3 cubic meters per dollar. It is thus no wonder that pressure is increasing on water supplies, at times pitting local communities against larger landed interests across the hemisphere.

China is not engaging with Latin America to consciously pillage the environment and create conflict with the peoples of the Americas. It just so happens—as was the case during the West's industrial surge in the nineteenth century discussed in chapter 2—that the ingredients China needs to fuel its own version of the industrial revolution are often located in Latin American locales, and their extraction tends to generate both environmental degradation and social conflict.

Dragons Are Not Demons

Contemporary Chinese investment in Latin America actually dates back to 1992, when one of China's oldest state-owned enterprises, Shougang, purchased the Marcona iron mine in Peru. It has been operating in Peru as Shougang Hierro Peru ever since. Marcona is one of the world's larger iron mines, with reserves of close to 1 billion tons. By some measures Shougang is the epitome of success in Latin America. In 2011, the influential business magazine *Latin Trade* ranked 779 publicly traded companies in Latin America based on revenue and profit. According to the article, "the final result shows Shougang Hierro Peru, majority owned by China-based iron and steel conglomerate Grupo Shougang, as the best company based on our six metrics."[13]

Looking at Shougang from a social and environmental angle, however, an article in a 2011 issue of the *Americas Quarterly* written by Barbara Kotschwar and colleagues at the Peterson Institute for International Economics said, "Shougang has seemingly fulfilled the worst expectations of Chinese companies."[14] Until recently,

Shougang Hierro Peru has been Exhibit A of how a Latin American country has failed at maximizing the benefits and mitigating the costs of Chinese investment in Latin America. That said, both Shougang and the Peruvian government have learned valuable lessons from Shougang's past experience. Both have been quick to attempt to rectify past wrongs and use the Shougang experience as one to improve upon.

Amos Irwin and I published an in-depth article comparing Shougang's performance with other domestic and foreign investors in a 2013 issue of the peer-reviewed *Journal of Environment and Development*. Based on extensive fieldwork, we found that Shougang was less apt to comply with local environmental regulations, complying only 72 percent of the time, relative to some Swiss and US firms that complied 86 to 90 percent of the time. When audited on its environmental behavior Shougang only put in place 71 percent of the auditor's recommendations, relative to a rate of 88 to 100 percent for the other firms. Shougang also fired union and indigenous workers who had a long history of striking for better wages and working conditions—and replaced these workers with Chinese miners. Shougang also skirted pledges it made to reinvest into the community.

However, we found that Shougang is not uniformly worse than its counterparts. Indeed, the US-based company Doe Run performed significantly worse on a number of counts, and is using a loophole in the US–Peru Free Trade Agreement to attempt to sue the Peruvian government after the government finally tried to make the firm clean up its act.[15] According to more recent research, Shougang has made significant improvement and now performs on par with most local and other foreign firms in terms of safety, environment, and labor standards. As a sign that the company is willing and able to adapt to Peruvian and global norms, in 2014 Shougang even agreed to participate in the Extractive Industries

Transparency Initiative (EITI)—an initiative that seeks to promote transparency and accountability within the global extractives sector.[16]

The fact is, Shougang's early growing pains in Latin America are an example of the exception, rather than the rule when it comes to the environmental performance of Chinese companies in Latin America. With Andres Lopez from the University of Buenos Aires in Argentina and Cynthia Sanborn of the University of the Pacific in Lima, Peru, I cochaired an eight-country study that looks at the environmental and social performance of Chinese trade and investment in Latin America. We did indeed find an association between the China Boom and an accentuation of environmental degradation and social conflict in Latin America. But when it came to the actual performance of Chinese companies, we found that Chinese firms perform no worse—and sometimes even better—than their counterparts in host countries and from abroad.

These findings are encouraging. When we first began researching the environmental impacts of globalization in the late 1980s and early 1990s, the chief concern was whether industrialized country firms operating in an context of strict environmental regulations at home would carry those practices to developing countries while relocating, or stoop to the lower environmental standards of developing countries.[17] In the case of China–Latin America investment, however, the environmental standards of the foreign investor (China) are *lower* than the standards of the host countries. Therefore we would expect numerous mistakes on the part of the Chinese side as their firms struggle to comply to standards abroad that are more stringent than at home. The Yale University–based Environmental Performance Index is an indicator project that attempts to measure a nation's level of environmental regulation and compliance. On a scale of 0 to 100, with 100 being the best, Switzerland has the best environmental regulation and compliance, with a score of 88; the United States ranks 33rd, with a score of 67.6. Most Latin American nations tend to rank in the 80s and 90s, with scores ranging from 50 to 60. China, though improving each year, was ranked number 118 with a score of 43 in 2013.[18]

It is therefore no small feat that when put to the test, some Chinese firms are showing the willingness and ability to outperform even Swiss and American firms. Cynthia Sanborn and Victoria Chonn document how Chinese firms, including Shougang itself, have banded together to learn from past mistakes and attempt to put in place best practices. The Association of Chinese Enterprises in Peru was formed in 2011, and comprises more than half of the 120 Chinese firms operating in that country. The group meets to share best practices and experiences. After the copper giant Aluminum Corporation of China (known as CHINALCO) was ordered to temporarily halt production when government inspectors found that acidic wastes were seeping into nearby lakes, the association went to the Peruvian government as a whole seeking workshops on Peruvian environmental regulation.[19]

Indeed, the case of CHINALCO stands in stark contrast to the early Shougang days, and to the performance of most other foreign firms. In 2013 CHINALCO opened the Toromocho project in Peru, investing over $3 billion—thus making the project one of the largest in the world. When angling for the project CHINALCO bidders were keenly aware of the stigma attached to Chinese investment given Shougang's previous problems, and thus went out of their way to pledge the Toromocho project as one that would establish itself as meeting or beating global standards for social and environmental responsibility. To that end, the firm has promised to deploy cutting-edge construction technology and a state-of-the-art acid water treatment plant, and relocate approximately 5,000 people in a responsible manner. Each family that moves to the New Morococha has been offered their own home (and title), running water, and a modern sewage system (wholly absent from the "old" Morococha), all paid for by CHINALCO. The firm also offers higher wages than its competitors and has entered into a government-sponsored "mesa" or roundtable that brings together the numerous stakeholders in the project (the firm, communities, civil society groups, the government, etc.) to navigate these issues.[20]

Another positive development is that Shougang, China Minmetals (another copper firm operating in Peru as Lumina copper), and oil giant CNPC have now agreed to participate in the EITI in Peru. The EITI is a cluster of governments, extractive companies, and civil society groups looking to increase transparency and accountability in the global mining sector. When a country or firm joins EITI, they are committed to adhering to global standards for reporting taxes and royalties in order to make more transparent their contributions to the host economy. Participating nations and firms must allow this information to be made public, so that civil society and governments can make firms and governments accountable. Peru has been part of EITI since 2005.[21] According to Elizabeth Economy and Michael Levi in their book *By All Means Necessary: How China's Resource Quest is Changing the World*,[22] China has had weak participation in the EITI. That appears to be changing, at least in Peru. According to Sanborn and Chonn Chinese firms were slower to participate because they needed to get the okay from their corporate headquarters back in China. In 2012 Lumina Copper, another Chinese firm in Peru, was the first to enter EITI, and Shougang and CNPC followed in 2014.[23]

In Cerda and Ushigua's Ecuador, Chinese companies have shown promise relative to their counterparts as well. Although Cerda and Ushigua are opposed to Andes Petroleum moving into their territory, Andes's record in Ecuador thus far shines in comparison to the record of other foreign companies in Ecuador. Andes operates in Sucumbíos, a place previously occupied for oil development by Texaco (now Chevron). This area has been subject to egregious levels of environmental contamination that make it close to impossible for people to earn a livelihood. Using the same loopholes in an investment treaty that Doe Run is attempting to sue Peru over, Chevron has brought an international case against Ecuador for trying to make Chevron assume liabilities for the environmental devastation in Sucumbíos. In contrast, Andes has had a much better relationship with the government on environmental issues, and nearby indigenous communities are actually hoping that Andes stays in the region in order to invest more.[24]

On an even higher note, China's SINOPEC is part of an innovative experiment in inshore oil drilling that aims to have minimal environmental and social impact. In Ecuador's Amazon Block 16, the Spanish firm Repsol and its junior partner (with a 20 percent stake) SINOPEC are experimenting with a new method of oil development in ecological and socially sensitive areas—termed "offshore inland" development. Championed by former Secretary of the Interior Bruce Babbitt, the basic idea of offshore inland development is to create "islands in the jungle" where oil companies have as little a footprint as possible. The most central element is not building new roads to the drilling and exploration sites, but rather helicoptering in key supplies as if the site is an offshore platform. The Camisea project in Peru is the first of this kind, has been operating for 10 years, and produces over 90 percent of Peru's natural gas.[25] The Block 16 project would not be considered a full-blown offshore inland project; Repsol did put a road from their site, but only to a nearby river, and consciously not connected to Ecuador's highway system in order to discourage new settlements near Yasuni. Equipment thus comes into the site through barges. SINOPEC'S subsidiary in Ecuador, Tiptop Energy, bought a 20 percent stake in the project from Repsol and has been partaking in and learning from this project.[26] It will be essential for SINOPEC to bring this knowledge and experience to the new concessions in the Amazon located near the Sápara peoples.

When governments and civil society organizations have pressured Chinese companies, the Chinese have even agreed to move the location of entire projects or decided against a project altogether. Bolivia's innovative and inclusive constitution grants local communities the power to approve mining projects under a majority vote. The Chinese metallurgy company Jungie was awarded concessions in Bolivia for a metals processing plant and tailings dam in the municipality of Tacobamba, just north of Potosi. The people of Tacobamba rejected the Jungie proposal, expressing their concerns over the potential impacts of sulfur and other pollutants that might result from the project. Jungie worked with the Bolivian government and the project was relocated to the municipality of Villa de Yocalla, a less remote area with other similar activity already in operation and where the local community voted in favor of the project.[27]

Perhaps the most difficult but bold and honorable move by a Chinese firm with respect to the environment was the complete withdrawal of China's largest hydroelectric company, Sinohydro, from the Agua Zarca dam project in Honduras. Like Peru, Ecuador, and Bolivia, Honduras has ratified the International Labor Organization's (ILO) 169 that recognizies the rights of indigenous people by granting them the right of prior informed consultation about projects impacting their territories. Indigenous peoples and environmental advocates claimed that they were not consulted adequately before the project commenced in 2011. Indeed, the project was wholly rejected in an assembly held by the mayor of the local community there.[28] Nevertheless, the Honduran government supplied military forces to protect the project and the military reportedly shot and killed the local indigenous leader there. Citing the project as "unpredictable and uncontrollable," Sinohydro has wiped its hands clean of this project entirely.[29] Sinohydro also faces stiff resistance from a coalition of global environmental campaigners. The Chinese company has won a concession to build a dam on Honduras's Patuca River, which may impact the ecological integrity and indigenous communities around the the Rio Platano World Heritage site—already seen as a threatened tropical rainforest biosphere that has been placed on UNESCO's endangered list because of illegal logging and poaching.[30]

China (Starting) to Scale Up

These cases are significant, but should not be overblown. Such practices are far from widespread, but they do show that when given the proper incentives by governments or civil society, Chinese companies are capable of adapting to domestic laws and global norms. Chinese officials are working to put in place guidelines for the social and environmental performance of its companies operating overseas. This is remarkable given China's level of income. Indeed, when the United States was at the same level of development as China it had yet to put in place bedrock environmental regulation at home, let alone for overseas operations. US companies, and the US-dominated World Bank, had notoriously bad records when it came to safeguarding the environmental and social impacts of aid and investment overseas. While US firms and the World Bank have cleaned up their act significantly as a result of government and civil society pressure around the world, they still make big mistakes and continue to be stigmatized for their tattered pasts.[31]

China has been setting and upgrading guidelines for overseas operations since 2007, when China's State Forestry Administration put in place the "Guide on Sustainable Overseas Silviculture by Chinese Enterprises" for Chinese logging companies. The guidelines require the preservation of high-value forests and endangered species, as well as consultations with local communities before investments occur. In 2008 China enacted the "Guidelines for Environmental and Social Impact Assessments of the China Export and Import Bank's Loan Projects." This is important given that the China Export-Import Bank (CHEXIM) provides financing for a vast amount of Chinese foreign direct investment in Latin America. CHEXIM's guidelines require that an environmental impact assessment be conducted. The China Development Bank (CDB) has similar guidelines. In 2013, China's Ministry of Foreign Commerce, along with the Ministry of Environmental Protection (MEP), issued the "Guidelines on Environmental Protection for Overseas Investment and Cooperation" that require all Chinese firms conducting business overseas to conduct environmental impact assessments and work with local communities.[32]

Perhaps the most interesting are the 2012 "Green Credit Guidelines," created by the China Banking and Regulatory Commission, the People's Bank of China (PBOC), and the Ministry of Environmental Protection. The guidelines require all bank finance in China—public or private—to adhere to a set of environmental and social norms. Article 21 applies specifically to financing for overseas operations:

> Article 21 Banking institutions shall strengthen the environmental and social risk management for overseas projects to which credit will be granted and make sure project sponsors abide by applicable laws and regulations on environmental protection, land, health, safety, etc. of the country or jurisdiction where the project is located. The banking institutions shall make promises in public that appropriate international practices or international norms will be followed as far as such overseas projects are concerned, so as to ensure alignment with good international practices.[33]

While it is remarkable that China is ramping up these guidelines, they still fall short in comparison with other such guidelines in existence. Moreover, thus far they are seen to suffer from a lack of transparency such that it is hard to evaluate the extent to which firms and banks are complying with them. For example, the CDB's guidelines incorporate four of the common social and environmental guidelines into its lending practices: environmental impact assessment, project review, public consultations with communities affected by the project, and an ex-post environmental impact assessment. However, the CDB does not incorporate into widely accepted guidelines a grievance mechanism, a requirement for adherence to international environmental laws and regulations, an independent review and assessment, or the establishment of covenants linked to compliance. A grievance mechanism and an independent review and assessment are important avenues for addressing public concerns and ensuring transparency throughout the process. CHEXIM goes beyond the CDB by requiring project review during the duration of the loan and establishing covenants linked to compliance. These additions are a step forward for socially and environmentally responsible loans because they directly link the loans to adherence to guidelines. However, in numerous conversations with companies by myself and colleagues related to this book and other projects, we find that company representatives on the ground in Latin America were not made aware of the guidelines. Other assessments have found that to the extent that such guidelines are used, the less often results are shared with host governments or communities.[34]

Nevertheless, Chinese regulators have shown a willingness to partner with other international institutions that have more experience evaluating and adapting to the social and environmental aspects of conducting international projects. In 2013 CHEXIM partnered with the Inter-American Development Bank (IDB) to form a $3 billion dollar fund for infrastructure and natural resource exploitation. After some negotiation, CHEXIM agreed to comply with the IDB's environmental and social safeguard policies and to receive technical support from IDB staff on how to conduct environmental and social safeguards for projects.[35] The IDB has already conducted some workshops with CHEXIM and other actors in China, and is even partnering with China's policy banks on other financing projects in Latin America where both parties will adopt IDB safeguards and learn from the experiences.

In late 2014, the China Chamber of Commerce of Metals Minerals & Chemicals Importers & Exporters developed a set of social and environmental guidelines with the German development agency Global Witness (a nongovernmental organization that focuses on natural resource management) and the Organization of Economic Cooperation and Development (OECD). Later in 2014, the China Chamber signed a memorandum of understanding with the OECD to develop further protocols under the guidelines and to hold training sessions so that participating firms can comply with the measures.[36]

Saving (for) the Future

It is not China's job to be the overarching managers of natural resources and social inclusion in the Americas. Latin American countries need to develop strong, stable, and predictable policies that ensure that natural resources are managed wisely. Natural resources can provide a source for long-run economic growth, but only if managed in a manner that is socially inclusive and not overly destructive of the environment. China, as an increasingly global player, should play its part. This chapter has demonstrated how there are many instances where China has played its part with the proper prompts from governments and civil society. At the end of the day it is the responsibility of Latin American governments to ensure that such prompts are in place for all economic activity within their borders, not just the Chinese.

As the statistics discussed in the first part of the chapter show, Latin American governments have fallen fall short of striking the right balance between commodity-led growth, social inclusion, and environmental sustainability during the China Boom. China's social and environmental bright spots in Latin America are overshadowed by the sheer scale and magnitude of commodity exploitation during the China Boom. China trade and investment was in sectors that were much more intensive with respect to land use change, air pollution, and deforestation than the rest of economic activity in Latin America. The high prices triggered by China trade and investment attracted even more demand from other countries into the same sectors, further accentuating environmental stress in the region. According to the World Bank, the economic costs of this activity averaged 8.6 percent of GDP on an annual basis in the Americas—significantly higher than in the 1990s, when such costs were put at just above 5 percent per year.[37]

In 2003, former World Bank economist Ramon Lopez published a landmark historical analysis in the reputable academic journal *World Development* titled "The Policy Roots of Socioeconomic Stagnation and Environmental Implosion: Latin America, 1950–2000." In that article Lopez attributes the relatively slow growth, poor social conditions, and significant environmental degradation in Latin America to a government "policy framework dominated by futile efforts to promote physical (and financial) capital accumulation almost at all costs."[38] In other words, the entire policy framework in Latin America is to promote as much short-term gain from economic activity like natural resource exploitation without accounting for the social and economic costs of such activity. Lopez is particularly concerned that the lack of clear property rights in the Americas, and the lack of incorporation of the environmental costs of economic activity provides explicit incentives to put extraction first. Lopez sums it up like this:

> Instead of concentrating their efforts in raising enough public revenues to finance the necessary investment in human and natural capital and the necessary institutional capacities to effectively enforce environmental regulation, governments have focused on the generation of an expensive and often incoherent system of short-run incentives to promote investments in physical capital.[39]

To Lopez, Latin American governments are not properly taxing the massive booms in commodity-led growth and investing the proceeds into policies for economic diversification, social improvement, and environmental protection. Lopez observes that the winners of the skewed policies are the owners of physical capital that form major lobby groups to maintain the status quo policy. This policy framework is reinforced because politicians win elections and gain international recognition by increasing short-term GDP. Finally, Lopez says that the nail in the coffin is a general ideology that sees government regulation as a hindrance on growth, rather than a tool to create the environment for long-run prosperity. This ideology is otherwise known as the Washington Consensus.

There is evidence that such trends only accentuated during Latin America's China Boom. In Brazil the famed "ruralistas" that have been reaping profits from the boom in cattle and soybean production since the turn of the century have been attributed for playing a key role in weakening Brazil's forest code for the Brazilian Amazon.[40] The new code granted amnesty to agricultural landowners who illegally deforested and allows those landowners to shrink the amount of forest they need to protect on their lands from 80 percent to 50 percent. Some estimate that the change in the code could lead to 190 million acres worth of deforestation.[41] These ruralistas are not Chinese, but have been emboldened by profits from Chinese demand during the boom.

As China's economy begins to slow, along with its demand for natural resources, there is pressure to increase the incentive for extraction. In this context in 2014, the government of Peru passed a law to expedite the approval of extractive projects that many see as a significant weakening of the environmental and social safeguards for such activity. The law puts new and shorter time limits on project approval, reducing the amount of time to conduct environmental impact assessments and to seek community input. It also limits the authority of environmental authorities to update and upgrade environmental assessments and puts mining ministries at key oversight junctures, creating conflicts of interest. While the China Boom looms in the background, there is no evidence that individual Chinese companies or the broader Association of Chinese Enterprises was directly involved in the lobby efforts.[42]

Whereas in Brazil and Peru there is evidence of downward pressure on environmental institutions from interest groups that have become stronger from the China Boom, downward pressure in Ecuador has a different source. Ecuador's government has been in a pinch for revenue since it partially defaulted on its international debt obligations in 2008, and since then China has become Ecuador's most important creditor. By 2014, over one-third of Ecuador's external debt went to China. Ecuador is dependent on natural resource extraction—and China—as a source for exports and foreign investment. Article 57 of Ecuador's new constitution enshrines ILO 169, and its Citizen Participation Law requires that without the support of the majority of locals, new projects must meet even higher environmental standards. According to members of the Sápara nation, however, majority approval was never sought for the new Andes Petroleum project that is generating so much controversy. Indeed, the Ecuadoran government confirms that their government never sought majority community approval, but signed an agreement with the president of the Sápara people, who has since been ousted because of the controversy surrounding that agreement.[43]

Brace Under Pressure

As the economies of Latin America begin to slow, there will be increased pressure to remove red tape with respect to social and environmental safeguards.

This is a mistake. Not only will it result in the degradation of the environment, but it will come at significant economic cost as well. In January of 2015 at the China-CELAC summit, China announced that it will aim to increase China–Latin America trade to $500 billion and Chinese investment in Latin America to $250 billion by 2025. That is a doubling of the current amount, and the majority of it will certainly be in primary commodities. As Figure 6.1 shows, many of the projects that are already planned cut right across some of the region's biodiversity hotspots, national parks, and places where ancient peoples earn their livelihoods. Both Latin America and China will need to safeguard the social and environmental impacts of this economic activity, for different reasons.

In Latin America's case, investing in natural capital is essential for the future of prosperity for their people and economies. As we saw in the last chapter, commodity-led growth is not sustainable from an economic point of view. As Lopez, Barbier, and many others have noted, commodity-led growth is not sustainable from a social and environmental point of view as well. Commodity-led growth needs to be properly governed so that the government can capture windfalls and invest them not only into the alternative

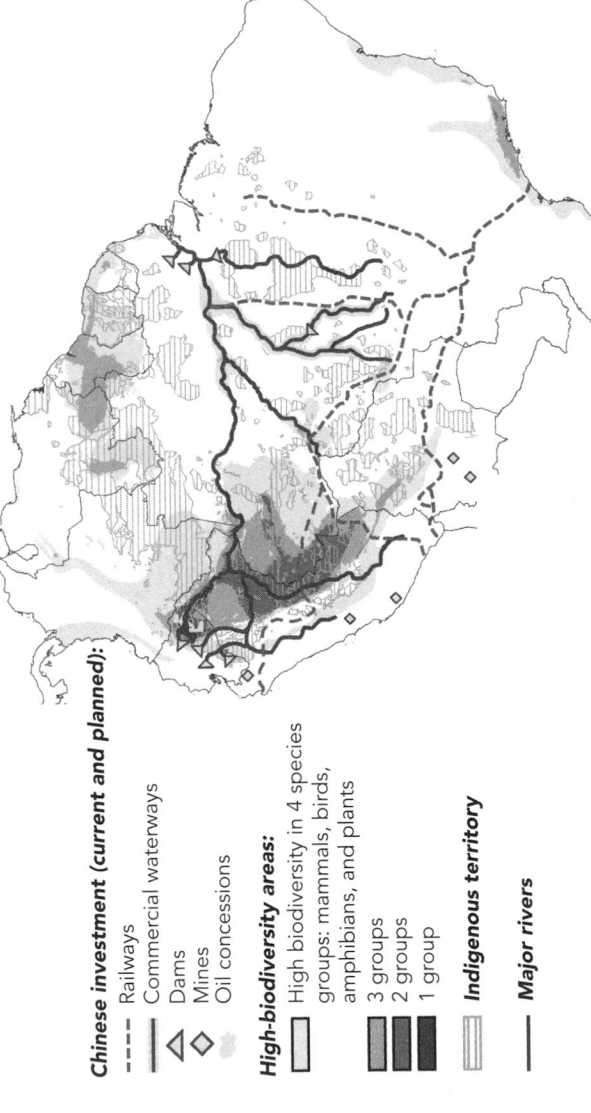

Figure 6.1 Chinese Investment, Biodiversity, and Indigenous People

forms of economic activity discussed in the last chapter; significant investment will need to go into people and the environment as well. Without it, Latin America's legacy of boom and bust cycles that increase social inequity and environmental degradation will never be broken and the prosperity of the Latin American people will always be limited.

For China it will make sense to upgrade, enforce, and make its social and environmental policies more transparent on economic and political grounds. Such efforts would help China to compete on the same terms as global competitors. But more than that, they could help mitigate risk to Chinese companies and lenders by strengthening *public* confidence in host countries, thus bolstering the political position of both the Chinese banks and recipient governments. This would help sustain existing markets while also positioning Chinese firms to secure future market access. Adopting and then adhering to stronger, broader, and deeper guidelines can help secure long-term relationships with host governments in regions across the world. The public record of protest and criticism in some countries makes clear that certain projects have been perceived by host country publics to flout environmental norms, resulting in denial or delay of contracts. To the extent that local skepticism and protests result in delays or even loss of projects, environment-related political risk can severely affect the bottom line of Chinese companies.

The large-scale Belo Monte dam project in Brazil is a case in point. Although Brazilian firms dominate the project, State Grid Corporation of China has taken over power distribution. Belo Monte is another example of a massive infrastructure project that has run up (and around) indigenous communities and environmental concerns. Massive protests and international scorn over the project are estimated to cost the developers $1.4 million per day and may delay the project for two years—and an extra

$1.02 billion.[44] Moreover, local publics in many countries increasingly look to international norms as benchmarks from which to evaluate other actors. Adopting established safeguards will help Chinese companies enter other markets as well, even in the industrialized world where standards are significantly higher than in Latin America. Establishing a good track record in Latin America and learning such norms can make firms more competitive across the world.

Projects like the Andes Petroleum concessions in Ecuador will be major testing grounds for the future. It has the potential to bring needed investment into that country. Ecuador has a strong constitution that creates space for such an investment to be conducted in a manner that reaps benefits for Ecuador and the Chinese companies and for communities like the Sápara—with minimal impacts on the environment. Striking such a balance could help Ecuador unlock a legacy of commodity dependence and social and environmental conflict that could be copied throughout the region. If China participates and helps guide such efforts, it stands to profit substantially from its billions of dollars of investments in natural resource projects across the hemisphere and learn what it takes to penetrate markets the world over. In so doing, China can truly live up to its image as being a Southern partner to Latin American governments rather than the Northern patron that has become stigmatized for foreign investment with disregard for the environment and surrounding peoples. This scenario would bring acclaim and pay dividends to all parties involved.

The other scenario, of course, is that countries of the region turn a blind eye to their innovative policies and constitutions in a desperate attempt to get any new investment possible. Especially when projects are in areas that are among the most biodiverse and culturally unique in the world, such an approach may not only cost Ecuadoran politicians elections and Chinese companies billions of dollars; it may trigger global activist campaigns that would spoil the public images and private investment profiles of Latin American and Chinese companies alike.

7

Saving the China Boom

"O Petróleo É Nosso!" ("The Oil Is Ours, not that of foreigners!") was the 1950s slogan credited to Brazilian President Getulio Vargas.[1] The slogan went well beyond oil, and symbolized the nationalistic impulses behind the state-led industrialization period. The region did an about-face in the 1980s, completely embracing foreign influence through the Washington Consensus. Carlos Salinas, president of Mexico in the late 1980s and early 1990s, boasted to Margaret Thatcher how he had embraced a program of "deregulation, privatization, and encouraging foreign investment."[2] One-size-fits-all mantras will not work in twenty-first-century Latin America. If the region wishes to save the China Boom and use it to trigger sustained prosperity, Latin American leaders will have to put processes over policies—processes that help each country discover its own path to prosperity. All paths will need a mix of both states and markets. A proper path will not pit states versus markets, but make them work together. A proper path will not pit China versus the United States, but benefit from both as well.

Latin America would do well to capitalize on the China Boom. China has re-emerged as a world economic power for the twenty-first century. As China has risen, it has increasingly purchased from and invested in Latin American primary commodities. Thus Latin

America rode China's coattails to experience its own China Boom. Today China is the number one trading partner for some of the region's largest economies, and China's development banks pour more money into the region than the World Bank or the Inter-American Development Bank (IDB).

As we have seen in this book, China has been guzzling oil from Venezuela, Ecuador, and Mexico to fuel its expanding fleet of cars, trucks, and container ships. China has wired more than half the world's consumer electronics products with copper from Chile and Peru. Many of China's new cities have iron ore from Brazil at their core. As standards of living have risen, the Chinese eat more beef—from cattle that are fed soya beans from Argentina and Brazil. In turn, Chinese companies have flocked to the Americas to invest in these commodities, backed by China's state-run development banks.

In the wake of the 9/11 attacks and then after the global financial meltdown that originated in the United States in 2008, Washington turned to other shores. Most of the countries in the region had made a strong transition to democracy, did not harbor terrorists, and had followed Washington's economic orders. While the United States wasn't paying attention, Latin America became incredibly strategic for China—as a source for many of the key natural resources it needs to grow its economy and feed the appetites of more than a billion people.

With the new friends have come new challenges, however. Chinese trade and investment in primary commodities caused prices and exchange rates to skyrocket in the region and made Latin American manufacturing industries less competitive on a global scale. Textiles, footwear, car-making; electronics from Argentina, Brazil, and Mexico; and Colombian sombreros have lost significant market share in world and regional markets.

Moreover, natural resource exploitation in Latin America goes hand in hand with environmental degradation and social conflict. The World Bank puts the economic costs of environmental degradation during the China Boom at 8.6 percent of annual GDP, dwarfing the 3.6 annual growth. Mining, oil exploration, and large-scale farming activities often necessitate the clearing of forests and the pollution of waterways; they are found in areas where many of the world's richest indigenous cultures reside. There are global advocacy campaigns reeling over Chinese oil exploration in the Ecuadorean Amazon and hydroelectric dams near biosphere reserves in Honduras.

Latin American governments fell far short in capturing their China windfall and investing some of the proceeds into industry and innovation, into people, and into protecting the environment. According to research by the International Monetary Fund (IMF), although the China-led commodity boom was among the longest and most lucrative in the region's history, most Latin American countries saved less of these windfalls than they had in past booms. Analagous studies by the United Nations show that the region's governments also failed to capture fiscal revenue in proportion to the windfall profits made in the sector during the China Boom as well.

The region should be praised for spending what little increases they did capture on combating poverty and inequality, enabling the region to reverse the uptick in inequality that occurred during the Washington Consensus period. However, Latin American governments did not invest in productive capital investments that generate innovation, industrial competitiveness, and employment generation over the long run. Economists have long said that developing countries need to invest 25 percent of GDP on an annual basis in order to raise living standards. Capital investments in Latin America during the Washington Consensus were a mere 18.8 percent annually, but only rose to 19.6 percent during the China Boom despite higher growth and government revenue.

Beginning in 2014, the Chinese economy began to rebalance from an export-led economy toward more of a consumer-based economy. With that transition has come slower growth and slower demand for Latin American commodities. Latin America has become so exposed to China that the China slowdown is among the strongest factors that will make Latin America return to the lower growth rates of yesteryear. What is more, after a painful recovery from the global financial crisis the United States has begun to become an attractive place to invest again, which could trigger a retreat from investment in Latin America at exactly the time the region will need it most.

Latin America will need to come to its own rescue, though it is in both China and even the United States' interest to help. Latin America will have to establish and strengthen institutions to capture more of the benefits of commodity-led growth and invest the proceeds into infrastructure, innovation, export competiveness, and environmental protection in a socially inclusive manner. At the same time, the region will need to better manage the financial instability that has long frustrated Latin American development.

Rebalancing Latin America's Economies

At the end of the day Latin America is responsible for its own economic and social management. Blaming its problems on China, the United States, or other external factors is not very useful, and only partly true at best. Economic downturns can be turned into opportunities for governments to exert leadership for the future. Latin America is endowed with great gifts that can be built upon for long-run development. The abundance of major natural resources can be a source of long-run wealth creation rather than a curse, and can form the core of new development strategy. Many Latin American countries developed relatively robust manufacturing sectors during the first three-quarters of the twentieth century, and some became leading lights in services as the century closed. These sectors too can be targets for a dynamic comparative advantage that will lead the region on a path to economic diversity, social inclusion, and sustainable development.

A renewed commitment to sustainable development in Latin America will require a rebalancing of the state and the market. While each period made its own contributions to development in the hemisphere, in the end the state-led industrialization period relied too heavily on an unchecked state. The Washington Consensus relied too heavily on an unchecked market. Like most of the other successful countries in the world, it is time for Latin American governments to build a partnership between states and markets. Moving into a new and more pragmatic era of balancing both the state and the market will take new vision and leadership. Leaders in the region will need to articulate a vision of the region where Latin Americans live in a society with a wider variety of economic opportunities and in a context of equality and environmental stewardship. To that end, Latin American leaders must design strategies with three key components. First, Latin America will have to greatly improve the ability of the state to capture its fair share of the benefits of economic activity during boom times. Second, countries in the region will have to work alone and together to invest the proceeds into economic diversification, social development, and environmental protection. Third, institutions will need to be created and improved to hold governments, the private sector, and households more accountable for their actions.

The good news is that these efforts will not need to be invented from scratch. On the contrary, many countries in the region have a burgeoning set of programs and institutions in each of these three areas. The challenge will be in scaling up and replicating them—and doing so in a manner that is efficient, transparent, and accountable. This will entail great leadership, and a long-run view that goes beyond political parties and the immediate future.

To that end, the most important effort will be for Latin American governments to retrieve a greater proportion of the benefits of economic activity during boom times. In chapter 5 it was noted that Latin American countries did not tax or save in proportion to the magnitude of the China Boom or relative to the region's peers or past. The region's governments will need to reform taxation regimes, as well as its systems of royalty payments and windfall programs for the commodity sector. It will also need to expand and scale up the stabilization funds, pension funds, national development banks, and sovereign wealth funds in order to properly manage and invest new revenues.

By and large, Latin America's taxation systems are not keeping pace with economic activity. According to the Economic Commision for Latin America and the Caribbean (ECLAC) the region's tax take is only 18 percent of GDP, compared to 34.3 percent of GDP among Organization for Economic Cooperation and Development (OECD) countries.[3] The region will need to increase revenues in this manner and expand the tax base to the engines of the economy. Too often, though, nations in the region compete with each other to attract foreign investment in the mining and manufacturing sectors by giving outright tax exemptions, holidays for a certain period, or tax rates lower than the domestic average and the average of their neighbors.[4] Moreover, the region relies more on indirect taxes—value-added and export taxes, and so forth—than on direct taxes on income and wealth. These indirect taxes in Latin America are often regressive. In Brazil, Bolivia, Uruguay, and many other Latin American countries, the level of inequality in incomes before taxes is lower than after indirect taxes are withheld. This has led

ECLAC to conclude that "the region's institutions do not succeed in reining in (ex ante) the market dynamics that lead to the concentration of income, and their capacity to correct it (ex post) through cash transfers and taxes is limited, especially compared with other countries."[5]

Of paramount importance alongside the basic tax system, countries in the region will need to upgrade institutions to capture windfalls from the commodities sector where fiscal revenue did not increase with the proportion of rents. Beginning with the first component just mentioned, and as I argued in chapter 5, Latin American countries failed to tax and save in proportion to the magnitude of the riches bestowed upon them due to the China Boom or relative to previous booms. Governments across the region will need to reform taxation regimes, as well as systems of royalty payments and windfall programs for the commodity sector. They will also need to expand and scale up on stabilization funds, pension funds, national development banks, and sovereign wealth funds in order to properly manage and invest massive new revenues. Most of the natural resources in Latin America are owned or managed by nation-states that grant concessions to the private sector (or state-owned companies) in exchange for royalty payments based on profits or the gross value of the product that is extracted. By and large, the region has better programs for the oil and gas sectors than for the mining and extractive sectors. This is in part because oil and gas companies are more often owned by the state or in public–private partnerships, and therefore reporting on rents and taxes is more easily monitored. In the oil and gas sector Latin American governments took in 34 to 78 percent of the rents during the China Boom, compared to 10 to 35 percent in mining. Bolivia, Chile, and Peru took bold steps during the China Boom to increase royalties and taxes in the mining sector and took in highs of 27 to 35 percent of mining rents in those countries.

Countries in the region will also have to better manage the short-term capital flows of a speculative nature that often follow commodity booms. Countries should move to develop local bond markets denominated in domestic currencies to smooth some of the risk associated with flexible exchange rates, capital flows, and debt problems in Latin America (discussed in chapter 5). Brazil and Mexico have the largest and most sophisticated local bond markets, with Chile and Colombia's gaining ground as well.[6] However, as also noted in chapter 5, the majority of debt in Latin America, especially in the corporate sector, is in the form of short-term finance in foreign currencies. Moreover, virtually all finance available to the region has proven to be procyclical—meaning that there is plenty of finance during a boom and too little finance during downturns. Countries in the region will need to put in place permanent and countercyclical regulations on short-term cross-border financial flows to stem financial instability, and steer investment toward more long-term and productive capital investments. Brazil, Colombia, and Peru put in place innovative regulations on capital flows of this sort during the surges of capital inflows during the China Boom that proved useful. However, such instruments will need to be stronger and expanded across countries.[7]

Latin American governments were able to manage accumulating foreign exchange reserves and making current expenditures on poverty alleviation and the reduction of inequality—both of which will remain central to raising living standards and maintaining financial instability. To the extent that transfer programs to the poor are also linked to health and education, they also build human capital for long-run growth. It is time to scale these programs up by an order of magnitude. For all their hype and real benefit, only 0.4 percent of GDP is targeted toward such programs in Latin America, and they cover just 120 million people.[8] Expanding such programs to the approximately 167 million still living in poverty—especially indigenous people who are discriminated against in general and often fall out of the reach of such programs—would thus come at little additional cost.

A few Latin American countries have passed some innovative legislation in this regard. In Brazil, 40 percent of revenue from oil and gas has to be earmarked toward education; 30 percent for health, sanitation, and infrastructure; and 30 percent for environmental protection. In Bolivia, 85 percent of the revenue from mining must be earmarked toward investment, with only 15 percent going toward current expenditures. Under participatory budgeting schemes in Peru, locals have set aside 20 percent of the revenue from the China Boom for education, 19 percent for health, 22 percent for transport infrastructure, and 13 percent for agriculture.[9]

It will take more than taxing, capturing more royalties, managing capital flows, and earmarked spending to generate the financing needed for long-run productive growth in the Americas. Special funds should be established to manage commodities while generating additional wealth for present and future generations. Here, Latin American governments have made significant strides that could be replicated and scaled up. The region is home to some of the most innovative stabilization funds, national development banks, and sovereign wealth funds across the developing world.

During earlier part of the China Boom, Chile upgraded its existing copper stabilization fund—and just in the nick of time. In 2006 Chile established the Economic and Social Stabilization Fund (FEES), which takes windfall profits from the copper sector and is held aside to help fund fiscal deficits when the copper price is low or when there is a general economic downturn. During the China Boom the FEES took in $24.6 billion, allowing Chile to have one of the larger stimulus packages in the wake of the 2008–2009 global financial crisis.[10]

Most countries either disbanded or demoted their development banks during the Washington Consensus period. The one big exception is the Brazilian National Development Bank (BNDES), whose capital increased fourfold during the China Boom. The bank has been reinvigorated to support long-run investments. And as in the case of Chile, BNDES played a big role during the 2008–2009 global financial crisis in terms of stabilization. The BNDES acted as a credit backstop for strategic firms as capital dried up in the immediate aftermath of the financial crisis.[11] That said, Brazil and the BNDES are examples of what I will discuss in a moment regarding the need to get the political economy right. Despite having a national development bank that provides more finance to Brazil than the World Bank provides to all of Latin America, Brazil's investment rate was an anemic 17.6 percent of GDP during the China Boom.[12]

Latin America also has some leadership in sovereign wealth funds (SWFs). SWFs are state-owned investment funds that are supported by revenues from commodities. SWFs take commodity revenues and invest them in stocks, bonds, and other global assets in the hope of increasing the wealth of the country and preparing for a day when nonrenewable commodities may no longer be available at a profit. Norway's SWF is seen as the flagship and helped that country transition away from oil production as the core of its economy. Eight Latin American countries have SWFs, including Brazil, Chile, and Peru. Trinidad and Tobego's Heritage and Stabilization Fund is seen as the most forward-looking, as it is one of the few in the region that has an explicit mandate to invest for future generations, as Norway's does.[13]

Reindustrialization for Socially Inclusive and Sustainable Development

Santiago Levy, one of the architects of Mexico's innovative Conditional Cash Transfer (CCT) programs who is now at the Inter-American Development Bank, often says that Latin America has to do better than producing healthy and better-educated poor people to work in restaurants in Dallas and New York, apple farms in the Pacific Northwest, or waiters in Cancun.[14] Levy is insinuating that Latin America has to invest in productive and employment-generating activity that can absorb these healthier and smarter people. Three areas vital for investment are infrastructure, innovation and upgrading, and the environment.

The Latin American region faces an annual infrastructure gap of 6.2 percent, with many of the region's major ports, railroads, and highways lacking significant upgrade since the state-led industrialization period.[15] A twenty-first-century infrastructure for Latin America cannot simply be repaving roads and extending railways from extractive industries to cities and ports. The region needs to incorporate an infrastructure network that facilitates new economic activity outside of the commodity sector as well. What is more, the digital infrastructure of the region is also in poor health. Only 35.4 percent of Latin Americans have access to the Internet, 5.2 percent to fixed broadband, and 5.6 percent to mobile broadband. That stands in stark contrast to Asia, where 48.5 percent have access to the Internet, 15 percent to fixed broadband, and 35.7 percent to mobile broadband.[16]

While chief economist of the World Bank, the eminent Chinese economist Justin Yifu Lin said that Latin America's inability to accelerate the development process was a result of the region's failure to maintain a process of industrial diversification and upgrading. Lin acknowledged that Latin America's state-led industrialization period left a bad taste in Latin American mouths because it was associated with political capture and corruption. But Lin stressed that policies for industrial diversification and upgrading for twenty-first-century Latin America should *not* be a return to the region's past, nor should they be an attempt to mimic China's brand of state-led industrialization. Lin marveled at the development of private markets and institutions in Latin America to signal how the region is far ahead of China on those fronts, and needed a leaner state role that facilitated structural change toward industrial upgrading, not dictated it. The key difference, to Lin, is that Latin American industrial strategies should build upon those sectors where it already has a comparative advantage. The problems with the past were due to the fact that Latin American governments tried to take too big a leap into industrialization. Rather than attempting to jump into the computer industry, Brazil should have tried to focus on a sector closer to its relative strengths—like refining soybeans or rolling steel from iron ore.

In addition to the World Bank, the Washington-based IDB has also come round to recognizing the need to focus on industrialization in Latin America. In 2014 it produced a landmark study called *Rethinking Productive Development: Sound Policies and Institutions for Economic Transformation* that stresses the need for the state to play a role in enhancing competitiveness and diversification. Like Lin, the IDB also emphasizes that such a set of policies is not a return to state-led industrialization: "the instruments of intervention are not public companies or subsidies to declining sectors or small and medium-sized enterprises (SMEs) of low competitive potential but rather policies of innovation, improvement of human capital, facilitating entrepreneurship and clusters, promoting internationalization, and, especially, an active public and private collaboration."[17]

The ECLAC has long emphasized the need to diversify production and increase productivity in the Americas. In some ways the ECLAC approach is more rooted and ambitious than the approaches of the World Bank or Inter-American Development Bank. One concern is that solely focusing on upgrading in industries directly related to commodity sectors will make economies more susceptible to swings in commodity prices, not less.[18] More broadly, however, ECLAC has also stressed that diversification by definition can mean the creation of whole new industries in an economy and sometimes may require linking new industry to necessary intermediate goods markets, labor markets, roads and ports, and final product markets.

What is common among all the major institutions arguing for a reinvigoration of upgrading is that nations should identify where the private market is failing to provide the incentives for investment in technological upgrading, and that the state can play a role in coordinating efforts to address those market failures. In enabling the technological capacity of new industries, markets do not give the correct investment signals when there are high and uncertain learning costs. In other words, technological dynamism that leads to diversification is not guaranteed by markets alone for many reasons such as weak capital markets, restrictive intellectual property laws, lack of information and poor coordination, imperfect competition and the need for scale economies, poor levels of research and development, and more. Historically, to correct for market failures nations have encouraged joint venturing with foreign firms to learn technological capabilities. In addition, they have invested heavily in higher education and publicly funded research and development. East Asian tigers—like developed countries before them—spent a great deal of effort providing education and training for their people. This was done by spending a significant amount of funds on education (including providing scholarships to obtain PhDs in developed countries), clustering schools in export processing zones, requiring that foreign firms hire nationals and train them on the job, and subsidizing training programs in domestic firms.[19]

Regardless of the specific approach, it is a major achievement that the region is debating what the most appropriate level of upgrading policies are—rather than whether to do them at all. Perhaps what is more important than the actual policy is putting in place a process to determine what the right upgrading policies should be. Past attempts at industrialization in the region had a one-size-fits-all approach: industrialize in all sectors at all costs. New, more nuanced approaches emphasize the need to put in place a process whereby policymakers (embedded within the private sector) can "self-discover" the binding constraints to economic growth in a particular economy. After such a "diagnostic" has taken place, then the policy process can commence.[20] This is exactly the approach taken by Robert Devlin and Graciela Moguillansky, two veteran economists of Latin American development. Devlin and Moguillansky drew on the examples of the Asian "tigers" of industrial development for their 2011 book *Breeding Latin American Tigers: Operational Principles for Rehabilitating Industrial Policies*. Drawing on the experiences of 10 countries outside Latin America, the authors show that the best policies emerge out of an alliance between the public and private sector where each party shares in the generation of information and support needed to identify market, institutional, and even ideological constraints to industrial development and in making strategies to address those constraints.[21] In more recent work for the World Bank, the authors report that industrial upgrading policy is "back" in Latin America, with some countries such as Brazil and Colombia even having formed "councils" for public–private alliances. While hailing this development as "major," they conclude that "industrial policies have returned to Latin America and their character is quite different from the much-maligned (not totally fairly) policies of the import substitution era. But the secret of successful industrial policies still depends on doing it right. Advances in this regard are significant, but there is considerable room yet for improvement."[22]

No strategy for capturing the benefits of commodity-led growth and investing some of the windfall into infrastructure and technological upgrading will succeed unless Latin America begins to see its ecosystems as "natural capital" that get equal footing alongside physical and human capital. As the home of 20 percent of the world's forested area and one-third of the world's fresh water resources—not to mention 30 percent of global copper, biodiesel, and other abundant deposits of oil, gas, minerals, and numerous products derived from the earth—Latin Americans need to better recognize that the stewardship of these resources is important from an economic as well as an altruistic perspective.

An important set of measures that would help capture the benefits of commodity production and raise revenue at the same time for reinvestment would be taxes on fossil fuel production. Here the region is lacking, but there are also some examples of leadership. In September of 2014 Chilean President Michele Bachelet introduced Latin America's first carbon tax. Chile will put a $5 levy on carbon dioxide emissions of larger power plants. Not only will the plan reduce carbon emissions and raise the cost of fossil fuel energy, it is estimated to bring in $160 million per year in government revenue for investment in renewable energy.[23] Mexico has a $3.50 tax on the sale of fossil fuels based on their carbon content and covers more than 40 percent of the country's greenhouse gas emssions. Costa Rica taxes gasoline and other environmental "bads" and parks some of the funds in a new environmental bank called BanCo2. The bank's mission is to invest in green development projects and mitigate the impacts of climate change and has helped Costa Rica reverse its deforestation trend.[24] In addition to taxing environmental bads, subsidies for fossil fuels could also be drastically reduced. Mexico, Argentina, Ecuador, and Venezuela top the list of countries with heavy subsidies in the fossil fuel sectors.[25]

Countries in Latin America will also need to upgrade their baseline environmental standards and safeguards—especially as they pertain to natural resource exploitation. As discussed in the last chapter, Peru has become a regional leader in transparency, joining the Extractive Industries Transparency Initiative. However, that country has begun to weaken its environmental regulation in pursuit of foreign investment in a weak economic environment. Such a short-term view will come back to bite in the long run. Overall stocks of natural resources will dry up as will the ability of ecosystems to absorb the waste from natural resource exploitation.

Many advocate the "Hartwick rule" (named after the work of eminent late economist John Hartwick) as a rule of thumb for natural-resource-based economies.[26] The Hartwick rule says that all of the rents from natural resource extraction need to be reinvested in productive and human capital such as infrastructure, innovation and industrialization, and education. This is essential to the future of Latin American economic development—but it won't be enough. The Hartwick rule is considered a relatively weak form of sustainable development because it assumes that there is easy substitution between natural capital and productive capital—that depleting a forest and its peoples can be easily replaced with investing in new industry or overseas investments that bring dividends equal to the losses of those natural resources.

Of course, the world's most biologically diverse areas that are also home to some of the richest and most ancient cultures in the world are not substitutable for conventional economic investments—to say the least. There will be times, even during downturns, that Latin Americans will have to draw a line in the sand—or the forest, or the mountains. There is just no way to put a price on the value that such people and places bring to humanity. Latin America's rich stock of plants, animals, and people could be the home to the discovery of wonder drugs that can help eradicate epidemics in the future. Forests in the region help absorb carbon dioxide emitted from factories, cars, and power plants across the planet. Some areas and peoples will need to be fundamentally protected from extractive activity, or at least be allowed to live alongside such extraction as in the case of some of the offshore inland projects discussed in the last chapter. In order to give the people that inhabit these regions their proper rights and voice, more countries will need to enshrine, codify, and enforce ILO 169 as Bolivia has.

Balancing the rights of people and nature with the need to expand infrastructure in Latin America is perhaps the greatest challenge. Latin America has a 6.2 percent annual infrastructure gap that is making the countries in the region lag economically. A twenty-first-century infrastructure is needed that expands information and communication technologies, energy and electricity, and roads, ports, and railways in a manner that increases regional trade and investment and better connects Latin American countries with the rest of the world. With some notable exceptions, infrastructure projects in the region have been largely national in design and extractive in their purpose. The mentality has been to increase access to extractive industry activity in order to expedite getting those resources to global markets. Such an approach only locks in commodity-dependent economic activity and social and environmental conflict. Latin Americans need to have a regional discussion on an infrastructure that will connect their economies to each other and the rest of the world in a manner that maximizes interconnectivity while minimizing social and environmental conflict. To this end, the upgrading of national and international safeguards for countries, development banks, and private-sector actors is essential. As shown in the last chapter, the World Bank and IDB have made strides in this area, but many national governments, national development banks, and Chinese actors are still significantly lacking.

Getting the Political Economy Right

Rebalancing Latin American economies for long-run economic development does not mean adopting the Beijing approach of state-led industrialization. Latin America has been there. Nor, however, will the Washington Consensus be the framework for the twenty-first century. Latin America has been there too. The state-led industrialization period had too much state and too little attention to people and the planet. The Washington Consensus had too little state and still not enough attention to people and the planet. Latin America needs to bring the state back in, but the state needs to be leaner, more effective, and more accountable—no easy task. Latin American governments know all too well that government programs can create more problems than they attempt to correct for. To build effective institutions the region's governments will need to better embed with the private sector while at the same time establishing built-in mechanisms that hold both the public and private sectors accountable for their actions. Only then will the region be able to deshackle itself from the capture of special interest groups and be able to use the state effectively toward sustainable development.

With the exception of some key natural resource sectors such as copper in Chile and oil and gas in most countries, the private sector will need to be the engine of sustainable growth for Latin America's future. That said, it is the utmost responsibility of the state to establish the proper playing field for markets to generate wealth in an equitable manner for present and future generations. I have argued that there are two key functions that Latin American governments need to improve to these ends: capturing more of the benefits of commodity-led growth and investing those benefits into economic diversification and social and environmental protection. This type of government activity, however, is prone to being captured by interest groups that wish to benefit from such programs—or by those that don't want to bear the costs.

As the World Bank has documented, Latin America is rife with two kinds of political capture that have long plagued the region and became accentuated during the China Boom. First is political patronage, where the beneficiaries of commodity-led growth are too closely knit with the government and influence government decision over government policy and the allocation of resources. This translates into large breaks for those in the natural resource sector in terms of taxes, environmental regulation, and kickbacks. Without institutions to weaken the relationship between the commodity sector and the state, Latin American governments will be hard pressed to put in place taxes, royalties whose proceeds go into funds, and banks for economic diversification and inclusive development. Related to this is "rent-seeking" behavior, where the beneficiaries of new government investments can distort government activity. Either through lobbying or corruption, private actors can take over government programs for their own benefit rather than the productive uses that such programs are geared toward.[27]

There are three guiding principles that need to be enshrined into government policy in order to avoid excessive patronage and rent-seeking that will distort Latin America's ability to capture the benefits of commodity-led growth and invest in a sustainable future. First, programs will need a higher level of embeddedness or partnerships with the private sector in order to design the proper institutions. Second, major checks will need to be imposed on the private sector to ensure that it does not distort the intent of government action. Third, civil society will need to be enabled to monitor both the state and the private sector and hold them each accountable for their actions.

The prominent sociologist Peter Evans has brought great insight into the need for the government to have "embedded autonomy" with the private sector in order to design tax and royalty systems that will be effective, and to be able to pinpoint the binding constraints the private sector experiences when attempting to move into sectors beyond primary commodities. Governments, especially those in Latin America, have a poor record of picking winners or sectors that should be targeted for innovation and industrialization strategies. Brazil was successful in developing Embraer, but for every Embraer there are a host of other companies we have never heard of because they did not succeed. Evans and others have documented that the state—whether through sovereign wealth funds, development banks, or fiscally funded programs—will be more effective if programs are designed by the private sector and the government working in partnership.

The private sector is much closer to the pulse of economic activity than governments are. The private sector can also help identify where government programs go wrong. That said, the private sector is less apt to invest or expand into sectors and activities outside its comfort zones. They see too much uncertainty due to lack of information and financial instability, and often simply suffer from myopia. In their cutting-edge work, economists Robert Devlin and Graciela Moguillansky conclude that "working together through a public-private alliance, and thus maximizing the input of national talent and capabilities, the public and private sectors are more likely to develop an intelligent strategy than either party can working alone."[28]

Again, Latin America will not have to reinvent the wheel. Countries in the region can draw on the success stories of examples in and out of the region. Devlin and Moguillansky document how public–private alliances in Singapore, South Korea, Malaysia, Spain, and the Czech Republic were formed to help identify the binding constraints for economic diversification and development. They also note that Brazil and Colombia have made strides in this area as well. As part of Brazil's broader set of industrial policy, they have set up a coordination council that consists of over twenty ministries, fourteen members of the business community, and the Brazilian National Development Bank. Colombia has had similar councils since the 1990s. That country's National Competitiveness Commission includes not only government and business representatives but also academics, unions, and other members of civil society.[29]

It is also paramount that public–private alliances do not get too close for comfort. Programs for long-run development need to have built-in mechanisms that ensure that they do not get taken over by rent-seeking corporations. For capturing the windfalls from commodity production it is imperative to have transparency about private-sector activity in the extractives sectors. ECLAC has recently highlighted this in saying that "the fact that the principal instrument for State participation is a tax on profits reported by the mining companies themselves highlights how important it is for governments to have independent mechanisms and specific indicators to make sure that the sector's profits and costs are transparent throughout price cycles."[30] Transparency is essential, as is accountability. Nations will need to credibly fine or penalize companies that are not complying. The IDB reckons that half the potential collection of taxes from wealthy individuals and corporations is lost to evasion in Latin America.[31]

In terms of executing projects for economic diversification, the most successful countries have partially circumvented rent-seeking by having strict discipline over the private actors in the public–private alliances. The late MIT economist Alice Amsden documented how East Asian industrialization efforts were more successful than their Latin American counterparts precisely because they put in place carrots and sticks for participating in public–private partnerships. The private sector does not get handouts to create industries and expand technological capacity. Indeed, private-sector actors would only receive support if they met strict performance standards. Key among those standards was exporting a certain percentage of new product after a certain time period. If firms did not export, they would not receive further tranches of government support. This accomplishes two things. First, it provides benchmarks and clear indicators that allow the government to cut firms and sectors out of programs before they infiltrate the government for more support. Second, it forces firms to shoot for the technological frontier and market competitiveness. Governments cannot control whether an American or German purchases a South Korean car; consumers will buy it based on price and quality. Therefore the test that allows a firm to get continued support is whether a firm can become globally competitive—a task that companies can't do by corruption, but only by putting government support to good use—by investing into innovation and competitiveness.

Latin American governments will not get the political economy right unless there are also mechanisms to hold the private sector *and* governments accountable. Direct civil society monitoring that highlights both the successes and limitations of government and company policies can bring issues to the attention of policymakers and the media. Civil society organizations should be enabled to expand their networks to monitor new economic actors in their region and link with their counterparts in China and across the world to bring further attention to government programs and private-sector behavior.

Academic research can also help derive a more empirically based understanding of these complex issues and serve as a neutral space where governments, companies, and civil society can establish a dialogue. Academics can also form international networks to compare findings with other analyses and disseminate their work more widely. Academic researchers and universities can also play a role in promoting educational and cultural exchange, joint research, and training for governments and other members of civil society. Finally, the media has a key role to play in monitoring and shedding light on the success and failure of government and corporate policies alike.

Latin American governments will not be working in a vacuum. Key to the success of renewed national development strategies will be the careful navigation of the China Triangle. Negotiating and partnering with both China and the United States will be essential for the region to achieve its goals. This will take leadership and new thinking in China and Latin America as well.

Navigating the China Triangle

The onus is on Latin American governments and regional bodies to establish an inclusive and sustainable development strategy for the region and its peoples. A key tenet of any comprehensive strategy will need to be constructive engagement with the two largest economies in the world, China and the United States. Latin America is increasingly strategic for China and will remain so for the United States. Latin American leaders will need to leverage the strategic importance of their region to form partnerships that will help support Latin American growth strategies, help reduce tensions, and bring benefits to each point in the China Triangle between Latin America, China, and the United States.

Engaging with China

The key ingredients of a new Latin American development strategy discussed in the previous chapter will be attractive to China—but Latin America will have to negotiate for them. A major component of a comprehensive development strategy will be negotiating a more balanced economic relationship with China than the commodities-for-manufactured goods trade that ensued during the China Boom. Latin America holds strategic assets to leverage when engaging with China. China, looking to advance its flagship companies overseas and provide financing to emerging market governments in order to diversify its assets, may be more willing to engage than it had during the China Boom.

There are three areas where China may buy in to a new development strategy in Latin America. First, China will continue to be a source of demand for Latin American commodities and possibly for a more diversified array of products if Latin America gets its policies right. Second, China may become an even larger presence in terms of foreign direct investment in Latin America. Third, China and its growing set of development banks and funds can be a source of much-needed finance for infrastructure, industrialization, and green development. There is some evidence that China stands ready, with 2015 as a turning point. In a May 2015 visit to Chile, Chinese Prime Minister Li Keqiang said that "industrial cooperation between China and Latin America arrives at the right moment," and "China has equipment manufacturing capacity and integrated technology with competitive prices, while Latin America has the demand for infrastructure expansion and industrial upgrading."[1]

In terms of demand for Latin American commodities and beyond, China is not going away. It is quite true that Chinese growth has slowed, but from 10 to 7 percent per year. A China slowdown to 7 percent growth, with a base of the approximately 13 trillion dollars it is today, is close to 900 billion dollars. Nine hundred billion dollars is roughly the size of the entire GDP of Indonesia, the world's 16th largest economy. The glory days of 10 percent growth in China occurred when the Chinese economy was less than half its 2013 size.

It is important to remind ourselves that China houses over one billion people, and hundreds of millions still live on less than $2.50

per day. In this light, China's per capita consumption of the core commodities that Latin America exports to China are still very low relative to industrialized countries. For crude oil China only consumes about 7 barrels of oil per person each year, compared to 35 barrels per person in Japan, 45 barrels per person in South Korea, and 61 barrels per person in the United States. If China's growth rate of oil consumption continues at the pace it has since its reforms began in the late 1970s it would be another 45 years before it reached the level of consumption that Japan has, let alone South Korea or the United States—implying that oil imports will be part of China's future for many years to come. The same holds true for copper and iron ore. For copper China only consumes roughly five kilograms per person per year, whereas the United States and Japan consume 8 to 12 kilograms per person per year. China consumes half the iron ore per capita as industrialized countries do as well. For both iron ore and copper it would take 50 years for China to consume at the same level as industrialized nations, assuming the same rate of growth since the late 1970s. If that level of growth is slower, of course there will be even more time to capitalize on Chinese demand for Latin American commodities.[2] It is also important to remember that in addition to China, other countries, such as India and Indonesia, will increasingly be a source of demand for Latin American commodities. In a joint study by the Asian Development Bank and the Inter-American Development Bank (IDB), researchers estimated that demand from China and other parts of Asia will continue to increase for most commodities for at least two to three decades.[3]

There may be demand for Latin American goods beyond the commodities sector as well. As China transforms itself toward a more consumption-based economy, it will need more consumer goods. While the manufacturing sector in Latin America has lost competitiveness during the commodity boom, Chinese transformation offers a second chance. If Latin American nations put a premium on innovation, industrialization, and export competitiveness, they may find openings in the Chinese economy that are not on offer elsewhere. Indeed, in 2014 the Brazilian aircraft giant Embraer signed 2.6 billion dollars worth of deals to sell small jets to small start-up regional airlines in China, showing that demand is picking up for China new jet-setting class.[4] Moreover, China's transformation may give Latin American consumer and other manufacturing products some breathing room in terms of export competitiveness through the exchange rate channel. As China becomes more of a consumer society and moves forward on financial reforms, it will ease its grip on the exchange rate. If managed properly the exchange rate will likely appreciate over the longer run. This will trigger more imports on the Chinese side and help make Latin American exports more competitive globally as well.[5] This is already proving evident for Mexico. From 2008 to 2013, only 24 percent of Mexican exports were directly threatened by China in world markets, down from 72 percent during the period from 2000 to 2006. These openings won't increase Latin American exports automatically, however; in the long run, they will only remain options for countries and companies that upgrade their competitiveness.[6]

China can also be a continued source of foreign direct investment into Latin America—and again, not only into the commodity sectors if Latin American countries and companies get their policies right. As markets in the natural resources, infrastructure and construction, and manufacturing sectors in China saturate the companies that led China's transformation in those sectors will be looking to go abroad. Indeed, this is already happening. Based on retained earnings from China's domestic boom and healthy lines of credit from the likes of the China Development Bank (CDB) and the China Export-Import Bank (CHEXIM), Chinese national champions are looking to merge with or acquire Latin American companies that will be suffering due to the slowdown, lower prices, and bloated balance sheets due to exchange rate depreciation.[7] As the exchange rate and wages increase in China, Latin America may not only be a destination for foreign investment in the primary commodities sector. Mexico and Central America will prove to be a platform to access to the US market as the United States gains momentum and those countries become more competitive. Indeed, Chinese textiles and copper tubing companies have already located in Mexico, and auto companies may soon follow. Chinese auto companies have already entered Uruguay, seeking access to the Argentine and Brazilian markets through Mercosur.

There is no sign that China is turning off the spigot in terms of finance to Latin American governments, either—though it may begin to take different forms. Since 2005 China's policy banks have provided upward of $119 billion to Latin American governments for infrastructure and mining projects. In January of 2015, China hosted the first China–CELAC (Community of Latin American and Caribbean States) summit and held the first ever conversation between China and the entire Latin American region. At that meeting China pledged to increase trade with Latin America to $500 billion and investment to $250 billion by 2025. To kick-start the pledge China established a number of funding arrangements totaling $35 billion, including $20-billion special loans for China–Latin America infrastructure cooperation, the $10-billion preferential loans for Latin American countries as well as the $5-billion China–CELAC Cooperation Fund that China promised previously. The $50-million China–Latin America Infrastructure Cooperation Special Fund has also started to invest in specific projects. China continues to see overseas finance and foreign direct investment as a way to diversify its holdings of US Treasuries. In addition to ramping up investments abroad through the CDB and CHEXIM, China is rapidly setting up new financial vehicles. In addition to the CELAC–China fund, China cofounded the $100 billion New Development Bank with the BRICS countries in 2015, and the $100 billion Asian Infrastructure Investment Bank. These vehicles may become the wave of China's financing future as they help China diversify risk. China may have overextended itself with nations like Argentina and Venezuela through bilateral loans. Multilateral finance may be a way to spread that risk.

The CELAC–China forum offers a fresh opportunity for a regional dialogue with China, rather than (or at least to supplement) bilateral economic relations. If managed properly this will allow the region to reach common goals for regional infrastructure, industrialization, and environmental protection that it can then engage with China about collectively. At the China–CELAC summit leaders from Latin America and China drew up a China–CELAC Cooperation Plan (2015–2019). The plan covers a wide range of issues, including peace and security; international affairs; trade, investment, and finance; infrastructure and transportation; energy and resources; education, culture, and sports; and environmental protection.

The China–CELAC Cooperation Plan is an unprecedented opportunity for Latin America to upgrade its industrial competitiveness and environmental protection. In addition to pledging to increase trade and investment and to create a number of funding vehicles to facilitate such trade, investment, and finance, China and CELAC pledge to "enhance collaboration to promote in CELAC countries the industrialization for value added goods," "with a view to supporting the internationalization and integration of SMEs [small and medium-sized enterprises] in global value chains." If that isn't enough, the plan also commits to "explore initiatives to the joint construction of industrial parks, science and technology, special economic zones and high-tech industrial parks between China and CELAC countries, especially in research and development (R&D) activities in order to improve industrial investment and the forming of industrial value chain," and "explore the possibility of inaugurating the China-LAC Industrial Development and Cooperation Forum in due time." China also commits to making major investments in Latin American infrastructure, and with a better eye on the sustainability of such projects "China-LAC Cooperation Fund, China-LAC Special Loan for Infrastructure, concessional loans offered by China as well as other financial resources, to support the key cooperation projects between China and CELAC countries, in a manner consistent with the social, economic and environmental development needs of the CELAC region, as well as with sustainable development vision."[8]

This plan is nothing short of incredible, and offers the best and balanced opportunity for Latin American economic development in 80 years. The plan also indicates that Latin American leaders have already come to realize the need to diversify their economies and make economic development more environmentally sustainable. However, the CELAC–China Cooperation Plan is organized and contains many of the exact initiatives that can be found in the Africa-China Cooperation Plan under the auspices of the Forum on China-Africa Cooperation (FOCAC) negotiated in Beijing in 2012—indicating that it is China that is the motivating force for industrialization and sustainable development in the region.[9]

China is handing Latin America an opportunity to upgrade in a sustainable manner on a silver platter. And if FOCAC is any indication, these plans are not mere communiqués for press conferences at the end of summits. China delivers. China's history of contemporary cooperation with Africa predates its cooperation with Latin America.[10] Indeed, China has had five ministerials with heads of Africa as a region as opposed to the first China–CELAC summit in 2015. China has delivered on a China-Africa Cooperation Fund and has kick-started a number of industrial parks across Africa, including in Ethiopia, Egypt, Nigeria, Mauritius, and Zambia. If these zones are primarily motivated by China and not Africa, why is China interested? Deborah Brautigam of Johns Hopkins University and Xiayang Tang of Tsinghua University attribute Chinese motivation for establishing industrial parks in Africa as being fivefold. First, the parks help increase demand for Chinese manufacturing exports. Second, by facilitating foreign investment, the zones serve as an export platform for Chinese firms wishing to cut tariff or transportation costs to the world's largest markets. Third, to the extent that the parks facilitate technological upgrading they help Chinese firms move up the value chain. Fourth, the zones help create economies of scale for overseas investment and help get small- and medium-sized Chinese firms overseas as suppliers to larger flagship firms. Fifth, the zones are a diplomatic tool envisioned to help other countries replicate China's success with such zones at home. Chinese firms are also motivated to locate to the zones because they can apply for special grants and long-term concessional loans to participate. What is more, China created a $1 billion fund for African SMEs that Chinese firms could participate in if locally registered as well. In the first assessment of these zones, though many of which are still in the works, Brautigam and Tang find that Chinese zones in Africa fall short in creating linkages to the rest of the economy that aid in the structural transformation of African economies. The authors stress that "each zone is embedded in a local policy framework and depends on local coordination outside the zone."[11] In other words, China can't do everything. Most African nations lack a home-grown strategy for industrial upgrading. Drawing from the Latin American experience, a key lesson for Latin America is that Chinese zones can enhance a homegrown strategy, but not act as a substitute for one.

Of course, a comprehensive development strategy for Latin America also has to put a premium on environmental protection. The plan says that China and CELAC will cooperate on global climate change negotiations and invest in more renewable energy in Latin America. What is more, the two pledge to "enhance collaboration in the protection of biodiversity and coastal ecological system, reserves management, environmentally sound technologies, water conservation, desertification combat and pollution control and treatment, among other issues, to improve the capacity for environment protection." As in the case with industrialization, China is offering a window and dialogue—backed by funding arrangements—to promote environmental protection. It will be up to Latin American nations in CELAC to make the environment as much of a priority as industrial diversification.

The current pattern of China–Latin America trade and investment is endemic to environmental degradation, high carbon emissions, and social conflict. New industry and infrastructure will need to be geared toward structural transformation that is environmentally sustainable. One area for joint cooperation is Latin America's lucrative clean energy potential. According to the IDB, Latin America will need to double its installed power capacity by 2030 at a cost of $430 billion. The IDB estimates that the region could produce orders of magnitude more electricity from solar, wind, geothermal, and biomass energy sources in Latin America.[12]

However, there is also major demand for infrastructure, amounting to 6.2 percent of GDP per year for the forseeable future. Infrastructure needs to be thought of in terms of regulatory infrastructure, Internet and communications, and energy and electricity, as well as roadways, railways, and ports. Moreover, a reinvigorated infrastructure for the region should focus on increasing both inter-Latin American trade and investment as well as exports—and seek to link newly created industrial clusters with cities, ports, and markets rather than the old model of simply building roads to the latest oil or mining concession. In addition, it will be imperative to adopt the most stringent social and environmental safeguards. Here CELAC and China would do well to adopt a strategy along the lines of the IDB's *Sustainable Infrastructure for Competiveness and Inclusive Growth*. Core to the IDB's strategy is to:

> Support the construction and maintenance of an environmentally and socially sustainable infrastructure: the strategy proposes including the critical components of environmental sustainability (climate change adaptation and mitigation, natural disaster risk reduction, and conservation of biodiversity) from the very start of the project cycle, so they represent a core focus of infrastructure planning. This strategy also stresses the need to design and manage infrastructure to boost its positive impacts on inclusion and poverty reduction.[13]

Putting clean energy investment and social environmental safeguards into the core of the CELAC–China economic cooperation agenda is in the interests of both parties. For Latin America this is important to maintain the stock of natural resources for economic growth in the long run and to maintain the rich biological and cultural diversity that the region enjoys. For China this is of utmost importance in order to reduce political and economic project risk. Projects that do not include stringent safeguards turn into political and economic nightmares—as Sinohydro has learned in Honduras—that create costly delays and tarnish company and country images.

The United States: From Patron to Partner

Now is a perfect time for the United States to hit the reset button on foreign economic policy in Latin America—and for Latin

America to do the same toward the United States. Both parties took each other for granted during the China Boom. After pushing hard to create the controversial Free Trade Area of the Americas (FTAA), the United States turned its focus to the Middle East and the Asian pivot. Latin American countries embraced China, with some inflaming the US–Latin America relationship with rhetoric of how they were deshackling themselves from a past dominated by US imperialism and the Washington Consensus. If the United States shifts from acting as a patron to a true partner of the Americas, both Latin America and the United States will be better off—and a more balanced relationship between Latin America, China, and the United States can coexist.

The United States is no longer in an economic or political position to create a Monroe Financial Doctrine or South American New Deal with Latin America as it did in the 1930s and 1940s (as discussed in chapter 2). However, the United States can reconstruct a similar sensitivity to Latin America that it had during that period. In so doing, the United States should articulate and reboot some of the major benefits that the United States brings to the Americas, and acknowledge and reform some of the mistakes that have been made by the United States in past decades.

A central tenet of US policy to Latin America during the New Deal was that Latin Americans deserved the policy space to determine their own economic destinies. The US government bolstered Latin American states in upgrading industrial capacities to ensure that their countries would grow and not be swayed by German penetration into the region. The US business community, led by Republican Nelson Rockefeller, supported industrial upgrading in Latin America for those reasons as well, but also because growth in the region created more demand for US products. US support was not simply a blessing, but was backed by the newly created US Export-Import Bank (US Ex-Im) that provided financing to steel mills and other industrial projects across the Americas.[14] A similar attitude and instruments will go a long way in the Americas— especially if coupled with an acknowledgment of past mistakes and a restatement of what the United States offers the region.

Embodied in the very name "the Washington Consensus" was the idea that Washington and the international financial institutions headquartered in Washington knew what was best for Latin American economic policy. Foreign economic policy then began telling Latin Americans what was good for them and codifying such ideas in IMF and World Bank programs, and in US trade agreements. In the twenty-first century, the United States should see Latin Americans as equals and declare a partnership with the region rather than the patronage that has defined US economic policy for decades. This is exactly what Roosevelt did, traveling to the region to declare the Good Neighbor policy and acknowledging that the United States had made mistakes in supporting dictators of the past. The United States should take credit for helping restore fiscal and monetary prudence in the region through the Washington Consensus years, but also acknowledge that growth was poor, financial instability more rife, and that some of our policies went too far.

In a renewed partnership the United States will need to emphasize how some aspects of the US–Latin America economic relationship have changed and are among Latin America's most strategic economic assets. The United States can take credit for some of the region's domestic policy achievements. It has a much more diversified trade and investment mix with Latin America than does China, plays a competitive role in development financing for the region, and, though not always followed, has a set of social and environmental guidelines that are among the strongest in the world.

In addition to taking credit for helping restore fiscal responsibility to the region, the United States should emphasize that it is still the largest trading partner to Mexico and Central America by orders of magnitude and is poised to regain its place as the largest trading partner with South America. As China's economy slows and transforms and the US economy finally recovers from its crisis, US demand for Latin American products will rebound. What is more, unlike Chinese demand, the US demand for Latin American products has been much more diversified—importing manufacturing and commodities alike. Indeed, though still relatively weak (especially in South America), Latin American manufacturing is more nested in North American production chains than with Asia. With the proper vision and policy space, this can be repaired. The United States not only imports a greater share of manufactured goods from Latin America, its foreign investment in the region is much more diversified as well. US automotive companies, electronics firms, big box retail, and banks can be found all across the Americas—not just US mining and energy companies. Expanding and moving into higher parts of these value chains should be at the core of any Latin American strategy for diversified growth.

Like trade and foreign direct investment (FDI), the United States plays key direct and indirect roles in providing financing for Latin American nations as well. One of Roosevelt's principle aims of the US Export-Import Bank was to provide finance to Latin American industrialization efforts while at the same time to create opportunities and partnerships with US firms. The US Export-Import Bank continues to provide upward of two billion dollars to Latin American governments on an annual basis. Nevertheless, the bank continues to be under vociferous attack by some members of the US Congress, who see it as too much government and a handout to big private companies. The majority of US Ex-Im Bank finance to Latin America goes into the manufacturing sector and downstream energy projects. Not only does it provide financing for industrialization in Latin America, it provides opportunities for

US exporters to play a role and become nested in such industrialization efforts. This 81-year program has become under appreciated in Latin America—its $2 billion per year is more financing than CHEXIM, and CHEXIM finance is heavily concentrated in commodity sectors.

The United States does of course play a major role in the World Bank and the Inter-American Development Bank. World Bank lending decreased to Latin America by 25 percent during the China Boom but still reached almost $80 billion, about the same amount as the China Development Bank. The IDB provided $92 billion to Latin America during the China Boom. Although these two development banks have tended to focus on micro-level health and educational interventions rather than infrastructure and industrialization, this has begun to change. Both institutions have set up infrastructure facilities, and both have given increased attention to the importance of industrial policy over the past few years.[15] What is more, there have been moves to lessen the policy conditionalities that were characteristic of the structural adjustment programs of the Washington Consensus period. World Bank and IDB finance is more likely to be conditioned on more general governance and transparency criteria rather than on controversial trade policy, privatization, and deregulation policies that plagued international financial institutions in the past.

Finally, at home and in its international policies, the United States boasts some of the strongest social and environmental standards. US environmental policies are the strongest in the Western Hemisphere, and the United States has helped craft a set of OECD guidelines for the environmental operations for overseas companies that are also strong. After decades of ignoring the environmental impacts of World Bank, Inter-American Development, and US Ex-Im projects, civil society pressure and a motivated new generation of bank leadership have put together environmental and social safeguards that are considered the gold standard of the profession. These institutions have pledged to reduce financing for coal and other fossil fuels and to provide financing for renewable energy development, water sanitation, biodiversity preservation, and adaption to climate change. Safeguard units in both institutions require consultations with indigenous communities and local groups before projects are executed, as well as environmental impact assessments that are made available for public comment.[16]

Alongside a rearticulation of these significant benefits of US–Latin American economic cooperation, the United States will have to acknowledge mistakes and make further reforms. Two key areas of reform would go a long way. First, the US Ex-Im Bank and World Bank are in need of reform and increased financing for Latin America. Second, US trade policy needs to be reset in the region. US treaties have a poor economic growth record, have restricted the ability of Latin American nations to put in place the proper policies for export competitiveness and industrial diversification, and have included loopholes that have allowed laggard firms to violate efforts to upgrade social and environmental standards.

The United States would do well to endorse reform and reboot financing to Latin America, not reduce or eliminate it. It was under similar duress in the hemisphere that the United States established the US Ex-Im Bank—but in the 1930s and 1940s it was in the face of potential threats stemming from European shores. In that atmosphere the Roosevelt administration founded the organization with strong injections of finance to Latin America. As World War II moved on, it was Nelson Rockefeller who convinced the Roosevelt administration to triple the funding for the US Ex-Im Bank.[17] Ironically, members of the same political party as Rockefeller who so championed the US Ex-Im Bank, Republican members of the US Congress, have worked hard to eliminate the bank in recent years.[18]

In an environment where the CDB and CHEXIM have entered Latin America and in some years have provided more finance to Latin American governments than the US Export-Import Bank, the World Bank, and the Inter-American Development Bank combined, the United States should be reforming and upgrading the US Ex-Im Bank, not eliminating it. It is true that the bank has often tilted its financing in support of larger US firms that could seek financing elsewhere. What is more, while it has very high social and environmental safeguards in place, they are not transparent in the disclosure of such safeguards. China in Latin America is an opportunity to reboot, recapitalize, and reform—not eliminate.

During the 1980s and early 1990s the Washington Consensus took the form of structural adjustment programs under the IMF and the World Bank. By the 1990s Washington's aim in Latin America was to solidify those programs through trade agreements. The flagship of these agreements was the 1994 North American Free Trade Agreement (NAFTA). As discussed in chapter 2, NAFTA did not live up to its expectations. NAFTA did increase trade and foreign direct investment into Mexico, but per capita growth rates and wages remained low. What is more, NAFTA cut Mexico's special economic zones off from the rest of the economy, creating enclaves of industry that rose and fell to the whim of the US market to which they were geared. When China entered the WTO and began selling similar products into the US market, Mexico's market share was considerably threatened in the United States.[19] There are signs that exchange rate depreciation and the suppression of wages in Mexico are making Mexico regain some of its competitiveness, as China's wages and exchange rate rises and the US economy picks up. This competitiveness will only be temporary unless Mexico upgrades beyond low-wage assembly work and diversifies so that manufacturing brings linkages to the rest of the economy.

The problem is that if Mexico wanted to implement many of the recommendations for industrial innovation and competiveness advocated by ECLAC, IDB, and now the World Bank, many of the rules under NAFTA would constrain its ability to do so. NAFTA's intellectual property rules make it much more difficult for companies and government to put in place innovation policies for industrial learning. Mexico has to adhere to tight patent and copyright rules, and cannot use many of the tools used by South Korea, China, and to some extent Brazil over the past decades. NAFTA's investment rules make it difficult for Mexican firms to create partnerships with foreign firms and reap some of the benefits of foreign investment. Nor does NAFTA provide the policy space for Mexico to manage speculative capital flows that can cause financial instability.[20] To his credit, US President Barack Obama, who did not support NAFTA, stated that NAFTA had many mistakes in his 2015 State of the Union address.[21] Obama billed the Trans-Pacific Partnership Agreement—a trade deal among NAFTA nations, Peru, Chile, and a number of Pacific Rim nations in Asia—as the renegotiation of NAFTA that he had promised on the campaign trail. Despite improvements in some areas, neither Obama nor Mexico proposed improvements that would allow more flexibility for industrial development and the management of financial stability.

When Obama's predecessor, George Bush, insisted on duplicating NAFTA's template for the Free Trade Area of the Americas, every nation in the Americas opted out except for Peru, Colombia, Chile, and some Central American nations. Brazil, the cochair of the negotiations, called off the negotiations because of US intransigence on intellectual property and investment rules. Not only was Brazil concerned that these rules would curtail their efforts in innovation and industrialization, but they were worried that US intellectual property rules would reduce access to medicines for

the majority of Brazilians. The United States also refused to negotiate agricultural subsidies and tariffs with Latin Americans under
the FTAA, despite the fact that such barriers to the US market were
the most significant for South American economies. Even with
agricultural subsidy reductions, the World Bank estimated that
free trade in the Americas would only raise incomes by 0.4 percent
of GDP. Those small benefits were seen as not worth the high costs
of lost policy space under the FTAA.[22]

Some of the nations that eventually signed bilateral trade deals
have suffered as well. Official estimates by the Inter-American
Development Bank and the International Monetary Fund show that
Colombia's and Peru's economies worsened from their trade deals
with the United States, and that Central American countries only
benefited by less than one-tenth of 1 percent of GDP.[23] In terms
of costs, these nations learned the hard way that crafty firms in
the United States have found loopholes that allow foreign firms to
circumvent efforts to upgrade social and environmental standards.
To Peru's credit, during the China Boom it has worked to upgrade
its environmental policies and reduce the deforestation of the
Amazon. Part of the upgrading process was to force companies to
install technologies to reduce the use of toxic materials in the work-
place. Doe Run (Renco Group), a New York–headquartered metals
and mining group, had long operated a metals smelter in La Oraya,
Peru—one of the most polluted cities in the world (also referred to
in chapter 6). After granting Renco two extensions on the cleanup,
Peru chose not to give Renco a third. Renco used provisions in the
US–Peru Free Trade Agreement to strike back—and is suing Peru
for $800 million dollars over its environmental regulations.[24]

As in NAFTA, the Peru deal allows for investor-state dispute
resolution (ISDS). Unlike at the WTO, where disputes are filed
and settled by nation-states and regulators, US deals in the hemisphere allow foreign firms to directly file claims for monetary

damages against host governments under ISDS—rather than getting approval and negotiators from the US government. Moreover, the rules allow foreign firms (not domestic ones) to file claims if the investor's expectations for the investment are not met. In other words, given that companies like Renco did not expect regulations to be upgraded, they can recast them as tantamount to expropriation. Not all US companies choose to behave like Renco, but Renco is not an isolated case of firms seeking loopholes around environmental regulation in the hemisphere. Conrado Olivera Alcocer, head of an environmental group in Peru, reported to *Bloomberg*, "this clause gives more power to foreign investors than the people of Peru."[25]

Renco and Peru are not isolated cases. Chevron corporation has sued Ecuador for over $2 billion to escape penalties from policies intended to reduce toxic waste and prevent further deforestation of the Amazon, and Metalclad Corporation has sued Mexico to avoid paying for toxic waste cleanup costs. Companies have targeted health regulations as well, evidenced by Philip Morris's notorious case against Uruguay to prevent health-based restrictions on cigarette sales.[26] Under the US investment treaty with Ecuador, the US oil company Burlington Resource Company used ISDS in response to policies by Ecuador's past two governments that attempted put in place windfall taxes to capture the benefits of commodity-led growth and invest them into alternative forms of economic activity. Burlington claimed that Ecuador's tax increase was "tantamount to expropriation," and the arbitral tribunal ruled in favor of Burlington.[27] Cases like these not only inflict damages on the countries that must defend regulation from foreign investors, but have a chilling effect on further regulation both within and in neighboring countries.[28]

To be seen as a partner, the United States will need to recognize that Latin America needs to capture the windfall profits of commodity exports and invest in infrastructure, industry, and the environment—and grant nations the flexibility to do so under trade and investment agreements. World Trade Organization law and process can be a better starting point for US trade policy reform in the region, and WTO provisions on intellectual property, investment, and financial services leave a lot more policy space for nations to put in place the proper innovation, industrialization, and financial stabilization policies. The WTO also has "special and differentiated treatment" as one of its core principles. Special and differentiated treatment is a long-standing trade law principle that recognizes that different provisions are appropriate at different levels of economic development—and grants exceptions or longer compliance periods, with certain provisions, for developing countries. While Asian bilateral and regional deals include special and differentiated treatment, not one US treaty does. Most importantly, under the WTO disputes are settled among nation-states, which are better equipped to balance the rights of citizens and corporations in both host and foreign states than investor-state dispute resolution.[29] This would allow the United States to screen those companies that want to abuse treaty commitments and reward those companies that uphold the higher standards found in US law, US executive orders, and OECD guidelines.

A Troika for the Hemisphere

The United States, China, and Latin America can also work together. As Latin America and other Western countries have, the United States should welcome and complement China's global development financing and make more room for China in the Bretton Woods institutions. Embracing China makes for a pretty sturdy system that would combine China's financial prowess alongside governance experience that the Bretton Woods institutions have accumulated. What is more, China and Latin America can take part in a comprehensive reform of these institutions. The three can also join hands at the Inter-American Development Bank, where each is a donor member. Such a compact of complementarity and cooperation will not only help Latin America finally achieve its development goals, but strengthen the economies of China and the United States and build more trust among the three parties.

The flagship institutions tasked to maintain economic stability and raise the living standards of the world's people were also founded in the Roosevelt era at the historic 1944 United Nations Monetary and Financial Conference held at the Mt. Washington Hotel in Bretton Woods, New Hampshire. The International Monetary Fund serves as a lender of last resort that helps provide monitoring of the financial stability of the global economy as a whole. The World Bank now provides long-term lending to poorer countries. In 1944, the world was still unaware of the need to provide a stable climate in order for the earth's ecosystems to reliably provide the world economy with the ecological services it needs to prosper. Today, these institutions now recognize the need to provide a stable ecological climate for the earth's economy.

The World Bank and other key Western-backed development banks have made significant achievements with respect to raising living standards and adapting to and mitigating changing climate. However, the World Bank and its counterparts continue to be criticized for falling short of their mission in terms of not having the capital to meet the growing needs in the world economy, not having the right governance in place for the twenty-first century, and not having appropriate recipes for development.

In terms of scale, the Western-backed financial institutions have not been able to increase their capital in proportion to the growing needs in the world. According to some estimates, development banks fall short of providing lending for poverty alleviation by $175 billion per year.[30] In Latin America, World Bank lending to the region declined by 25 percent during the China Boom. The World Economic Forum projects that by 2020, about $5.7 trillion will need to be invested each year into green infrastructure in developing countries—a significant portion in Latin America.[31] Not only will this require shifting the current $5 trillion into a greener direction, they will need to increase by $700 billion more each year to truly make the shift toward a more sustainable world environment.[32]

The governance structure of the World Bank is skewed away from including the very countries the World Bank hopes to serve. There has long been a gentlemen's agreement that the World Bank would be run by a citizen of the United States, while the head of the International Monetary Fund would be a European. Moreover, The United States holds veto power over all decisions in the World Bank, IMF, and other institutions, while China and Latin American countries have very little say.[33]

Finally, Western-backed financial institutions have been criticized and stigmatized from all sides of the political spectrum for falling short their mission. Critics argue that the World Bank has practiced a one-size-fits-all policy recipe that countries must adhere to in order to receive funding. The World Bank has also received scrutiny for having a mixed record on financing for climate change. The bank has backed off from the most draconian structural adjustment programs, but maintains a fairly conservative line. While the bank has begun to pay lipservice to the need for industrialization, it has provided little lending in this area. Despite breakthroughs on climate change and the environment, the World Bank has still managed to involve itself in some of the world's dirtiest projects.[34] Although the World Bank has gold standard social and environmental standards, there are now global advocacy campaigns claiming that the World Bank is in the midst of watering those standards down.[35]

China's new development banks have arisen from at least two motivations. China has accumulated an enormous store of wealth and savings that it seeks to diversify by making big investments across the world. Second, China feels slighted by the West for not being given a greater role in the Bretton Woods institutions. In 2010, the IMF passed significant reforms that would have given China and other emerging economies a greater say. Those reforms, however, have been stalled in the US Congress.

Since China wasn't let into existing institutions, it has begun to create its own. These institutions now have levels of capital at their disposal that rival that of the Western-backed development bank. The World Bank holds just over $200 billion in capital and has just over $500 billion in assets. The CDB holds $100 billion in capital, and has over $1 trillion in assets. The CDB and CHEXIM now provide more loans to Latin American governments than the World Bank and the Inter-American Development Bank—and more loans to Asia than the World Bank and the Asian Development Bank.

As discussed earlier, in 2015 China set up an additional $35 billion in funds for Latin America under the new China–CELAC Cooperation Plan. In 2014 China set up the Asian Infrastructure Investment Bank with $50 billion in capital, and the Silk Road Fund with $40 billion. Also in 2014, China established the New Development Bank with Brazil, Russia, India, and South Africa that has initial capital of $100 billion. China has long had the China-Africa Development Fund, which has $2 billion. There is no sign that China is stopping, either.

The United States has long criticized China for not shouldering more of the world's burdens as China's economy and power have risen. The *New York Times* reports, however, that the United States has been threatened by China's new banks and has sought to undermine them: "Instead, in quiet conversations with China's potential partners, American officials have lobbied against the development bank with unexpected determination and engaged in a vigorous campaign to persuade important allies to shun the project, according to senior US officials and representatives of other governments involved."[36] Indeed, the United States rebuked the United Kingdom in 2015 when it joined the Asian Infrastructure Investment Bank, publicly bemoaning the fact that the United States had not been consulted and expressing concerns over the United Kingdom's "constant accommodation" of China.[37]

Latin America—and indeed the world at large—cannot afford for this burgeoning set of development banks to become a source of geopolitical strife between the United States and China. Rather than opposing an expanded role for China and other emerging markets in the Western-backed financial institutions and rejecting China's subsequent financial arrangements, the United States should embrace them as a welcome complement that can help solve the world's ills.

One arena where China, the United States, and Latin America can work together is at the Inter-American Development Bank, where each is a member. Indeed, there is some movement afoot. In 2012 CHEXIM and the IDB set up a joint investment platform that includes three regional equity funds: the LAC-China Infrastructure Fund that will focus on infrastructure projects, the LAC-China Mid Cap Fund that will target midsized companies, and the Natural Resources fund that will fund projects in agriculture, mining and energy. The IDB agreed to focus on China's financing priorities, and CHEXIM agreed to follow the IDBs' social and environmental standards. Hans Schulz, a senior IDB official, said with respect to the new platform: "Given Latin America's rich endowment of natural resources and sensitive biodiversity, it is paramount that investments flowing to the region are carried out in an environmentally and socially responsible manner and that the highest standards of corporate governance are applied."[38] One of the first projects was a $132.6 million wind farm in Uruguay.[39] This is an example of how China's finance and skill in large infrastructure investment can be combined with state-of-the-art safeguarding. This will be an important testing ground where each party can learn to work with each other, rather than against.

Moving Forward

Barring a political or economic crisis, China's demand for Latin American natural resources, its interest in investing in Latin American resources and manufacturing platforms, and its interest in providing finance to Latin American governments will not likely subside for the forseeable future. Indeed, in 2015 China pledged to increase trade with Latin America to $500 billion and investment to $250 billion, and crafted a comprehensive new cooperation plan with the region to implement those and many other commitments that could be highly beneficial for Latin America's economies.

While engaging with its newfound economic partner, Latin America should not disengage with the United States. The United States is still the region's largest trade and investment partner, and the composition of that trade is more diversified across a number of sectors, not just natural resources. What is more, the World Bank, US Export-Import Bank, and the Inter-American Development Bank match China's financing to the region during most years. US law and these development banks boast higher social and environmental standards than their Chinese counterparts. The perceived competition with China gives Latin America more bargaining power with the United States to increase efforts by the US Ex-Im Bank and the World Bank and to upgrade social and environmental standards and transparency in those institutions. It also gives the region leverage to work with the United States to create more flexibilities and close harmful loopholes in US trade and investment treaties. Work to this end is in the United States' best interests, as a growing and secure partner in Latin America is far better for US economic and national security than a patronized, disgruntled, and unstable Latin America.

In the end, however, the onus is on the Latin Americans themselves. To fully benefit from its new relationship with China and its longstanding ties with the United States, the region's governments will need to put in place policies to capture the windfalls from commodity-led growth and invest the proceeds into economic diversification and export competitiveness, social inclusion, and environmental protection. Trade, investment, and finance with China and the United States can be key tenets of such a strategy, but in the end it is Latin America's responsibility to put the right policies in place. A failure to do so cannot be blamed on China or the United States. As Cassius said to Brutus in Shakespeare's *Julius Caesar*, "The fault, dear Brutus, is not in our stars, But in ourselves."

NOTES

Chapter 2

1. See Magnus Mörner and Harold Sims, *Adventurers and Proletarians: The Story of Migrants in Latin America* (Pittsburgh: University of Pittsburgh Press, 1985).

2. See Angus Maddison, *Contours of the World Economy, 1–2030 AD*, Essays in Macro-Economic History (Oxford: Oxford University Press, 2007); Kenneth Pomeranz, *The Great Divergence* (Princeton, NJ: Princeton University Press, 2000).

3. Bilge Erten and Jose Antonio Ocampo, "Super Cycles of Commodity Prices Since the Mid-Nineteenth Century," *World Development* 44 (April 2013): 14–30.

4. The term was coined by Carlos Diaz-Alejandro in C. Diaz-Alejandro, "Latin America in the 1930s," in *Latin America in the 1930s*, ed. R. Thorpe (London: Macmillan, 1984). For analyses of this era see P. Basu and D. McLeod, "'Terms of Trade Fluctuations and Economic Growth in Developing Economies," *Journal of Development Economics* 37, nos. 1–2 (1992): 89–110; Christopher Blattman, Jason Hwang, and Jeffrey Williamson, "Winners and Losers in the Commodity Lottery: The Impact of Terms of Trade Growth and Volatility in the Periphery, 1870–1939," *Journal of Development Economics* 82, no. 1 (2007): 156–79.

5. See J. Coatsworth and A. Taylor (eds.), *Latin America and the World Economy Since 1800* (Cambridge, MA: Harvard University Press, 1988); and Luis Bertola and Jose Antonio Ocampo, *The Economic Development of Latin America Since Independence* (Cambridge, Cambridge University Press, 2012), 46.

6. Bertola and Ocampo, *The Economic Development of Latin America Since Independence*, 95.

7. Bertola and Ocampo, *The Economic Development of Latin America Since Independence*, 120.

8. See Jeffry Frieden, *Global Capitalism: Its Fall and Rise in the Twentieth Century* (New York: Norton, 2007).

9. See John Gerard Ruggie, "International Regimes, Transactions, and Change: Embedded Liberalism in the Postwar Economic Order," *International Organization* 36, no. 2 (1982): 379–415; Eric Helleiner, *States and the Re-emergence of Global Finance* (Ithaca, NY: Cornell University Press, 1994).

10. Stephen Marglin and Juliet Schor, *The Golden Age of Capitalism: Interpreting the Post War Experience* (Oxford: Oxford University Press, 1992).

11. Prebisch's classic work is Raul Prebisch, *The Economic Development of Latin America and Its Principal Problems* (New York: United Nations, 1950). For a full account of his life and work see Edgar J. Dosman, *The Life and Times of Raúl Prebisch, 1901–1986* (Montreal: McGill-Queen's University Press, 2008).

12. Lewis's classic work is Arthur W. Lewis, "Economic Development with Unlimited Supplies of Labor," *Manchester School of Economic and Social Studies* 22, no. 2 (1954): 139–91. His views on the larger structure of the world economy, however, can be found in his book *The Evolution of the International Economic Order* (Princeton, NJ: Princeton University Press, 1978).

13. Albert O. Hirschman, *The Strategy of Economic Development* (New Haven, CT: Yale University Press, 1958); Hollis Chenery, "A Structuralist Approach to Development Policy," *American Economic Review* 65, no. 2 (1975): 310–16.

14. See Eric Helleiner, *Forgotten Foundations of Bretton Woods: International Development and the Making of the Postwar Order* (Ithaca, NY: Cornell University Press, 2014).

15. Helleiner, *Forgotten Foundations*, 43.

16. Helleiner, *Forgotten Foundations*, 46.

17. Alice Amsden, *The Rise of the Rest: Challenges to the West from Late Industrializing Countries* (New York: Oxford University Press, 2000). See also Bertola and Ocampo, *The Economic Development of Latin America Since Independence*, Chapter 4.

18. Bilge Erten and Jose Antonio Ocampo, "Super Cycles of Commodity Prices Since the Mid- Nineteenth Century," *World Development* 44 (April 2013): 14–30; and World Bank, World Bank Development Indicators, http://data.worldbank.org/data-catalog/world-development-indicators, accessed October 24, 2014.

19. Erten and Ocampo, "Super Cycles," 198. Robert Devlin, *Debt and Crisis in Latin America* (Princeton, NJ: Princeton University Press, 1989).

20. Amsden, *Rise of the Rest*; see also Robert Wade, *Governing the Market* (Princeton, NJ: Princeton University Press, 1992) and Erten and Ocampo, "Super Cycles," 226.

21. Peter Evans, *Embedded Autonomy: States and Industrial Transformation* (Princeton, NJ: Princeton University Press, 1985). See also Amsden, *Rise of the Rest*.

22. The term was originally coined by John Williamson "What Washington Means by Policy Reform," in *Latin American Readjustment: How Much has Happened*, ed. John Williamson (Washington, DC: Institute for International

Economics, 1989). As noted in the text, Williamson's original ten-step program was much less harmful than the policies adopted by the countries themselves.

23. Williamson, "What Washington Means by Policy Reform," 4.

24. Erten and Ocampo, "Super Cycles," 256.

25. Author's calculations based on World Bank Development Indicators, GDP per capital from 1980 to 2002 compared to 1960 to 1980. Discounting the lost decade Mexico's rate was still just 1.5 percent annually. For Mexican productivity data see Federal Reserve Bank of the United States, St. Louis, "Total Factor Productivity Level at Current Purchasing Power Parities for Mexico," http://research.stlouisfed.org/fred2/series/CTFPPPMXA669NRUG, accessed November 6, 2014.

26. Erten and Ocampo, "Super Cycles," 250.

27. Author's calculation based on World Bank Development Indicators; also see C. A. Hidalgo, B. Klinger, A.-L. Barabasi, and R. Hausmann, "The Product Space and Conditions and the Development of Nations," *Science* 317, no. 5837 (July 2007): 482–87.

28. Erten and Ocampo "Super Cycles," 247.

29. There is a large literature on this inherent nature of Latin American economies. See Erten and Ocampo, "Super Cycles," 218; Ricardo Ffrench-Davis, and Gabriel Palma, "The Latin American Economies, 1959–1990," in *The Cambridge History of Latin America*, vol. 6, *Latin America: Economy and Society since 1930*, ed. L. Bethell (Cambridge: Cambridge University Press, 1998).

30. For a summary of these vulnerabilities and gains see Robert Devlin and Graciela Moguillansky, *Breeding Latin Tigers* (Washington, DC: World Bank/United Nations, 2011); for environmental analyses see Edward Barbier, "The Policy Roots of Socio-Economic Stagnation and Environmental Implosion: Latin America 1950–2000," *World Development* 31, no. 2 (2003): 259–80; and Ramon Lopez, "Agricultural Expansion, Resource Booms and Growth in Latin America: Implications for Long-Run Economic Development," *World Development* 32, no. 1 (2004): 137–57.

31. Pomeranz, *The Great Divergence*, 84.

32. Angus Maddison, www.ggdc.net/maddison/maddison-project/home.htm, accessed September 22, 2015.

33. For the various explanations of China's decline as a world power see David Landes, "Why Europe and the West? Why Not China?," *Journal of Economic Perspectives* 20, no. 2 (2006): 3–22; Pomeranz, *The Great Divergence*, 84. More secure property rights were also seen as a factor; see Douglass C. North and Robert Paul Thomas, *The Rise of the Western World: A New Economic History* (Cambridge: Cambridge University Press, 1973).

34. Author's calculations based on Maddison, www.ggdc.net/maddison/maddison-project/home.htm.

35. See Maddison, www.ggdc.net/maddison/maddison-project/home.htm.

36. The best introduction to the Chinese economy in English is Barry Naughton, *The Chinese Economy: Transitions and Growth* (Cambridge, MA: MIT Press, 2007). See also Justin Yifu Lin, *Demystifying the Chinese Economy* (Cambridge: Cambridge University Press, 2012), and Gregory Chow and Dwitght Perkins, *The Routledge Handbook of the Chinese Economy* (London: Routledge, 2014).

37. Manufacturing/GDP data from World Bank World Development Indicators; growth rates are author's calculations based on Maddison, www.ggdc.net/maddison/maddison-project/home.htm.

38. See Naughton, *Chinese Economy*, 39, and Peng Xizhe, "Demographic Consequences of the Great Leap Forward in China's Provinces," *Population and Development Review* 13, no. 4 (1987): 639–70.

39. Naughton, *Chinese Economy*, 86.

40. Henry Sanderson and Michael Forsythe, *China's Superbank: Debt, Oil and Influence—How the China Development Bank is Rewriting the Rules of Finance* (New York: Bloomberg, 2013).

41. See Sanderson and Forsythe, *China's Superbank*, 11; Carl Walter and Fraser Howie, *Red Capitalism: The Fragile Financial Foundation of China's Extraordinary Rise* (New York: Wiley, 2011).

42. Liang Chuan "Infrastructure Development in China," in *International Infrastructure Development in East Asia—Towards Balanced Regional Development and Integration*, ERIA Research Project Report 2007–2, ed. N. Kumar (Chiba: IDE-JETRO, 2008), 85–104; for US estimates see US Department of Transportation, "System Mileage Within the United States," www.rita.dot.gov/bts/sites/rita.dot.gov.bts/files/publications/national_transportation_statistics/html/table_01_01.html, accessed October 22, 2014.

43. Organization for Economic Cooperation and Development (OECD), "FDI in Figures" (Paris: OECD, 2013), www.oecd.org/daf/inv/FDI%20in%20figures.pdf, accessed November 5, 2014.

44. For a striking video by the *Economist* magazine on internal migration in China see http://chinamoviesenglish.wordpress.com/2013/02/01/the-economist-the-worlds-largest-internal-migration, accessed November 14, 2014.

45. See Zhongxiu Zhao, Huang Xiaoling, Ye Dongya, and Paul Gentle, "China's Industrial Policy in Relation to Electronics Manufacturing," *China & World Economy* 15, no. 3 (2007): 33–51. For similar discussion of the Chinese auto sector development see Kelly Sims Gallagher, *China Shifts Gears: Automakers, Oil, Pollution and Development* (Cambridge, MA: MIT Press, 2006).

46. See Kevin P. Gallagher and Lyuba Zarsky, *The Enclave Economy: Foreign Investment and Sutainable Development in Mexico's Silicon Valley* (Cambridge, MA: MIT Press, 2007); Kevin P. Gallagher and Roberto Porzecanski, *The Dragon in the Room: China and the Future of Latin American Industrialization* (Redwood City, CA: Stanford University Press, 2010).

47. Data in this paragraph from Nicholas Lardy, *Markets over Mao: The Rise of Private Business in China* (Washington, DC: Peterson Institute for International Economics, 2014).

48. See the Commission on Growth and Development chaired by Nobel Economist Michael Spence, http://web.worldbank.org/WBSITE/EXTERNAL/EXTABOUTUS/ORGANIZATION/EXTPREMNET/0,,contentMDK:23225570~pagePK:64159605~piPK:64157667~theSitePK:489961,00.html, accessed November 4, 2014.

49. China State Environmetnal Protection Agency and Bureau of National Statistics, *Green GDP Accounting Study Report 2004*, www.gov.cn/english/2006–09/11/content_384596.htm, accessed November 4, 2014. See also Fergus Ororke, "China's Revived Green GDP Program Still Faces Challenges," *Green Biz Asia*, 2013, www.cleanbiz.asia/news/chinas-revived-green-gdp-program-still-faces-challenges#.VGfJjYdPK3V, accessed November 4, 2014.

50. See Jose Antonio Ocampo and Kevin P. Gallagher, *Capital Account Liberalization in China: The Need for a Balanced Approach* (Boston: Global Economic Governance Initiative, Boston University, 2014) for a discussion of Latin America's lessons for China in this area.

Chapter 3

1. Jessica Brice, "Brazil Slowing as Lula China Policy Sows Doubts," *Bloomberg News*, September 22, 2014.

2. Author's calculations based on World Bank (2014) World Development Indicators Database, http://data.worldbank.org/data-catalog/world-development-indicators, accessed September 22, 2015.

3. All export data in this chapter are author's calculations from the United Nations (2014) Commodity Trade Statistics Database, http://comtrade.un.org/, accessed September 3, 2014.

4. World Bank, *World Development Indicators* (Washington, DC: World Bank, 2015).

5. Elizabeth Economy and Michael Levi, *By All Means Necessary: How China's Resource Quest is Changing the World* (New York: Oxford University Press, 2014), 22.

6. Brendan Coates and Nghi Luu, "China's Emergence in Global Commodity Markets" (Washington, DC: US Treasury, 2012), www.treasury.gov.au/~/media/Treasury/Publications%20and%20Media/Publications/2012/Economic%20Roundup%20Issue%201/Downloads/01%20China%20Commodity%20demand.ashx, accessed November 25, 2014.

7. See United Nations Economic Commission for Latin America and the Caribbean, *People's Republic of China and Latin America and the Caribbean: Ushering in a New Era in the Economic and Trade Relationship* (Santiago: United Nations Economic Commission for Latin America and the Caribbean, 2012).

8. Rebecca Ray and Kevin P. Gallagher, *2013-China-Latin America Economic Bulletin* (Boston: Boston University Global Economic Governance Initiative, 2014).

9. Iacob Koch-Weser, *Chinese Mining Activity in Latin America* (Washington, DC: Inter-American Dialogue, 2013).

10. William Shurtleff and Akiko Aoyagi, "History of Soy in Latin America," Soy Info Center, www.soyinfocenter.com/HSS/latin_america1.php, accessed November 14, 2014.

11. United Nations Economic Commission for Latin America and the Caribbean, *China and Latin America and the Caribbean: Building a Strategic Economic and Trade Relationship* (Santiago: United Nations Economic Commission for Latin America and the Caribbean, 2012).

12. See Susan Thomas, "Copper Miners' Blind Spot: Chinese Collateral Financing Deals," *Bloomberg*, April 16, www.reuters.com/article/2014/04/16/copper-financing-idUSL6N0N158020140416, accessed November 14, 2014.

13. US Energy Information Administration (USEIA) (2014), "China Key Energy Statistics," www.eia.gov/beta/international/country.cfm?iso=CHN, accessed September 24, 2015 (Washington, DC: USEIA); www.eia.gov/countries/analysisbriefs/China/china.pdf, accessed November 4, 2014.

14. USEIA, "China Key Energy Statistics."

15. Enrique Dussel Peters, "The Mexican Case," in *China and Latin America: Economic Relations in the Twenty-First Century*, eds. Rhys Jenkins and Enrique Dussel Peters (Bonn: German Development Institute, 2012).

16. Zhang Yuwei, "Baking in Beijing Rises for Mexico's Bimbo," *China Daily*, June 20, 2012, www.grupobimbo.com/en/press-room/news/964/971/baking-in-beijing-rises-for-mexicos-bimbo.html, accessed November 23, 2014.

17. See Enrique Dussel Peters, *Mexican Firms Investing in China*, Discussion Paper No. IDB-DP-255 (Washington, DC: Inter-American Development Bank, 2012).

18. Antoni Estevadeordal, Mauricio Mesquita Moreira, and Theodore Kahn, "LAC Investment in China: A New Chapter in Latin America and the Caribbean-China Relations" (Washington, DC: Inter-American Development Bank, 2014).

19. Ryan Berger, "Charticle: The Fast Ramp Up, The Economics of the China-Latin America Relationship," *Americas Quarterly* 6, no. 1 (Winter 2012), www.americasquarterly.org/charticles/charticle_winter2012.html, accessed September 22, 2015.

20. Zhu Rongji, "Report on the Outline of the Tenth Five-Year Plan for National Social and Economic Development, Beijing, State Council," 2001, http://en.people.cn/features/lianghui/zhureport.html, accessed September 22, 2015.

21. Peter Elstrom, "Huawei's $30 Billion China Credit Opens Doors in Brazil, Mexico," *Bloomberg*, April 24, 2011, www.bloomberg.com/news/2011-04-25/huawei-counts-on-30-billion-china-credit-to-open-doors-in-brazil-mexico.html, accessed September 30, 2015.

22. Kevin Gallagher and Amos Irwin, "Exporting National Champions: China's Outward Foreign Direct Investment Finance in Comparative Perspective," *China & World Economy* 22, no. 6 (2014): 1–21.

23. FDI data calculations from Rebecca Ray and Kevin P. Gallagher, *2013-China-Latin America Economic Bulletin*.

24. Gustavo Bittencourt (coord.), Enrique Dussel Peters, Célio Hiratuka, and Martha Castilho, "El impacto de China en América Latina. Comercio e inversiones" (Montevideo: RED MERCOSUR, 2012); Enrique Dussel Peters, *Chinese FDI in Latin America: Does Ownership Matter?* (Medford, MA: Working Group on Development and the Environment in the Americas, Tufts University, 2012).

25. Gallagher and Irwin, "Exporting National Champions."

26. W. Zhang, "China Outbound Foreign Direct Investment Survey" (Beijing: China Council for the Promotion of International Trade Report, China Council for the Promotion of International Trade, 2013); Gallagher and Irwin, "Exporting National Champions"; and Nicholas R. Lardy, *Markets Over Mao: The Rise of Private Business in China* (Washington, DC: Peterson Institute for International Economics, 2014).

27. Economy and Levi, *By All Means Necessary*.

28. Andres Lopez and Daniela Ramos, "Argentina y China: Nuevos Encadenamientos Mercantiles Globales Con Empressas Chinas," in *La Inversion Extranjera Directa de China en America Latina*, ed. Enrique Dussel Peters (Mexico City: National Autonomous University of Mexico, 2014).

29. K. Wu, "China's Overseas Oil and Gas Investment: Motivations, Strategies, and Global Impact," *Oil, Gas, and Energy Law Intelligence* 6, no. 1 (2008): 1–9.

30. Lopez and Ramos, "Argentina y China."

31. Evan R. Ellis, *China on the Ground in Latin America* (New York: Palgrave, 2014).

32. Alexandre Barbosa, Angela Cristina Tepasse, and Marina Neves Biancalana, "Las Relaciones Economicas entre Brasil y China a partir del desempeno de las empresas State Grid y Lenovo," in *La Inversion Extranjera Directa de China en America Latina*, ed. Enrique Dussel Peters (Mexico City: National Autonomous University of Mexico, 2014).

33. Ray and Gallagher, *2013-China-Latin America Economic Bulletin*; data purchased from from Dealogic, www.dealogic.com. See also Ellis, *China on the Ground in Latin America*.

34. Cynthia Sanborn and Victoria Chonn Ching, "Making Ways for Mines: Chinese Investment in Peru," *ReVista, the Harvard Review of Latin America* 13, no. 2 (Winter 2014), published by the David Rockefeller Center for Latin American Studies, Harvard University, http://revista.drclas.harvard.edu/book/making-way-mines, accessed September 30, 2015.

35. Margaret Myers, "China Eyes Latin America to Fill Its Kitchen Cupboard," *Caixin*, January 8, 2014 http://english.caixin.com/2014-01-08/100626498.html, accessed March 25, 2015.

36. Sumner Lemon, "Lenovo Completes Purchase of IBM's PC Unit," *Tech Hive*, May 2, 2005, www.techhive.com/article/120670/article.html, accessed November 20, 2014.

37. CCE stands for three companies: Digibrás Indústria Do Brasil S.A., Digiboard Eletrônica Da Amazônia Ltda, and Dual Mix Comércio De Eletrônicos Ltda. See "Lenovo Acquires CCE to Build PC+ Leader in Brazil," http://news.lenovo.com/article_display.cfm?article_id=1628, accessed November 25, 2014.

38. Ellis, *China on the Ground in Latin America*.

39. Inter-American Dialogue, "Chinese Automakers in Latin America Shift into High Gear," July 22, 2014, http://chinaandlatinamerica.com/2014/07/22/chinese-automakers-in-latin-america-shift-into-high-gear/, accessed November 25, 2014.

40. Gustavo Bittencourt and Nicolas Reig, "China y Uruguay: El Caso de las Empresas Automotrices Chery y Lifan," in *La Inversion Extranjera Directa de China en America Latina*, ed. Enrique Dussel Peters (Mexico City: National Autonomous University of Mexico, 2014).

41. Bittencourt and Reig, "China y Uruguay."

42. Ellis, *China on the Ground in Latin America*.

43. *Bloomberg*, "Huawei's $30 Billion China Credit Opens Doors."

44. Ray and Gallagher, *2013-China-Latin America Economic Bulletin*.

45. Erten and Ocampo, "Super Cycles," 14–30.

46. Rhys Jenkins, "The 'China Effect' on Commodity Prices and Latin American Export Earnings," *CEPAL Review* 103 (April 2011): 73–87.

47. Gustavo Adler and Nicolas Magud, *Four Decades of Terms-of-Trade Booms: Saving-Investment Patterns and a New Metric of Income Windfall*, IMF Working Paper, WP/13/103 (Washington, DC: International Monetary Fund, 2013).

48. World Bank, *China and India's Challenge to Latin America* (Washington, DC: World Bank, 2011).

49. International Monetary Fund, *Regional Economic Outlook: Western Hemisphere Fears and Challenges* (Washington, DC: International Monetary Fund, 2014).

50. World Bank, *Latin America's Long-Term Growth: Made in China?* (Washington, DC: World Bank, 2011), 22.

51. Nora Lustig, *Taxes, Transfers, Inequality and the Poor in the Developing World. Round 1*, CEQ Working Paper No. 23 (New Orleans: Center for Inter-American Policy and Research and Department of Economics, Tulane University and Inter-American Dialogue, 2014).

Chapter 4

1. Economic Commission for Latin America and the Caribbean, *The Economic Infrastructure Gap in Latin America and the Caribbean* (Santiago: United Nations Economic Commission for Latin America and the Caribbean, 2011).

2. Brian Faughnan and Elizabeth J. Zechmeister, "Americas Barometer: What Do Citizens of the Americas Think of China?," 2013, Latin American Public Opinion Project, Vanderbilt University, www.vanderbilt.edu/lapop/insights/ITB007en.pdf, accessed December 1, 2014.

3. Yuan Chen, "The Shape and Significance of Jiang Zemin's 'Going Abroad' Policy" (in Chinese). Literature of the Chinese Communist Party No. 1, 2009, http://mall.cnki.net/magazine/article/DANG200901013.htm, accessed December 1, 2014.

4. For the full details of the interesting background of Chen Yun and Chen Yuan see Henry Sanderson and Michael Forsyth, *China's Superbank: Debt, Oil, and Influence: How China Development Bank Is Rewriting the Rules of Finance* (New York: Bloomberg Books, 2013).

5. Geoff Dyer with Jamil Anderlini and Henny Sender, "China's Lending Hits New Heights," *Financial Times*, January 17, 2011, www.ft.com/intl/cms/s/0/488c60f4-2281-11e0-b6a2-00144feab49a.html?siteedition=intl#axzz3KlvwXIwQ, accessed December 1, 2014.

6. The Development Bank of Latin America (CAF) is indigenous to Latin America but is also a major source of finance to the region.

7. Deborah Brautigam, *The Dragon's Gift: The Real Story of China in Africa* (Oxford: Oxford University Press, 2009).

8. Edward Steinfeld, *Forging Reform in China: The Fate of State-Owned Industry* (Cambridge: Cambridge University Press, 1998), 71.

9. Concessional loans are loans with lending rates lower than those that are commercially available.

10. Erica Downs, *Inside China, Inc.: China Development Bank's Cross-Border Energy Deals,* John L. Thornton China Center Monograph Series No. 3 (Washington, DC: Brookings Institution, 2011); Sanderson and Forsythe, *China's Superbank.*

11. Andrew Sheng, "Central Bank Currency Swaps Key to International Monetary System," *East Asia Forum*, April 1, 2014, www.eastasiaforum.org/2014/04/01/central-bank-currency-swaps-key-to-international-monetary-system/, accessed December 1, 2014.

12. Russo Camila, "Argentina Gets Reserves Boost from China Currency Swap," *Bloomberg News*, October 30, 2014, www.bloomberg.com/news/2014-10-30/argentina-gets-reserves-boost-from-china-currency-swap.html, accessed December 1, 2014; BBC News, "China and Brazil Sign $30bn Swap Agreement," 2013, www.bbc.com/news/business-21949615, accessed December 1, 2014.

13. The original report is Kevin P. Gallagher, Amos Irwin, and Katherine Koleski, "New Banks in Town: Chinese Finance in Latin America" (Washington, DC: Inter-American Dialogue, 2012). The interactive database can be found at www.thedialogue.org/map_list, accessed December 1, 2014.

14. See Gallagher et al., "New Banks in Town" for analysis.

15. Deborah Brautigam and Kevin P. Gallagher, "Bartering Globalization: China's Resource-Secured Finance in Africa and Latin America," *Global Policy* 5, no. 3 (September 2014): 346–52.

16. Inter-American Development Bank, "China to Provide $2 Billion for Latin America and the Caribbean Co-financing Fund," March 16, 2013, www.iadb.org/en/news/news-releases/2013-03-16/china-co-financing-fund,10375.html, accessed December 8, 2014.

17. See Gallagher et al., "New Banks in Town."

18. China gave aid to Castro's Cuba and Allende's Chile in the 1960s and 1970s. Barbara Stallings, *Chinese Aid to Latin America: Trying to Win Friends and Influence People* (Providence: Brown University, mimeo).

19. See Stallings, *Chinese Aid to Latin America.*

20. Brautigam, *The Dragon's Gift*, 47.

21. Marianna Parraga, "UPDATE 2-Venezuela Oil Sector Gets $1.5 Bln Loan from Japan," *Reuters*, June 28, 2011, www.reuters.com/article/2011/06/28/venezuela-japan-oil-idUSN1E75R19420110628, accessed December 1, 2014.

22. See Gallagher et al., "New Banks in Town," and related database China-Latin America Finance Database (www.thedialogue.org/map_list), accessed September 30, 2015).

23. Brautigam and Gallagher, "Bartering Globalization."

24. Downs, *Inside China, Inc.*; Julie Jiang and Jonathan Sinton, *Overseas Investments by Chinese National Oil Companies* (Paris: International Energy Agency, 2011).

25. Brautigam and Gallagher, "Bartering Globalization."

26. Downs, *Inside China, Inc.*

27. John Pomfret, "China Invests Heavily in Brazil, Elsewhere in Pursuit of Political Heft," *Washington Post*, July 26, 2010, www.washingtonpost.com/wp-dyn/content/article/2010/07/25/AR2010072502979.html?sid=ST2010092006580, accessed December 4, 2014.

28. See Rory Carrol, "China Pours its Wealth into Latin America," *The Guardian*, April 17, 2010, www.theguardian.com/world/2010/apr/18/china-brazil-south-america-trade, accessed December 4, 2014.

29. Brautigam, *The Dragon's Gift*, 115.

30. LIBOR stands for the London Interbank Offered Rate, and represents the average interest rate offered by London's major banks. Financial institutions across the world set their rates relative to LIBOR, so it serves as a good benchmark for comparison.

31. World Bank Treasury, "IBRD Lending Rates and Loan Charges," 2010, http://treasury.worldbank.org/bdm/htm/ibrd.html, accessed September 1, 2015; Republic of Argentina, "Form 18-K: Annual Report," US Securities and Exchange Commission, December 31, 2010, www.sec.gov/Archives/edgar/data/914021/000090342311000486/roa-18k_0928.htm, accessed December 4, 2014.

32. Deborah Brautigam, "Aid 'With Chinese Characteristics': Chinese Foreign Aid and Development Finance Meet the OECD-DAC Aid Regime," *Journal of International Development* 23, no. 5 (2011): 756.

33. See Kevin P. Gallagher and Amos Irwin, "China's Economic Statecraft in Latin America: Evidence from China's Policy Banks," *Pacific Affairs* 88, no. 1 (March 2015): 99–121.

34. Gallagher and Irwin, "China's Economic Statecraft."

35. Embassy of the People's Republic of China in the Republic of Ecuador, "Ecuadorian Embassy Holds Meeting to Explain Coca-Codo Sinclair Dam Project" (in Chinese), 2010, http://ec.china-embassy.org/chn/jmwl/t560094.htm, accessed December 5, 2015.

36. J. P. Morgan, "Index Group: EMBI+ (JP Morgan)," Financial Bonds Information, 2011. www.cbonds.info/cis/eng/index/index_detail/group_id/1/, accessed December 20, 2011.

37. See Gallagher and Irwin, "China's Economic Statecraft."

38. Ngaire Woods, *The Globalizers: The IMF, the World Bank, and Their Borrowers* (Ithaca, NY: Cornell University Press, 2006).

39. See Gallagher et al., "New Banks in Town."

40. Simon Romero, "Deals Help China Expand Sway in Latin America," *New York Times*, April 15, 2009, www.nytimes.com/2009/04/16/world/16chinaloan.html?_r=0, accessed September 30, 2015.

41. Nathan Gill, "Ecuador Credit Rating Raised by Moody's on China, Finances," *Bloomberg News*, September 13, 2012, www.bloomberg.com/news/2012-09-13/moody-s-raises-ecuador-rating-on-china-loans-improved-finances.html, accessed December 8, 2014.

42. Francisco Rodriquez, "Lost in Translation," Venezuela Economic Watch, Bank of America, Merrill Lynch, 2015; and El Universal, "Venezuela, China Amend Loans Agreement Repaid With Oil," November 26, 2014, www.eluniversal.com/economia/141126/venezuela-china-amend-loans-agreement-repaid-with-oil, accessed December 8, 2014.

43. The International Capital Markets Association (a group of private investors) and the US Treasury came up with guidelines for new bond issuances that would make sure that the kind of interpretation that occurred in the Argentina case were not replicated: "Sovereign Debt Information," www.icmagroup.org/resources/Sovereign-Debt-Information/, accessed December 8, 2014. The IMF also has a new series of recommendations to rectify the problem as well: "Strengthening the Contractual Framework to Address Collective Action Problems in Sovereign Debt Restructuring," www.imf.org/external/pp/longres.aspx?id=4911, accessed September 15, 2015.

44. Ken Parks, "Argentina Central Bank Borrows $814m Under China Currency Swap," *Wall Street Journal*, October 30, 2014, http://blogs.wsj.com/frontiers/2014/10/30/argentina-central-bank-borrows-814m-under-china-currency-swap/, accessed December 9, 2014.

45. Associated Press, "China and Chile Sign Currency Swap Agreement," May 25, 2015, http://news.yahoo.com/china-chile-sign-currency-swap-agreement-221303419.html;_ylt=AoLEVvP6iIRViFAAkMAPxQt.;_ylu=X3oDMTByOHZyb21tBGNvbG8DYmYxBHBvcwMxBHZoaWQDBHNlYwNzcg—.

46. "Agreement on the New Development Bank, Fortaleza, July 15," http://brics6.itamaraty.gov.br/media2/press-releases/219-agreement-on-the-new-development-bank-fortaleza-july-15, accessed December 9, 2014; "Treaty for the Establishment of a BRICS Contingent Reserve Arrangement, Fortaleza, July 15," http://brics6.itamaraty.gov.br/media2/press-releases/

220-treaty-for-the-establishment-of-a-brics-contingent-reserve-arrangement-fortaleza-july-15, accessed December 9, 2014.

47. Yu Lintao, "Vibrant Integration," *Beijing Review*, January 19, 2015, www.bjreview.com.cn/world/txt/2015-01/19/content_664488.htm, accessed March 25, 2015.

48. *CRI English*, "$30 Bln Fund to be Launched for China-Latam Production Capacity Co-op," May 20, 2015, http://english.cri.cn/12394/2015/05/20/2361s8 79525.htm, accessed June 18, 2015; see also *China Daily*, "China, Brazil, Sign $27 Billion in Trade Agreements," May 20, 2015, www.chinadaily.com.cn/world/2015livistsa/2015-05/20/content_20766430.htm, accessed September 30, 2015.

Chapter 5

1. Alejandra de Vengoechea, "Alarma en Colombia por la falsificación en China de sombreros vueltiaos," *ABC Internacional*, 2013, www.abc.es/internacional/20130129/abci-colombia-falsificaciones-sombreros-201301261745.html, accessed October 14, 2014.

2. Juan Carlos Diaz, "El Sombrero Vueltiao de Tuchin tiene imitacion 'Made in China,'" *El Tiempo*, 2013, www.eltiempo.com/archivo/documento/CMS-12487862, accessed October 14, 2014.

3. Juan Carlos Dias, "Rechazo masivo al sombrero vueltiao 'Made in China,'" *El Tiempo*, 2013, www.eltiempo.com/archivo/documento/CMS-12503087, accessed October 14, 2014.

4. Ministerio de Comercio, Industria y Turismo Superintendencia de Industria y Comercio, "Resolucion numero 439 de 2013," 2013, www.sic.gov.co/recursos_user/documentos/normatividad/Resoluciones/20013/Resolucion_439_2013.pdf, accessed September 30, 2015.

5. Joshua Goodman, "Chinese Knockoff Sombrero Drags Colombian Tribe Into Trade Fight," *Bloomberg News*, January 27, 2013, www.bloomberg.com/news/articles/2013-01-27/chinese-knockoff-sombrero-drags-colombian-tribe-into-trade-fight, accessed February 6, 2015.

6. Goodman, "Chinese Knockoff Sombrero."

7. For more technical discussions of the resource curse and empirical proof of the resource curse see Jeffrey D. Sachs and Andrew M. Warner, "The Big Rush, Natural Resource Booms And Growth," *Journal of Development Economics* 59, no. 1 (June 1999): 43–76.

8. For a good overview and examples of nations that have escaped the resource curse see M. Humphreys, J. D. Sachs, and J. E. Stiglitz (eds.), *Escaping the Resource Curse* (New York: Columbia University Press, 207).

9. Kevin P. Gallagher and Lyuba Zarsky, *The Enclave Economy: Foreign Investment and Sustainable Development in Mexico's Silicon Valley* (Cambridge, MA: MIT Press, 2007).

10. Albert O. Hirschman, *The Strategy of Economic Development* (New Haven, CT: Yale University Press, 1958).

11. See Kevin P. Gallagher and Roberto Porzecanski, *The Dragon in the Room: China and the Future of Latin American Industrialization* (Redwood City, CA: Stanford University Press, 2010).

12. Rebecca Ray and Kevin P. Gallagher, *China-Latin America Economic Bulletin*, 2015 Edition (Boston: Boston University, Global Economic Governance Initiative, 2015).

13. Enrique Dussel Peters and Kevin P. Gallagher, "NAFTA's Uninvited Guest: China and the Future of North American Integration," *CEPAL Review* 110, no. 8 (August 2013): 83–108. CEPAL stands for Economic Commission for Latin America and the Caribbean.

14. Numerous studies document the impacts of Chinese competition on Mexico and Central America; see Enrique Dussel Peters, *Economic Opportunities and Challenges Posed by China for Mexico and Central America* (Bonn: German Development Institute, 2005); R. Jenkins, "China's Global Growth and Latin American Exports," Working Papers, RP2008/104 World Institute for Development Economic Research, www.wider.unu.edu/publications/working-papers/research-papers/2008/en_GB/rp2008-104, accessed September 30, 2015; R. Jenkins, "Measuring the Competitive Threat from China for Other Southern Exporters," *The World Economy* 31, no. 10 (2008): 1351–66; R. Jenkins and E. D. Peters (eds.), *China and Latin America: Economic Relations in the Twenty-First Century* (Bonn: German Development Institute, 2009); R. Jenkins, E. D. Peters, and M. M. Moreira, "The Impact of China on Latin America and the Caribbean," *World Development* 36, no. 2 (2008): 235–53; C. Freund and C. Ozden, "The Effect of China's Exports on Latin American Trade with the World," in *China's and India's Challenge to Latin America*, eds. D. Lederman, M. Olarreaga, and G. E. Perry (Washington, DC: World Bank, 2009); K. P. Gallagher, J. C. Moreno-Brid, and R. Porzecanski, "The Dynamism of Mexican Exports: Lost in (Chinese) Translation?," *World Development* 36, no. 8 (2008): 1365–80; R. Devlin, A. Estevadeordal, and A. Rodríguez-Clare (eds.), *The Emergence of China: Opportunities and Challenges for Latin America* (Washington, DC, and Cambridge, MA: Interamerican Development Bank, David Rockefeller Center for Latin American Studies, Harvard University, 2006).

15. Rhys Jenkins and Alexandre de Freitas Barbosa, "Fear for Manufacturing? China and the Future of Industry in Brazil and Latin America," in *From the*

Great Wall to the New World, China and Latin America in the 21st Century, eds. Julia Strauss and Ariel Armony (Cambridge: Cambridge University Press, 2012).

16. Rhys Jenkins, "Chinese Competition and Brazilian Exports of Manufactures," *Oxford Development Studies*, February 14, 2014, http://dx.doi.org/10.1080/13600818.2014.881989, accessed February 17, 2015. Hiratuka has also found a loss of Brazilian competitiveness in regional and world markets; see C. Hiratuka and S. Cunha, "Qualidade e Diferenciac_a~o das Exportac_oes Brasileiras e Chinesas: Evoluc_a~o Reciente no Mercado Mundial e na ALADI, IPEA Texto para Discussa~o 1622, Brasilia," 2011, www.ipea.gov.br/portal/index.php?option=com_content&view=article&id=9803, accessed September 30, 2015.

17. Dani Rodrik, "The Perils of Premature Deindustrialization," *Project Syndicate*, October 11, 2013, www.project-syndicate.org/commentary/dani-rodrikdeveloping-economies--missing-manufacturing#6WhDjt8DoLx8DgKo.99, accessed February 17, 2015.

18. Dani Rodrik, "Premature De-Industrialization," National Bureau of Economic Research Working Paper No. 20935 (Cambridge, MA: National Bureau of Economic Research, 2015).

19. Jenkins and Barbosa, "Fear for Manufacturing?"

20. Camara de la Industria del Calzado, "Antidumping a calzado de origen China," 2008, www.calzadoargentino.org.ar/comercioexterior-antidumping.asp.

21. "Argentina: Termination with Duties of an Anti-Dumping Investigation Concerning Footwear from China," Global Trade Alert, 2010, www.globaltradealert.org/measure/argentina-termination-duties-anti-dumping-investigation-concerning-footwear-china, accessed April 14, 2015.

22. "China-Argentina Trade Differences Increase and Are Openly Aired," *MercoPress*, April 23, 2010, http://en.mercopress.com/2010/04/23/china-argentina-trade-differences-increase-and-are-openly-aired, accessed October 4, 2010.

23. "China-Argentina Trade Differences Increase and Are Openly Aired."

24. "China Soya Ban Angers Argentina," *BBC News*, April 6, 2010, http://news.bbc.co.uk/2/hi/8604372.stm, accessed October 4, 2015.

25. Chun-Wei Yap, "Argentina's Hot New Export? Polo Boots for Chinese Women," *Wall Street Journal*, 2011, http://blogs.wsj.com/chinarealtime/2011/05/18/argentinas-new-hot-export-polo-boots-for-chinese-women/, accessed April 12, 2015.

26. "China Ends Freeze on Argentina Soy-Oil Imports, Says Buenos Aires," *MercoPress*, June 26, 2010, http://en.mercopress.com/2010/06/26/china-ends-freeze-on-argentina-soy-oil-imports-says-buenos-aires, accessed April 12, 2015.

27. The editors, "Global Insider: Argentina China Trade Relations," *World Politics Review*, February 2, 2011, www.worldpoliticsreview.com/trend-lines/7752/global-insider-china-argentina-trade-relations, accessed September 30, 2015.

28. Feiwen Rong, "China Agrees to Reopen Market to Argentina Soybean Oil Imports, People Say," Bloomberg News, October 20, 2010, www.bloomberg.com/news/articles/2010-10-11/china-agrees-to-reopen-market-to-argentine-soybean-oil-imports-people-say, accessed September 30, 2015.

29. Silvio Carvalho Neto et al., "International Competitiveness of a Footwear Industry Cluster in Franca: Brazil," *IP Research and Communities*, March 1, 2008, www.freepatentsonline.com/article/Journal-Academy-Business-Economics/192587646.html, accessed April 12, 2015.

30. Neto et al., "International Competitiveness of a Footwear Industry Cluster."

31. Claudia Trevisa, "Brasileiros vao a China em busca de emprego," *Folha de Sao Paulo*, October 5, 2013, www1.folha.uol.com.br/fsp/dinheiro/fi0510200313.htm, accessed April 14, 2015.

32. "Brazil: Definitive Antidumping Duties on Imports of Shoes Originating in China," *Global Trade Alert*, September 30, 2009, www.globaltradealert.org/measure/brazil-definitive-antidumping-duties-imports-shoes-originating-china, accessed April 14, 2015.

33. "Brazil: Definitive Antidumping Duties."

34. "Surcharge to China Footwear Boosts Footwear Production in Franca," *Folha de Sao Paulo*, March 17, 2010, www.en.investe.sp.gov.br/news/post/surcharge-to-china-footwear-boosts-production-in-franca/, accessed April 14, 2015.

35. Richard Smith, ed., "Brazil–Footwear: Suspected Circumvention of Antidumping Measures," *Assintecal*, November 2, 2011, www.fashionnetasia.com/en/businessresources/3358/brazil_footwear_suspected_circumvention_of_antidumping_measures.html, accessed June 13, 2015.

36. Jonathan Wheatley, "Corporate Bonds: An Emerging Bubble," *Financial Times*, February 15, 2015, www.ft.com/intl/cms/s/0/d31fe990-b2a4-11e4-b234-00144feab7de.html?siteedition=intl#axzz3Rw7HScNh, accessed February 16, 2015.

37. Jose Antonio Ocampo, *Latin America's Mounting Economic Challenges*, Baker Institute for Public Policy Issue Brief 10-17-14 (Houston: Rice University, 2014).

38. Economic Commission for Latin America and the Caribbean, *Capital Flows to Latin America and the Caribbean: Recent Developments* (Santiago: Economic Commission for Latin America and the Caribbean, 2014).

39. Nicholas Lardy, *Sustaining China's Growth After the Financial Crisis* (Washington, DC: Peterson Institute for International Economics, 2012).

40. See IMF, *World Economic Outlook and Global Financial Stability Reports* (Washington, DC: International Monetary Fund, 2011, 2012).

41. For a full discussion of capital flows and the IMF changes in the wake of the financial crisis see Kevin P. Gallagher, *Ruling Capital: Emerging Markets and the Reregulation of Cross-Border Finance* (Ithaca, NY: Cornell University Press, 2015).

42. John Paul Rathbone, "Currency Fears Spread in Latin America," *Washington Post*, February 13, 2013, www.washingtonpost.com/world/the_americas/currency-fears-spread-in-latin-america/2013/02/12/535357ce-7548-11e2-aa12-e6cf1d31106b_story.html, accessed February 16, 2015.

43. Jose De Gregorio, *How Latin American Weathered the Global Financial Crisis* (Washington, DC: Peterson Institute for International Economics, 2014).

44. Bertrand Gruss, *After the Boom: Commodity Prices and Economic Growth in Latin America and the Caribbean*, Working Paper WP/14/154 (Washington, DC: International Monetary Fund, 2014).

45. Ocampo, *Latin America's Mounting Economic Challenges.*

46. "Emerging Markets—Brazil's Real Crosses 2.80 Mark, Weakest in 10 Years," *Reuters*, February 10, 2015, www.reuters.com/article/2015/02/10/markets-emerging-idUSL1N0VK17U20150210, accessed February 16, 2015.

47. Bertrand Gruss and Fabiano Rodriquez Bastos, "Mind the Dragon: Latin America's Exposure to China," *IMF Direct*, 2014, http://blog-imfdirect.imf.org/2014/11/11/mind-the-dragon-latin-americas-exposure-to-china/, accessed February 16, 2015.

48. For a good analysis of fiscal budgets, capital flows, and the Eurozone see Mark Blyth, *Austerity: The History of a Dangerous Idea* (New York: Oxford University Press, 2013).

49. Jenkins and Barbosa, "Fear for Manufacturing?"

50. G. Adler and N. Magud, "Four Decades of Terms-Trade Booms: Saving-Investment Patterns and a New Metric of Income Windfall," IMF Working Paper 10/103 (Washington, DC: International Monetary Fund, 2013).

51. World Bank, *World Bank Development Indicators* (Washington, DC: World Bank, 2015).

52. Economic Commission for Latin America and the Caribbean, *Compacts for Equality: Towards a Sustainable Future* (Santiago: Economic Commission for Latin America and the Caribbean, 2014).

Chapter 6

1. For a report on the People's Climate March and photos of marchers see "Hundreds of Thousands Turn Out for People's Climate March in New York City," www.huffingtonpost.com/2014/09/21/peoples-climate-march_n_5857902.html, accessed November 12, 2014. For a gallery of protestors see "26

Amazing Photos from the People's Climate Marches Around the World," www.mtv.com/news/1937882/peoples-climate-marches-around-the-world/, accessed January 15, 2015.

2. Rebecca Ray and Adam Chimienti, "A Line in the Equatorial Forests: Chinese Investment and the Environmental and Social Impacts of Extractive Industries in Ecuador," Discussion Paper #5 (Boston: Global Economic Governance Initiative, Boston University, 2015).

3. See Ann Helwege, "Challenges with the Resolution of Mining Conflicts in Latin America," *Extractive Industries and Society* 2, no. 1 (2014): 73–84.

4. See Dara O'Rourke and Sarah Connolly, "Just Oil? The Distribution of Environmental and Social Impacts of Oil production and Consumption," *Annual Review of Environment and Resources* 28 (2003): 587–617.

5. Philip Fearnside, "Soybean Cultivation as a Threat to the Environment in Brazil," *Environmental Conservation* 1, no. 1 (March 2001): 23–38.

6. See Ray and Chimienti, "A Line in the Equatorial Forests"; Helwege, "Challenges with the Resolution of Mining Conflicts"; O'Rourke and Connolly, "Just Oil?"; and Fearnside, "Soybean Cultivation."

7. William Laurance et al., "Reducing the Global Environmental Impacts of Rapid Infrastructure Expansion," *Current Biology* 25, R1–R4 (March 30, 2015): 259–R62.

8. This statement rests on the assumption that all goods are perfectly substitable. Norway saved windfalls from oil exploration and invested into alternative economic activities that generate similar amounts of economic growth. However, when it comes to the environment all goods are not perfectly substitutable—some ecosystems take thousands of years to reach their current level, and of course some civilizations that live on such lands, if eviscerated, can never come back.

9. Edward B. Barbier, "Agricultural Expansion, Resource Booms and Growth in Latin America: Implications for Long-Run Economic Development," *World Development* 32, no. 1 (2004): 137–57. See also Edward B. Barbier, *Scarcity and Frontiers: How Economies Have Developed Through Natural Resource Exploitation* (Cambridge: Cambridge University Press, 2011).

10. See Chapter V of Economic Commission for Latin America and the Caribbean, *Compacts for Equality: Towards a Sustainable Future* (Santiago: Economic Commission for Latin America and the Caribbean, 2014).

11. According the World Bank, "Natural resource depletion is the sum of net forest depletion, energy depletion, and mineral depletion. Net forest depletion is unit resource rents times the excess of roundwood harvest over natural growth. Energy depletion is the ratio of the value of the stock of energy resources to the remaining reserve lifetime (capped at 25 years). It covers

coal, crude oil, and natural gas. Mineral depletion is the ratio of the value of the stock of mineral resources to the remaining reserve lifetime (capped at 25 years). It covers tin, gold, lead, zinc, iron, copper, nickel, silver, bauxite, and phosphate." For a full discussion of the methodology and for the data see World Bank, *The Changing Wealth of Nations: Measuring Sustainable Development for the New Millenium* (Washington, DC: World Bank, 2011).

12. See Glen Peters et al., "Growth in Emission Transfers via International Trade from 1990 to 2008," *Proceedings of the Natural Academy of Sciences* 108, no. 21 (2011): 8903–08; and Rebecca Ray et al., *China in Latin America: Implications for South-South Cooperation and Sustainable Development* (Boston: Global Economic Governance Initiative, Boston University, 2015).

13. "Shougang: Latin America's Best Company," *Latin Trade*, October 4, 2011, http://latintrade.com/shougang-latin-americas-best-company/, accessed January 20, 2015.

14. Barbara Kotchswar et al., "Do Chinese Mining Companies Exploit More?" *Americas Quarterly*, Fall Issue 2011, http://americasquarterly.org/do-chinese-mining-companies-exploit-more, accessed January 20, 2015.

15. Amos Irwin and Kevin P. Gallagher, "Chinese Mining in Latin America: A Comparative Perspective," *Journal of Environment & Development* 22, no. 2 (2013): 207–34.

16. Cynthia Sanborn and Victoria Chonn, "Chinese Investment in Peru's Mining Industry: Blessing or Curse?," Working Group on Environment and Development Discussion Paper 2015-4 (Boston: Global Economic Governance Initiative, Boston University, 2015).

17. For a review of this literature see Kevin P. Gallagher, "Economic Globalization and the Environment," *Annual Review of Environment and Resources* 34 (2009): 279–304.

18. "Country Rankings," *2014 Environmental Performance Index*, http://epi.yale.edu/epi/country-rankings, accessed January 20, 2015.

19. Sanborn and Chonn, "Chinese Investment in Peru's Mining Industry."

20. Sanborn and Chonn, "Chinese Investment in Peru's Mining Industry."

21. See EITI website, https://eiti.org/, accessed January 20, 2015.

22. Elizabeth Economy and Michael Levi, *By All Means Necessary: How China's Resource Quest Is Changing the World* (New York: Oxford University Press, 2014).

23. Sanborn and Chonn, "Chinese Investment in Peru's Mining Industry."

24. Ray and Chimienti, "A Line in the Equatorial Forests."

25. Ray and Chimienti, "A Line in the Equatorial Forests."

26. Ray and Chimienti, "A Line in the Equatorial Forests."

27. Alejandra Saravia Lopez and Adam Rua, "An Assessment of the Environmental and Social Impacts of Chinese Trade and Investment in the Bolivian Economy," Working Group on Development and Environment Discussion Paper 2015-8 (Boston: Global Economic Governance Initiative, Boston University, 2015).

28. Global Initiative for Economic, Social, and Cultural Rights, *Joint Parallel Report to the Committee on Economic, Social and Cultural Rights on the occasion of the consideration of the Second Periodic Report of the People's Republic of China during the Committee's 52nd Session*, Duluth, MN, 2014, http://globalinitiative-escr.org/wp-content/uploads/2014/02/131216-GI-ESCR-and-WNESL-Parallel-Report-CESCR-China-2014.pdf, accessed January 20, 2015.

29. Peter Bosshard, "China's Global Dam Builder at a Crossroads," *International Rivers*, 2014, www.internationalrivers.org/blogs/227/china%E2%80%99s-global-dam-builder-at-a-crossroads, accessed January 20, 2015; BankTrack, "Aqua Zarca Dam," www.banktrack.org/show/dodgydeals/agua_zarca_dam, accessed September 22, 2015.

30. Chris Davis, "Chinese Dam Business in South America on the Rise," *China Daily*, January 20, 2014, http://usa.chinadaily.com.cn/world/2014-01/20/content_17244423.htm, accessed January 20, 2015.

31. For a review of the World Bank and US firms and the environment see Bruce Rich, *Mortgaging the Earth: The World Bank, Environmental Impoverishment, and the Crisis of Development* (New York: Island Press, 1994), and *Foreclosing the Future: The World Bank and the Politics of Environmental Destruction* (New York: Island Press, 2013).

32. Kevin P. Gallagher, Amos Irwin, and Katherine Koleski, *The New Banks in Town: Chinese Finance in Latin America* (Washington, DC: Inter-American Dialogue, 2012); World Resources Institute, *Environmental and Social Policies in Overseas Investments: Progress and Challenges for China* (Washington, DC: World Resources Institute, 2012).

33. China Banking Regulator Committee, *Notice of the CBRC on Issuing the Green Credit Guidelines*, 2012, www.cbrc.gov.cn/EngdocView.do?docID=3CE646AB6 29B46B9B533B1D8D9FF8C4A, accessed January 20, 2015.

34. See also Friends of the Earth, *Credit Where Credit Is Due: Assessing the Implementation of China's Green Credit Guidelines* (San Francisco: Friends of the Earth, 2014).

35. Inter-American Development Bank, *Environmental and Social Management Report LAC-China Investment Funds* (Washington, DC: Inter-American Development Bank, 2013).

36. Becky Davis, "Chinese Mining Group Sets Guidelines for Overseas Interaction," *New York Times*, October 24, 2014, www.nytimes.com/2014/10/25/business/

international/chinese-mining-group-sets-guidelines-for-overseas-interaction. html?_r=0, accessed January 20, 2015.

37. World Bank, *World Development Indicators* (Washington, DC: World Bank, 2015).

38. Ramon Lopez, "The Policy Roots of Socioeconomic Stagnation and Environmental Implosion: Latin America 1950–2000," *World Development* 31, no. 2 (February 2003): 270.

39. Lopez, "The Policy Roots of Socioeconomic Stagnation," 271.

40. "Environmental Law in Brazil: Compromise or Deadlock?," *The Economist*, June 2, 2012, www.economist.com/node/21556245, accessed January 20, 2015.

41. Simon Romero, "Brazil's Leader Faces Defining Decision on Bill Relaxing Protection of Forests," *New York Times*, May 16, 2012, www.nytimes.com/2012/05/17/world/americas/brazils-president-dilma-rousseff-faces-defining-decision-over-forest-bill.html?pagewanted=all, accessed January 20, 2015.

42. Sanborn and Chonn, "Chinese Investment in Peru's Mining Industry."

43. Ray and Chimienti, "A Line in the Equatorial Forests."

44. Stephan Nielsen and Mario Sergio Lima, "Protest Over Brazil Hydro Drives Delay and Boosts Cost," *Bloomberg Business Week*, June 6, 2013, http://www.bloomberg.com/news/articles/2013-06-05/protests-over-brazil-hydropower-leads-to-delays-and-boosts-costs, last accessed September 30, 2015.

Chapter 7

1. John Wirth, *The Politics of Brazilian Development, 1930–1954* (Redwood City, CA: Stanford University Press, 1970), 271.

2. Noted in speech by Margaret Thatcher, January 29, 1990, "Speech at Dinner for Mexican President (Carlos Salinas)," www.margaretthatcher.org/document/108001, accessed June 30, 2015.

3. Economic Commission for Latin America and the Caribbean, *Compacts for Equality: Towards a Sustainable Future* (Santiago: Economic Commission for Latin America and the Caribbean, 2014).

4. United Nations Conference for Trade and Development, *Tax Incentives for Foreign Direct Investment* (Geneva: United Nations Conference for Trade and Development, 2000); I also witnessed this first-hand in interviews for my book with Lyuba Zarsky, *The Enclave Economy: Foreign Investment and Sustainable Development in Mexico's Silicon Valley* (Cambridge, MA: MIT Press, 2007).

5. Economic Commission for Latin America and the Caribbean, *Compacts for Equality*, 37.

6. Serge Jeanneau and Camilo E. Tovar, "Domestic Bond Markets in Latin America: Achievements and Challenges," *BIS Quarterly Review*, 2006, www.bis.org/publ/qtrpdf/r_qt0606e.pdf, accessed February 20, 2015.

7. See my book *Ruling Capital: Emerging Markets and the Reregulation of Cross-Border Finance* (Ithaca, NY: Cornell University Press, 2015).

8. Economic Commission for Latin America and the Caribbean, *Compacts for Equality*.

9. Economic Commission for Latin America and the Caribbean, *Compacts for Equality*.

10. Economic Commission for Latin America and the Caribbean, *Compacts for Equality*.

11. Nelson Barbosa, "Financial Regulation and the Brazilian Response to the 2008–2009 Financial Crisis," *Brazilian Journal of Political Economy* 31, no. 5 (2011): 848–52, special edition 201; Joe Leahy, "Brazil's BNDES—Lender of First Resort for Brazil's Tycoons," *Financial Times*, January 15, 2015, www.ft.com/intl/cms/s/0/c510368e-968e-11e4-922f-00144feabdc0.html?siteedition=intl#axzz3SbF3m LRR, accessed February 20, 2015.

12. See Aldo Musacchio and Steve Larrarini, *Reinventing State Capitalism: Leviathan in Business, Brazil and Beyond* (Cambridge, MA: Harvard University Press, 2014). BNDES has been less than effective and is in need of reform.

13. Sovereign Wealth Fund Institute, "Heritage and Stabilization Fund," 2015, www.swfinstitute.org/swfs/heritage-and-stabilization-fund/, accessed February 23, 2015.

14. See Santiago Levy, *Good Intentions, Bad Outcomes: Social Policy, Informality and Economic Growth in Mexico* (Washington, DC: Brookings Institution Press, 2008). See also 2009 Boston University lecture by Levy, "Can Income Transfer Programs for the Poor Eradicate Poverty?," www.bu.edu/gdp/events/past-events/santiago-levy/, accessed February 20, 2015.

15. D. Perrotti and R. Sánchez (2011), "La brecha de infraestructura en América Latina y el Caribe," Recursos Naturales e Infraestructura series, No. 153 (LC/L.3342) (Santiago: Economic Commission for Latin America and the Caribbean, 2011).

16. Economic Commission for Latin America and the Caribbean, *Compacts for Equality*. Developing Asia includes Hong Kong, Indonesia, Malaysia, the Philippines, the Republic of Korea, Singapore, and Thailand.

17. Inter-American Development Bank, *Rethinking Productive Development: Sound Policies* (Washington, DC: Inter-American Development Bank, 2014), xix.

18. Economic Commission for Latin America and the Caribbean, *Structural Change for Equality: An Integrated Approach to Development* (Santiago: Economic Commission for Latin America and the Caribbean, 2012).

19. See Alice Amsden, *The Rise of the Rest: Challenges to the West from Late Industrializing Countries* (Oxford: Oxford University Press, 2001).

20. See Ricardo Hausman and Dani Rodrik, "Economic Development as Self-Discovery," Working Paper No. 8952 (Cambridge, MA: National Bureau of Economic Research, 2002); Dani Rodrik, *Industrial Policy for the 21st Century* (Vienna: United Nations Industrial Development Organization, 2005).

21. Robert Devlin and Graciela Moguillansky, *Breeding Latin American Tigers: Operational Principles for Rehabilitating Industrial Policies* (Santiago, Chile and Washington, DC: ECLAC and World Bank, 2011).

22. Robert Devlin and Graciela Moguillansky, *What's "New" in the New Industrial Policy of Latin America*, World Bank Policy Research Paper 6191, 38 (Washington, DC: World Bank, 2012), 38.

23. "Chile Becomes the First South American Country to Tax Carbon," *Reuters*, September 26, 2014, http://in.reuters.com/article/2014/09/27/carbon-chile-tax-idINL6N0RR4V720140927, accessed March 3, 2015.

24. "Chile to Implement Carbon Tax Complimenting the Latin American Trend of Environmental Reform," *Panoramas*, www.panoramas.pitt.edu/content/chile-implement-carbon-tax-complimenting-latin-american-trend-environmental-reform, accessed March 3, 2015.

25. Economic Commission for Latin America and the Caribbean, *Compacts for Equality*, 246.

26. J. M. Hartwick, "Intergenerational Equity and the Investing of Rents from Exhaustible Resources," *American Economic Review* 67, no. 5 (1977): 972–74.

27. World Bank, "Natural Resources in Latin America and the Caribbean: Beyond Booms and Busts?," 2010, http://documents.worldbank.org/curated/en/2010/01/12511333/natural-resources-latin-america-caribbean-beyond-booms-busts, accessed March 3, 2015.

28. Devlin and Moguillansky, *Breeding Latin American Tigers*, 240.

29. Devlin and Moguillansky, *What's "New" in the New Industrial Policy of Latin America*.

30. Economic Commission for Latin America and the Caribbean, *Compacts for Equality*, 278.

31. Gustavo Canavire-Bacarreza, Jorge Martinez-Vazquez, and Violeta Vulovic, *Taxation and Economic Growth in Latin America* (Washington, DC: Inter-American Development Bank, 2013).

Chapter 8

1. Clifford Krauss and Keith Bradsheer, "China's Global Ambitions, With Loans and Strings Attached," *New York Times*, July 24, 2015, www.nytimes.com/2015/07/26/business/international/chinas-global-ambitions-with-loans-and-strings-attached.html?_r=0, accessed September 23, 2015.

2. See Kevin P. Gallagher, "Taking the China Challenge: China and the Future of Latin American Development," *Latin America 2060: Consolidation or Crisis?* (Boston: Boston University, Pardee Center for the Study of the Longer Range Future, 2011).

3. Inter-American Development Bank and Asian Development Bank, "Shaping the Future of the Asia and the Pacific-Latin America and the Caribbean Relationship" (Washington, DC: Inter-American Development Bank and Asian Development Bank, 2012).

4. Clement Tan, "Embraer Shifts to China Startups to Sell Smallest Jets," *Bloomberg Business*, November 11, 2014, www.bloomberg.com/news/articles/2014-11-11/embraer-shifts-to-china-startups-to-sell-smallest-jets, accessed March 9, 2015.

5. Michael Pettis, *The Great Rebalancing: Trade, Conflict, and the Perilous Road Ahead for the World Economy* (Princeton, NJ: Princeton University Press, 2013).

6. See chapter 6 for definitions of "threat." New calculations from Rebecca Ray and Kevin P. Gallagher, "China-LAC Economic Bulletin, 2015" (Boston: Global Economic Governance Initiative, Boston University, 2015).

7. Personal communication with advisors to Ministry of Foreign Commerce, China, October 11, 2014.

8. See China-CELAC Cooperation Plan (2015–2019), www.itamaraty.gov.br/index.php?option=com_content&view=article&id=6743:documentos-aprovados-na-i-reuniao-dos-ministros-das-relacoes-exteriores-do-foro-celac-china-pequim-8-e-9-de-janeiro-de-2015&catid=42:notas&Itemid=280&lang=pt-BR#china, accessed September 30, 2015.

9. Forum on China-Africa Cooperation, "The Fifth Ministerial Conference of the Forum on China-Africa Cooperation Beijing Action Plan (2013–2015)," 2012, www.focac.org/eng/zxxx/t954620.htm, accessed March 9, 2015.

10. See Deborah Brautigam, *The Dragon's Gift: The True Story of China in Africa* (New York: Oxford University Press, 2010), for the best treatment of China's history in Africa.

11. See Deborah Brautigam and Xiayang Tang, " 'Going Global in Groups': Structural Transformation and China's Special Economic Zones Overseas," *World Development* 63, no. 3 (2014): 78–91, quotation from 85.

12. See Walter Vergara, Claudio Alatorre, and Leandro Alves, *Rethinking Our Energy Future: A White Paper on Renewable Energy*, Discussion Paper No. IDB-DP-292 (Washington, DC: Inter-American Development Bank, 2013).

13. Inter-American Development Bank, *Sustainable Infrastructure for Competiveness and Inclusive Growth* (Washington, DC: Inter-American Development Bank, 2013), ii.

14. Eric Helleiner, *Forgotten Foundations of Bretton Woods: International Development and the Making of the Postwar Order* (Ithaca, NY: Cornell University Press, 2014).

15. See discussion regarding Justin Lin at the World Bank and the IDB's new reports on industrial policy in the previous chapter.

16. Kevin P. Gallagher and Fei Yuan, *Safeguarding Sustainable Development? Multilateral Development Banks in Latin America* (Boston: Global Economic Governance Initiative, Boston University, 2015).

17. Helleiner, *Forgotten Foundations of Bretton Woods.*

18. Brian Wingfield, "US Export-Import Bank: From Apple Pie to Endangered Species," *Bloomberg News*, 2014, www.bloombergview.com/quicktake/u-s-export-import-bank, accessed March 9, 2015.

19. See Gallagher and Zarsky, *The Enclave Economy;* Gallagher and Porzecanski, *The Dragon in the Room;* and Peters and Gallagher, "NAFTA's Uninvited Guest," 83–108.

20. See Kevin P. Gallagher, "Trading Away the Ladder? Trade Politics and Economic Development in the Americas," *New Political Economy* 13, no. 1 (March 2008): 37–59.

21. Barack Obama, State of the Union Address Transcript, January 20, 2015, www.nytimes.com/2015/01/21/us/politics/obamas-state-of-the-union-2015-address.html?_r=0, accessed March 16, 2015.

22. World Bank, *Global Economic Prospects* (Washington, DC: World Bank 2005), Table 6.2; see also Gallagher, "Trading Away the Ladder?," 37–59; and "Exchanging Development for Market Access? Deep Integration and Industrialization under Multi-Lateral and Regional-Bilateral Trade Agreements," *Review of International Political Economy* 12, no. 5 (2005): 750–75.

23. Alvin Hilaire and Yongzen Yang, *The United States and the New Regionalism,* WPIEA2062003 (Washington, DC: International Monetary Fund, 2003); Lima Duran, Carlos J. de Miquel, and Andres Schuschny, *Trade Agreements of Colombia, Ecuador, and Peru with the United States: Trade, Production, and Welfare Effects* (Washington, DC: Inter-American Development Bank, 2007), 88.

24. Andrew Martin, "Coup d'Etat to Trade Seen in Billionaire Toxic Lead Fight," *Bloomberg*, May 10, 2013, www.bloomberg.com/news/articles/2013-05-09/rennert-800-million-toxic-lead-fight-roils-global-trade, accessed March 12, 2015.

25. Martin, "Coup d'Etat to Trade Seen in Billionaire Toxic Lead Fight."

26. For a more comprehensive discussion about ISDS see Gus Van Harten, *Sovereign Choices and Sovereign Constraints: Judicial Restraint in Investment Treaty Arbitration* (New York: Oxford University Press, 2013) and *Investment Treaty Arbitration and Public Law* (New York: Oxford University Press, 2007).

27. International Center for the Settlement of Investment Disputes, *Burlington Resource Inc. v. Republic of Ecuador,* ICSID Case No. ARB/08/5 (Washington,

DC: International Center for the Settlement of Investment Disputes, 2012); Ximena Herrera-Bernal, "Impuestos sobre ganancias extraordinarias (Windfall taxes) y medidas provisionales: cuatro casos recientes," *International law, revista colombiana de derecho internacional* 15 (2009): 125–54.

28. Van Harten, *Sovereign Choices and Sovereign Constraints*; and *Investment Treaty Arbitration and Public Law*.

29. For broader proposals and analyses on these issues see Kevin P. Gallagher,*The Clash of Globalizations: Essays on the Political Economy of Trade and Development Policy* (London: Anthem Press, 2013).

30. On poverty see Jeffrey Sachs, *The End of Poverty* (New York: Penguin Books, 2007); on climate finance see Amar Bhattarcharya, Jeremy Oppenheim, and Lord Nicholas Stern, "Driving Sustainable Development Through Better Infrastructure: Key Elements of a Transformation Program," Washington, DC: Brookings Institution, 2015, www.brookings.edu/research/papers/2015/07/sustainable-development-infrastructure-bhattacharya, accessed September 30, 2015.

31. World Economic Forum, *Green Investment Report 2013* (Geneva: World Economic Forum, 2013).

32. World Resources Institute, 2013, "How Can We Pay for Green Growth?," Washington, DC: World Resources Institute, www.wri.org/blog/2013/02/how-can-we-pay-green-growth-new-report-provides-answers, accessed March 16, 2015.

33. Ngaire Woods, *The Globalizers: The IMF, World Bank, and their Borrowers* (Ithaca, NY: Cornell University Press, 2006).

34. See Bruce Rich, *Foreclosing the Future: The World Bank and the Politics of Environmental Destruction* (Washington, DC: Island Press, 2013).

35. See "World Bank Safeguards Review," *Bank Information Center*, 2015, www.bicusa.org/issues/safeguards/, accessed March 13, 2015.

36. Jane Perlez, "US Opposing China's Answer to World Bank," *New York Times*, October 9, 2014, www.nytimes.com/2014/10/10/world/asia/chinas-plan-for-regional-development-bank-runs-into-us-opposition.html?_r=0, accessed March 14, 2015.

37. Geoff Dyer, "Superpowers Circle Each Other in Contest to Control Asia's Future," *Financial Times*, March 13, 2015, www.ft.com/intl/cms/s/0/f59ed7d4-c90a-11e4-bc64-00144feab7de.html#axzz3nGxtRb00, accessed with subscription, September 13, 2015.

38. "Three Fund Members Selected for New IDB-China Ex Im Bank Equity Investment Platform," *Inter-American Development Bank*, 2012, www.iadb.org/en/news/news-releases/2012-10-17/investment-platform-for-latin-america-and-the-caribbean,10162.html, accessed March 9, 2015.

39. Stephen Nielson, "IDB, China Fund to Provide \$133 Million for Uruguay Wind Project," *Bloomberg*, October 31, 2013, www.bloomberg.com/news/articles/2013-10-31/idb-china-fund-to-provide-133-million-for-uruguay-wind-project, accessed April 21, 2015.

INDEX

exports to China: of Argentina, 42, 46, 103; of Bolivia, 46; of Brazil, 47, 105, 170; of Colombia, 46, 47; commodities, 7, 43–47, 96, 98, 120, 123, 168; compared to rest of world, 43, 44f; of Ecuador, 7, 47, 75; employment created, 98–99; manufactured, 47, 169–170; of Mexico, 7, 42, 47; oil, 7, 42, 47, 66, 75, 145; of Paraguay, 46; share of total exports, 98; soy and soy products, 42, 45, 46, 86, 103, 105; technology, 47; of Venezuela, 7, 47

external shocks, 5, 28

Extractive Industries Transparency Initiative (EITI), 126–27, 129, 158–59

FCCV (Fondo Conjunto Chino-Venezolano). See China-Venezuela Joint Fund

Federal Reserve, US, 107

FEES. See Economic and Social Stabilization Fund

financial crises: of 1980s, 5, 24, 25, 38–39; bailouts, 5, 25; in late twentieth century, 5, 28, 38–39. See also global financial crisis of 2008–2009

financial instability, during China Boom, 105–12, 115–16

fiscal revenues: earmarked for social programs, 152; increasing, 149–150; as proportion of GDP, 149; royalties, 114, 149, 162; shortfalls, 137; spending, 114, 152, 159. See also taxes

Five Principles of Peaceful Coexistence, 82

FOCAC. See Forum on China-Africa Cooperation

Fonden. See Venezuelan National Development Fund

Fondo Conjunto Chino-Venezolano. See China-Venezuela Joint Fund

food sector: in China, 46; Chinese investment, 52; exports to China, 48; multinationals, 48. See also agriculture; soy and soy products

food security, 56

foreign investment: in China, 35–36, 48–49; in commodity lottery period, 3–4, 19; incentives, 149; liberalization, 25; in manufacturing, 23; short-term, 28, 151; in United States, 147; volatility, 28, 151. See also multinational corporations

foreign investment from China: in Africa, 12, 71, 72, 174; in agriculture, 55–56; in banking, 58; controversies, 118, 138–39, 141–43; data sources, 51; in energy and mining, 42, 47, 52, 53–55, 65, 72, 118, 125–26, 171; financing,

51, 52, 53, 58, 65; flows, 51–52; in food sector, 52; in future, 139, 140f, 142–43, 168, 170–73, 191; "go out" strategy, 50–51, 67, 73; growth, 7, 51–52; in industrial parks, 12, 172–73; lack of conditions, 12, 65–66, 82; in manufacturing, 12, 49–50, 56–57; by private-sector firms, 52–53; in railroads, 2, 103; sectors, 52, 65; by state-owned enterprises, 52, 53–55; stocks, 52. See also infrastructure investment from China

Forum on China-Africa Cooperation (FOCAC), 173

fossil fuels. See energy and mining; greenhouse gas emissions

free trade agreements. See trade agreements

Free Trade Area of the Americas (FTAA), 6, 41, 177, 183–84

Geely, 52

General Motors, 49

Georgi, Deborah, 102

Glendon, Sarah, 85

global financial crisis of 2008–2009: impact in Latin America, 94, 153; impact on US policies, 8; recovery from, 2, 59, 107, 147; stimulus packages, 59, 107, 152

Global Witness, 135

Goldman Sachs, 105

governments. See debt, government; fiscal revenues

Great Depression, 4, 20

Great Wall, 55

Green Credit Guidelines, 133

greenhouse gas emissions, 39, 117, 158. See also climate change

gross domestic product (GDP). See economic growth

growth. See commodity-led growth; economic growth

Grupo Bimbo, 48

Grupo Shougang, 125–27, 128, 129

Guadalajara, Mexico, 37, 94

Haiti, Chinese aid after earthquake, 73

Hartwick rule, 159

Heritage and Stabilization Fund, Trinidad and Tobago, 153

Heritage Foundation, 84

Hewlett-Packard, 56

Hirschman, Albert O., 22, 95, 98

Honduras: hydroelectric projects, 131–32, 176; indigenous peoples, 131

Huawei, 42, 52, 58
human capital. *See* education
hydroelectric projects, 76, 131–32, 141–42, 176

IAD. *See* Inter-American Dialogue
IBM, 37, 56
IBRD. *See* International Bank for
  Reconstruction and Development
ICBC. *See* Industrial and Commercial Bank
  of China
IDB. *See* Inter-American Development Bank
IFIs. *See* international financial institutions
IMF. *See* International Monetary Fund
immigration: to China, 104; to Latin America,
  1, 16, 19, 126; to United States, 13, 16
imports. *See* trade
import substitution policies, 4. *See also* state-
  led industrialization
incomes: in China, 38, 168–69; increases,
  62, 113; per capita, 18t, 19. *See also*
  poverty; wages
India, Japanese loans, 73–74
indigenous peoples: in Bolivia, 121; in Brazil,
  121; in Colombia, 121; consulting with,
  138–39, 181; in Ecuador, 117–18, 121, 129,
  138–39, 142; in Honduras, 131; mine workers,
  126; in Peru, 121, 126; poverty, 152; protecting, 159–160; rights, 131, 160; territories, 118,
  121, 140f, 159–160
Industrial and Commercial Bank of China
  (ICBC), 34–35, 58
industrialization: of China, 74; diversification,
  155–56, 164; economic and social effects, 99;
  premature deindustrialization, 99–105, 100f,
  112; reindustrialization, 153–57, 172–73; US
  support, 22–23, 177–78, 179–180; of West,
  3, 18, 30. *See also* manufacturing; state-led
  industrialization
inequality: in China, 39; in commodity lottery
  period, 19; decreases, 2, 8, 62–63; increases,
  2, 4, 5, 19; reducing, 112, 114, 146, 151–52;
  regressive taxes and, 149–150; in state-led
  industrialization period, 4; in Washington
  Consensus period, 2, 5, 27. *See also* poverty
inflation, 5, 25, 26, 29
infrastructure investment: in China, 34, 35;
  gaps, 12, 65, 73, 154, 160; in green infrastructure, 188, 190; from international financial
  institutions, 188; policy recommendations,
  11, 154, 160, 175–76; road building, 121–22;
  in state-led industrialization period, 4;
  transportation, 160

infrastructure investment from
  China: amounts, 7, 171; dams, 76, 141–42;
  from development banks, 71–72, 190–91;
  financing packages, 76; in future, 11, 168,
  173; goals, 72, 73; growth, 64, 65; supporting
  commodity industries, 160; in Venezuela, 71
intellectual property rules, 183–84, 186. *See
  also* patents
Inter-American Development Bank
  (IDB): China Cofinancing Fund, 71; China
  Export-Import Bank and, 134–35, 190–91;
  development finance amounts, 67, 70, 70f;
  energy reports, 175; environmental safeguards, 14, 135, 190; interest rates, 78; investment data, 48; lending to Latin America,
  65, 72, 180; policy recommendations, 155,
  187; sustainable infrastructure development
  strategy, 176; trade studies, 169
Inter-American Dialogue (IAD), 7, 55, 69
interest groups, political capture, 161–62
interest rates: in Brazil, 105–6; capital flows
  and, 28; in China, 35; on Chinese loans,
  58, 71, 78–81; on government debt, 80, 81;
  in Latin America, 107–8; LIBOR, 203n30;
  spreads, 58, 78–79, 81; in United States,
  107; of Western development banks,
  78, 79, 80
International Bank for Reconstruction and
  Development (IBRD), 78–79. *See also*
  World Bank
international financial institutions (IFIs): alter-
  natives, 86–87; capital, 187–88, 189; Chinese
  role, 186–87, 189, 190; conditionality, 5, 25,
  65–66, 82–84, 180; criticism of, 84, 187–88;
  environmental and social safeguards,
  180–81, 187, 188; financing for Latin
  America, 65, 78; reforms, 84, 187; social welfare goals, 72, 83, 187; structural adjustment
  programs, 182, 188; US influence, 84, 188.
  See also development banks; International
  Monetary Fund; Washington Consensus;
  World Bank
International Labor Organization (ILO) 169,
  131, 138, 160
International Monetary Fund (IMF): conditionality, 5, 82–84; on exchange rates,
  108–10, 111; founding, 187; governance,
  188; growth estimates, 8; on investments
  from windfall profits, 146; lending to Latin
  America, 25; reforms, 189; savings data, 9;
  trade data, 60
Internet access, 154

multinational corporations: Chinese, 52, 58, 119, 126–27, 128–130, 131, 132–35, 141, 170–71; Latin American, 48; patents, 115. *See also* foreign investment

Myers, Margaret, 55–56

NAFTA. *See* North American Free Trade Agreement

National Development and Reform Commission (NDRC), China, 50

natural gas, 44, 130–31

natural resources: as natural capital, 157–58, 159; resource curse, 8–9, 91–94, 112, 116. *See also* commodities; energy and mining; environmental degradation; oil; water

Naughton, Barry, 33–34

NDRC. *See* National Development and Reform Commission

Nemak, 49

neoliberal economic policies, 25–26, 26t, 83–84, 137. *See also* Washington Consensus

Netherlands, investment in Latin America, 50

New Development Bank, 86–87, 172, 189

Nicaragua, canal project, 64

North American Free Trade Agreement (NAFTA): critics, 183; impact in Mexico, 27, 37, 94, 95, 97, 182–83; intellectual property rules, 183; trade within, 49, 57; Washington Consensus in, 6

Norway: oil revenues, 9; sovereign wealth fund, 153

Obama, Barack, 14, 64, 183

Ocampo, Jose Antonio, 111

Occidental Petroleum, 54

OECD. *See* Organization for Economic Cooperation and Development

official aid, 72–73, 78, 79

oil: Chinese consumption, 44, 47, 169; Chinese imports, 7, 42, 47, 66, 75, 145; loans backed by, 66, 69, 74–75, 76–77, 85–86; prices, 23–24, 85–86, 110

oil companies, Chinese, 42, 53–54, 75, 118, 129, 130–31

oil production: Chinese investment, 47, 65, 118; environmental impact, 118, 120–21, 129–130; exploration, 65; improved methods, 130; rents and taxes, 150

Olivera Alcocer, Conrado, 185

Organization for Economic Cooperation and Development (OECD), 77, 79, 135, 149, 180, 186

Ortega, Daniel, 64

PAE. *See* PanAmerican Energy

Panama, Chino-Panameños, 1, 16

Panama Canal, 16

Panama Railroad Company, 1

PanAmerican Energy (PAE), 53–54

Paraguay: agriculture, 46; exports to China, 46

Pastrana, Andres, 89

patents, 115, 115t, 183. *See also* intellectual property rules

patronage, 162

PBOC. *See* People's Bank of China

Pengxin Group, 55

People's Bank of China (PBOC), 35, 67, 68–69, 86, 133

People's Republic of China (PRC). *See* China

Peru: banks, 58; Chinese investment in, 55, 58, 125–26, 128–29; Chinese official aid, 73; environmental regulations, 126–27, 138, 158–59, 184; financial regulations, 151; free trade agreement with United States, 126, 184–85; indigenous peoples, 121, 126; investment levels, 114; mining, 55, 125–26, 138, 150; natural gas projects, 130–31; natural resources, 42; social expenditures, 152; trade with China, 7, 46; Twin Ocean Railroad Connection, 2

Pestana, Eligio Antonio, 90

Peters, Enrique Dussel, 52

Peters, Glen, 124

Petrobras, 69, 74, 81, 87

PetroChina, 75

Petro Ecuador, 75

petroleum. *See* oil

Philip Morris, 185

policy banks, 34, 51, 65, 67–68, 74. *See also* development banks; *and individual banks*

policy recommendations: for Chinese investment, 142; constructive engagement with China, 167; cooperation in China Triangle, 186–191; for development banks, 155, 187; environmental regulations, 158–59; infrastructure investment, 11, 154, 160, 175–76; for Latin America, 10–11, 144, 160–65, 191, 192; rebalancing economies, 147–153; reindustrialization, 153–57; tailored to each country, 144; for United States, 13, 14–15, 176–186, 191–92

political capture, 161–62

political economy, 153, 160–65

political risk, 141

pollution. *See* environmental degradation

Porzecanski, Roberto, 96

poverty: in China, 38; government programs, 62–63, 112, 114, 146, 151–52; reducing, 38, 62–63, 112, 114. *See also* inequality

PRC (People's Republic of China). *See* China

Prebisch, Raul, 4, 20–21

premature deindustrialization, 99–105, 100f, 112

private sector: in China, 52, 58; in Latin America, 154–55; partnership with state, 148–153, 155, 156, 157, 161, 162–64. *See also* multinational corporations

productivity growth: in China, 38; in Latin America, 23, 27, 112

public opinion, 66

railroads, 1, 2, 19, 35, 103

Randon, 49

Ray, Rebecca, 97, 98, 124

regulations: capital controls, 109–10, 151; deregulation, 26, 28; financial, 20, 34–35, 151; health, 185. *See also* environmental regulations

reindustrialization, 153–57, 172–73

Renco Group, 184, 185

renewable energy, 158, 175, 190

rent-seeking behavior, 162, 164

reprimarization of exports, 96

Repsol, 54, 130

research and development, 115, 115t, 156, 173. *See also* technology

resource curse, 8–9, 91–94, 112, 116. *See also* commodities; natural resources

risk: diversification by China, 171–72; managing, 66, 73–75, 77; political, 141

roads, 121–22. *See also* infrastructure investment

Rockefeller, Nelson, 14, 177, 181

Rodrik, Dani, 99–100

Roosevelt, Franklin D., 14, 22–23, 178, 179, 181

Salinas, Carlos, 144

Sanborn, Cynthia, 127, 128, 129

Santos, Juan Manuel, 90

Sápara people, 117–18, 121, 138–39, 142

savings, 38–39, 113. *See also* investment

Schulz, Hans, 190

Securities and Exchange Commission (SEC), US, 51, 69

services. *See* banks; telecommunications industry

Servitje, Daniel, 48

Shen Zhiliang, 84

Shougang, 125–27, 128, 129

Shougang Hierro Peru, 125–27

Silk Road Fund, 189

Sinohydro, 131–32, 176

SINOPEC. *See* China Petroleum and Chemical Corporation

socially inclusive development, 135, 147, 159–160, 176, 181

social safeguards, 13, 14, 133, 134–35, 141, 180–81, 182

Socma, 57

South Asia: economic growth, 114; Japanese loans to India, 73–74

South Korea: computer industry, 24–25; oil consumption, 169. *See also* Asian tigers

sovereign debt. *See* debt, government

sovereign wealth funds (SWFs), 11, 149, 150, 153

soy and soy products: Chinese demand, 46, 86; Chinese investment in, 55, 56; environmental impact, 121; exports to China, 42, 45, 46, 86, 103, 105; prices, 59; trade disputes, 103. *See also* agriculture; food sector

stabilization funds, 152

Stallings, Barbara, 73

Standard Bank of Argentina, 58

State Grid Corporation, 54, 141

state-led industrialization: advocates, 4, 20–22, 144; in China, 17, 30, 31–32; economic growth, 4, 23; end of, 25, 39; goals, 4, 17; infrastructure investment, 4; results, 20, 24; shortcomings, 23–25, 154; US support, 22–23

state-owned enterprises: Chinese, 31, 34, 37, 51, 52, 53–55; Latin American, 23, 69, 150

state role in economy, partnership with markets, 148–153, 155, 156, 157, 161, 162–64. *See also* state-led industrialization; Washington Consensus

Suarez, Eder, 89, 90

sustainable economic development, 148–49, 158–160, 167–68, 173, 175, 176, 188

SWFs. *See* sovereign wealth funds

Taiwan, computer industry, 24–25. *See also* Asian tigers

Tang, Xiayang, 174

taxes: carbon, 158; from commodities production, 114, 149, 150, 159, 162, 164; evasion, 164; indirect, 149–150; reforms, 149, 150; windfall, 185. *See also* fiscal revenues

technology: Chinese industry, 36–37; computer industries, 24–25, 37, 47, 49, 56–57, 94; exports to China, 47; foreign competition, 24–25, 37; imports from China, 49; infrastructure, 154, 160; Internet access, 154; patents, 115, 115t, 183; raw materials, 46; sharing, 12